Bullying Prevention for Schools

A Step-by-Step Guide to Implementing a Successful Anti-Bullying Program

ALLAN L. BEANE

JOSSEY-BASS
A Wiley Imprint
www.josseybass.com

Published by Jossey-Bass
A Wiley Imprint
989 Market Street, San Francisco, CA 94103-1741—www.josseybass.com

Jossey-Bass books and products are available through most bookstores. To contact Jossey-Bass directly call our Customer Care Department within the U.S. at 800-956-7739, outside the U.S. at 317-572-3986, or fax 317-572-4002.

Jossey-Bass also publishes its books in a variety of electronic formats. Some content that appears in print may not be available in electronic books.

Library of Congress Cataloging-in-Publication Data
Beane, Allan L.
 Bullying prevention for schools : a step-by-step guide to implementing the bully free program / Allan L. Beane.
    p. cm.
 Includes bibliographical references and index.
 ISBN 978-0-470-40701-1 (pbk.)
 1. Bullying in schools–Prevention–Handbooks, manuals, etc. 2. Bullying–Prevention–Handbooks, manuals, etc. 3. School violence–Prevention–Handbooks, manuals, etc. I. Title.
 LB3013.3.B433 2009
 371.5'8–dc22
                                                                                          2009017421

Printed in the United States of America
FIRST EDITION
PB Printing   10 9 8 7 6 5 4 3 2

Contents

About This Book

Several years ago, the pain of being mistreated visited our home. When our son, Curtis, was in seventh grade, he was bullied and eventually isolated by several students. My wife and I decided to transfer him to another school system. He found acceptance and a sense of belonging at the new middle school. Then at age fifteen, Curtis was in a car accident that changed his life.

My wife and I had to give the surgeons permission to remove two fingers and one-third of his right hand. He had two other fingers repaired and one rebuilt. When he went back to school, many of his classmates encouraged and supported him. But many were cruel to him. Once again, I asked myself, "How can kids be so cruel?" There was a cry from within me for answers. I wanted to know if I could stop cruelty from developing, and I wanted to stop it after it had already developed.

There was also a cry from within my son, and it was deeper and more intense than mine. The bullying had a tremendous impact on his self-esteem, confidence, and emotional health even into his adult years. At the age of twenty-three, he suffered from depression and anxiety. He developed posttraumatic stress from the car wreck and the persistent peer mistreatment. He also sought the company of the wrong people. He got desperate to escape his pain by taking an illegal drug. He had a heart problem that no one knew about, and the drug killed him.

Now you understand why I am passionate about preventing and stopping bullying and why I am writing this book for you. I understand the pain expressed by children who are mistreated and the heartache their parents experience. I want to stop the pain. I also have witnessed the frustration of professionals who seek to prevent and stop bullying. They have a tremendous need for a step-by-step guide to implementing a program that will prevent and stop bullying.

In response to my son's bullying, I wrote my first book, *The Bully Free Classroom*. I wrote this book you are holding because I do not want any student to experience what our son did. I especially do not want them to take the path he took. After his death, I wrote several books and developed numerous other materials and resources (bracelets, brochures, posters, and others) that now make up the Bully Free Program. My wife, Linda Beane, and I coauthored one book, *Bully Free Bulletin Boards, Posters, and Banners*. Thousands of schools in the United States and other countries now use our materials and resources, and Linda and I work full time helping schools implement the Bully Free Program. We have dedicated the rest of our lives to preventing and stopping bullying. Our efforts have expanded into presenting school assembly programs, presenting to parents, training school personnel, and training others who work with young people. Visit our Web site, www.bullyfree.com, for more information.

Bullying can be found in every neighborhood, school system, and school. To prevent and reduce it requires a systematic effort in each school. Ideally, there will be a school-system-wide commitment to preventing and stopping bullying. There must be adult involvement, including parents and others in the community. But this kind of commitment doesn't always exist. I have actually had school superintendents tell me that bullying didn't exist in their school system. Adults denying that bullying exists or ignoring bullying is the worst thing that can happen to children, a school, and a community. When adults harness the energy of school personnel, parents, community representatives, and children, bullying can be prevented and stopped, or at least significantly reduced. I often wonder if we can ever eliminate it—considering the nature of human beings. However, I am extremely hopeful. Using this book is the first step toward making that a reality.

I hope you find this book informative and helpful.

Allan L. Beane
April 2009

Acknowledgments

I offer my grateful thanks to everyone who has helped by providing advice, information, and comments during the preparation of this book. Special acknowledgment and thanks are due to my wife, Linda Beane, for her proofreading and her desktop publishing knowledge and skills. I deeply appreciate her insight, love, and support during this project. Special thanks are also due to Darlene Gibson for her thorough proofreading of an earlier manuscript. I want to express my sincere gratitude to Kate Bradford and Nana Twumasi at Jossey-Bass for their editorial assistance, knowledge, skills, ideas, encouragement, and support during the preparation of this manuscript.

This book is dedicated to our son, Curtis Allan Beane,
who was bullied in seventh grade and high school. It is also
dedicated to our daughter, Christy Turner; our son-in-law, Mike;
and our grandchildren, Emily Grace Turner, Sarah Gail Turner,
Jacob Allan Turner, and Jimmy Andrew Turner. They have
been the light in the darkness caused by Curtis's death.
We hope this book, and those who use it, will bring light
into the darkness of students who are mistreated.

The Author

Allan L. Beane, Ph.D., is an internationally recognized expert, speaker, and author on bullying. He is the president of Bully Free Systems LLC in Murray, Kentucky. He has over thirty-four years of experience in education that includes teaching special education, teaching regular education, serving as vice president of a university, and serving as director of a school safety center. He has served as an expert and consultant in criminal cases and lawsuits involving bullying and has been an expert guest on Fox News and CNN's *Nancy Grace Show*. He and material from his anti-bullying program have been featured in many national magazines and journals, such as *USA Today, USA Weekend, Time for Kids, Newsweek for Teens, School Transportation News,* and *Parenting* magazine. Beane's son was bullied in seventh grade and high school. His son's life inspired him to develop his anti-bullying program, the Bully Free Program, which has been adopted around the United States. His books, *The Bully Free Classroom* (Free Spirit Publishing) and *Protect Your Child from Bullying* (Jossey-Bass), are available in several languages. He often gives keynote addresses, speaks to students and parents, and provides training for school personnel and others. For more information, visit his Web site at www.bullyfree.com.

Introduction

Bullying is a form of overt and aggressive behavior that is intentional, hurtful (physically or psychologically, or both), and persistent (repeated). Bullied students are teased, harassed, and assaulted (verbally or physically, or both) by one or more peers and often socially rejected by their peers. In any bullying, there is an imbalance of strength (power). Students should not be made to feel they are alone in coping with their mistreatment. One of the most effective deterrents to bullying is adult authority and supervision. Unfortunately, adults in our schools cannot tackle this problem alone. Efforts to combat bullying must be a collaboration among school personnel, volunteers, students, parents, law enforcement, community agencies and organizations, and others. The Bully Free Program includes such collaboration. Anti-bullying programs should include not only policies and procedures, but also prevention and intervention strategies that are administrative and teacher centered, as well as curriculum.

Increasingly adults are realizing the importance of creating school environments that are bully free—where all students feel a sense of belonging and acceptance and everyone treats others the way he or she wants to be treated. The purpose of this book is to help you create this kind of environment in your school by explaining how to develop, implement, and evaluate the Bully Free Program in your school system or school. The aim of the Bully Free Program is to create peaceable, caring environments in which students and adults feel psychologically, emotionally, and physically safe and all adults and students model self-control, acceptance of others, kindness, empathy, and respect. Even if your school system or school has already initiated an anti-bullying program, this book can be used to fill gaps in it.

This book provides a step-by-step action plan that requires the collaboration of parents, school personnel, volunteers, students, and key community representatives. Ideally, the Bully Free Program will be implemented in all of the schools in a district. Some aspects of the program can also be used in community programs for children and youth. Implementing this program only at certain grade levels will not sufficiently tackle the problem. It is wonderful to have caring teachers who have a passion for stopping bullying, but they cannot do this alone. They need the help of many others—administrators, custodians, bus drivers, bus monitors, cafeteria workers, volunteers, students, parents, school resource officers, counselors, school psychologists, and key community representatives. Therefore, this book is designed to guide implementation of the school-wide Bully Free Program because research indicates that such an approach can effectively reduce bullying. Of course, it is best if a program can be implemented throughout the school system because bullying often occurs at all grade levels, including preschool.

Steps to Program Planning and Implementation

Any anti-bullying program should be implemented throughout the school district or system. If this isn't possible, it should be schoolwide and in as many schools as possible. The program should also be comprehensive and multifaceted in that it permeates policies, procedures, activities, events, instructional activities, operating procedures, codes of conduct, discipline procedures, and other areas. The program should be an ongoing curriculum and strategies approach and not viewed as a one-time event or add-on program. However, the program should also go beyond the curriculum and become a way of living in every school. After all, it is the little things we do and say every day that will make a difference.

This book is based on the assumption that at least a schoolwide program is desired. However, the following steps in this book can be easily adapted for a systemwide program:

Step 1: Establish and train the Bully Free Program team and develop the program time line.

Step 2: Provide bully free awareness training for school personnel and volunteers.

Step 3: Provide a bully free awareness assembly for all students.

Step 4: Provide a bully free awareness presentation for parents and community.

Step 5: Develop a program evaluation plan and determine the status of bullying in the school.

Step 6: Develop the Bully Free Program mission statement, objectives, slogan, and logo.

Step 7: Implement a bully free curriculum.

Step 8: Develop and implement the Bully Free Program administrative strategies plan and policies.

Step 9: Establish the bully free rules and behavioral expectations.

Step 10: Develop the discipline rubrics and adopt prosocial (nonpunitive) strategies.

Step 11: Develop the response plan.

Step 12: Identify the high-risk locations and times and develop and implement a coordinated and monitored supervision plan and schedule, as well as a reporting and information exchange system.

Step 13: Train school personnel, volunteers, and other key individuals to adhere to policies, procedures, discipline rubrics, prosocial strategies, and response plans.

Step 14: Conduct a meeting with adults and an assembly program for students to increase awareness and involvement.

Step 15: Develop and implement a student involvement and empowerment plan.

Step 16: Develop and implement parent and community involvement and education plans.

Step 17: Review and confirm the implementation and completion of program components and activities.

Step 18: Readminister the survey instruments, analyze pre- and post-data, and make improvements.

Step 19: Celebrate success and plan for next year.

Appendixes

The appendixes include a description of the Bully Free Program, an overview of bullying, examples of documents to be developed by the Bully Free Program team, forms, and survey instruments. All of the material in the appendixes may be copied and used by your school.

Bully Free Program Implementation Files

Several files have been provided online in electronic form to facilitate the efforts of the Bully Free Program team. These files are located at www.bullyfree.com. When you visit the Web site, click on "Click here to access our training resources." Then click on "Resources for Bully Free Program Committee." Type *bfp1* when you are asked your user name and *bullyfree* when you are asked your password.

Task Checklists

To assist you in completing each step, a task checklist is provided at the end of each step. The checklist will help the team track its progress. The checklists have space to add tasks and to write notes regarding team decisions.

To effectively promote peer acceptance, a systemwide or schoolwide plan is needed that uses the program components and strategies discussed in this book. I hope this book will give you the information, desire, and confidence necessary to prevent and stop bullying. This book will help you give it your best shot. As Helen Keller said, "When we do the best we can, we never know what miracle is wrought in our life, or in the life of another."

Step 1

Establish and Train the Bully Free Program Team and Develop the Program Time Line

In order for the Bully Free Program to achieve the expected results in your school, the steps set out in this book need to be implemented systematically and as described here. Since planning is the beginning of action and input from all stakeholders is important, a team structure should be used to systematically implement and assess the effectiveness of the Bully Free Program. If this is a systemwide effort (there will be a program in several schools), I recommend that two types of teams be established: a systemwide Bully Free Program team and a Bully Free Program team in each school. Establishing such teams communicates the school system's commitment to preventing and stopping bullying. If a systemwide team is appointed, it should serve as the steering committee and be made up of the chairs of the school teams. The superintendent should appoint a chair of the systemwide team.

From here on, this book will address the role of the schoolwide Bully Free Program team. A school team serves as the working committee in the school.

Establishing the School's Bully Free Program Team
Membership
A team should be formed in each school desiring to implement the program. The team chair should be appointed by the appropriate person in the school system. The chair must be dedicated to preventing and stopping bullying and must have the ability to provide effective leadership. This person often serves as the Bully Free Program coordinator. The chair should then work with the school officials to identify the team members.

The team should have no more than about a dozen members. Although it may be tempting to limit the membership of this team to school personnel because it is easier to get everyone to a meeting, wide representation on the team is important. The broader the scope of representation, the more likely the team will be successful. Although parents are very busy and have difficulty meeting during the day, they can play an important role in planning and implementing the Bully Free Program. They also can assist in enlisting the support of other parents and other community representatives. Sometimes it is not realistic to have a student representative on the team. In many school systems, all the students ride buses and can't meet with the team, which usually meets after school. If circumstances make it feasible for student representation, we encourage it.

Some schools have used an existing committee to serve as the program's team when there seems to be appropriate representation on the committee. For example, schools have used discipline committees and school safety committees.

I offer one note of caution on membership. Just because a person volunteers to be on the Bully Free Program team does not mean this person should be on it. Sometimes adults who are bullies want to be on the team, and sometimes individuals with negative attitudes who always want to have their way want to be on it. Therefore, be very selective in choosing members.

Nevertheless, whether you are using an existing committee or forming a new team, the following people should be considered for membership:

- A school principal or assistant principal who provides leadership so the program has priority and its momentum is maintained
- A teacher representative from each grade who serves as a program liaison with other teachers in that grade and an ongoing consultant to them
- A guidance counselor or school psychologist who serves as a program liaison with other counselors and school psychologists
- A special education director or teacher who serves as a program liaison with other special education personnel
- A parent who serves as a program liaison with other parents and helps coordinate efforts to involve parents in the program

Others may be asked to be on the team or to attend team meetings from time to time—for example:

- A member of the nonteaching staff (secretary, cafeteria worker, bus driver)
- A school resource officer or school-based law enforcement officer
- A volunteer supervisor
- A school nurse
- A community representative (for example, the parks and recreation director or YMCA director)
- A student (for students in middle school or higher grades)
- A representative from the after-school program

These individuals should feel passionate about preventing and stopping bullying. The members of the school's team should also be willing to give the project the time it requires, listen to those they represent, and take the initiative to obtain the opinions and ideas of those they represent.

The representation of the team members may vary from one school to another. For example, some schools may decide to have one teacher represent more than one grade level.

Desirable Team Member Behaviors

The individuals selected should demonstrate willingness to:

- Accept that all members are equal in value and power.
- Be on time and give full attention to each session.
- Commit to the tasks of the team.
- Share and value different ideas and viewpoints.
- Seek ideas and strategies that all can agree on.
- Communicate often to keep everyone informed.
- Recognize the efforts as well as the accomplishments of team members.
- Actively listen to team members and ask information-seeking questions.
- Leave their position, title, and degrees outside the team meetings.
- Assist in keeping the team on task and make effective use of time.
- Encourage and explore the use of creative ideas from all team members.
- Be prepared for each team meeting and complete assignments on time.
- Learn from and value the knowledge and experience of team members.
- Support and implement the team's plan.

These desirable characteristics should be periodically reviewed by the team members and used to discuss the effectiveness of the team in working together.

Responsibilities of the School's Team

The school's team is considered the working committee and is responsible for planning and ensuring the implementation of the Bully Free Program using the steps presented in this book. It also has responsibility for maintaining commitment to the Bully Free Program and maintaining the program's momentum in the school. Strategies for maintaining commitment and momentum are presented in Step 8.

The Bully Free Program team should become knowledgeable about bullying and become familiar with all of the Bully Free Program materials and resources.

Planning and Conducting the First Team Meeting

The team chair should establish a date, time, and location for the first meeting. He or she should make sure the meeting is held in an easily accessible location, preferably with nearby parking or public transportation. The room should have good lighting, tables, and comfortable chairs. Appropriate refreshments should also be made available (consider those who may have special dietary needs, including food allergies).

Prior to the first meeting, the chair should determine which of the members of the team will write and disseminate the minutes to the members and others deemed appropriate to receive minutes. It is best for the chair to select this person and ask him or her to serve in this capacity before the meeting.

A copy of this book should be ordered for each team member. This book is not only a guide; it contains numerous documents that team members need to examine prior to certain meetings and also serves as a record book for tracking the team's progress and recording important team decisions.

I suggest ordering one of each of the grade-appropriate Bully Free Program kits and a support materials kit that your school will use (www.bullyfree.com) so that they are available at the first meeting. At some point, a brief period of time may be scheduled for members to examine these.

The chair and principal or superintendent should send a letter and a copy of this book to team members thanking them for agreeing to serve on the team and inviting them to attend the first team meeting; specify the date, time, and place; and ask them to become familiar with this book and bring it with them to the first meeting (and all other meetings as well). They should also be told to read Appendix A. The letter should also mention the mission of the team: to make sure the Bully Free Program is successfully implemented.

At the first meeting, each member should be asked to introduce himself or herself. The chair should thank them for agreeing to be on the team and explain why they were selected. Next, the recorder/secretary should be introduced. The team should then determine the best way to disseminate the meeting minutes.

The chair should explain the mission of the team: to implement the Bully Free Program by following the steps described in this book. The chair should note that each team member will become very familiar with the program and should strive to become very knowledgeable about bullying.

Next, a time and place for future team meetings and ground rules should be determined—for example:

- We will meet for two hours only unless everyone agrees to meet longer.

- We will start on time.

- We will do our best not to be late.

- We will not leave the meeting early.

Ground rules are important to the functioning of teams. Sometimes teams are ineffective because the ground rules are not enforced or they might not be clear.

The suggestions of team members regarding ground rules could be written on a flip chart and discussed. How often the team meets will depend on the availability of the members and the eagerness of the team to implement the program. My recommendation is that the team meet at least once a month, and perhaps more often initially. To move the team more quickly through the steps, groups of two or three team members could be given assignments focusing specifically on certain steps.

Too often individuals in education are asked to work together as a team without teaching them effective team member behaviors. Corporations using the team model rarely make this mistake, and we in education can learn from their effective approaches.

At the first meeting, team members should examine the list of desirable behaviors and briefly discuss them. Also discussed should be the importance of attending team meetings. If a person mentions that he or she will have to miss several meetings, speak to him or her after the meeting about finding a replacement. If a team member mentions that he or she must occasionally miss a meeting, the chair, in consultation with the appropriate school officials, can appoint an alternate who will attend the meetings this team member misses. Once the alternate has been appointed, send copies of all minutes to both the team member and the alternate.

Train the Bully Free Program Team

It is important for the team to become knowledgeable about bullying and the steps to implementing the Bully Free Program. One possibility for training is to work with one of my associates or me at Bully Free Systems LLC to implement the program. Of course, this is not a requirement. If your school is interested in such training, contact information is available at www.bullyfree.com.

The recommended training objectives are listed below, and related recommended reading appears in parentheses after each objective. The readings can be found in the appendixes to this book as well as online at www.bullyfree.com. There is also a tremendous body of information about bullying on the Internet.

After the training, each team member should be able to:

- Discuss the major components and elements of the Bully Free Program (see Appendix A's summary on last two pages).
- Define bullying (see Appendix B).
- Discuss how males and females are similar and different in their bullying behavior (see Appendix B).
- Discuss how frequently bullying occurs (see Appendix B).
- Discuss when and where bullying occurs (see Appendix B).
- Discuss why students keep bullying a secret (see Appendix B).
- Discuss the impact bullying has on its victims and those who bully—both immediate and long-term consequences (see Appendix B).
- Discuss the warning signs (see Appendix B).
- Discuss some typical adult responses to bullying (see Appendix B).
- Discuss the steps to implementing the Bully Free Program.

Team members can be trained by studying material on their own and discussing it at a series of team meetings or through a retreat or workshop.

- *Series of team meetings.* If the team wishes to discuss the aforementioned items and the material appearing in Appendixes A and B during a series of team meetings, ask them to read selected material prior to each meeting. Selected team members could present the content to the team.

- *Retreat or workshop.* Some schools have offered a two-day retreat or workshop for team members. The retreat usually covers the objectives as well as a snapshot of the steps for implementing the program. I am often asked to provide this training at the retreat. When this training strategy is used, the first two or three hours of the training focus on the nature of bullying and the rationale for preventing and stopping bullying. Therefore, sometimes all school personnel are invited to attend the first two or three hours. This has the effect of training the team (Step 1) and completing Step 2, which is to provide awareness training for all school personnel. (Visit www.bullyfree.com for more information about workshops.)

Preparing for the Next Meeting

The chair of the team should ask the team to review this book and to come prepared at the next meeting to establish a Bully Free Program time line. They should be asked to review the following example and be prepared to design a tentative time line. This example also appears in the files located at www.bullyfree.com.

Example of Bully Free Program Time Line

Year One

August and September

- Select the program coordinator and identify and train the Bully Free Program team. (Step 1)
- Provide bully free awareness training for all school personnel and volunteers. (Step 2)
- Provide a bully free awareness assembly for all students. (Step 3)
- Provide a bully free awareness presentation for parents and the community. (Step 4)
- Develop a program evaluation plan and determine the status of bullying in the school by collecting baseline data (examine existing data and administer bully free surveys). (Step 5)

October and November

- Develop the Bully Free Program mission statement, objectives, slogan, and logo. (Step 6)
- Implement the bully free curriculum. (Step 7)
- Develop and implement the Bully Free Program administrative strategies plan and policies. (Step 8)
- Establish the bully free rules and behavioral expectations. (Step 9)
- Develop the discipline rubrics and adopt prosocial (nonpunitive) strategies. (Step 10)

(continued on next page)

Example of Bully Free Program Time Line, Cont'd.

December and January

- Develop the response plan. (Step 11)
- Identify high-risk locations and times for bullying; then develop and implement a coordinated and monitored supervision plan and schedule, as well as a reporting and information exchange system. (Step 12)

February and March

- Train school personnel and volunteers to adhere to policies, procedures, discipline rubrics, prosocial strategies, and response plans. (Step 13)
- Conduct a meeting with adults and an assembly program for students to increase awareness and involvement. (Step 14)
- Develop and implement a student involvement and empowerment plan. (Step 15)
- Develop and implement parent and community involvement and education plans. (Step 16)

April

- Review and confirm the implementation and completion of all program components and activities. (Step 17)
- Readminister the survey instruments, analyze pre- and post-data, and make improvements. (Step 18)

May

- Celebrate success, and plan for the next year. (Step 19)

June and July

- Provide staff development focused on bullying and the program.

Year Two

August

- Train new staff and update other school personnel.

September

- Begin regular meetings of the Bully Free Program team to maintain the program's momentum.
- Collect baseline data for second year.
- Implement all components and elements of the Bully Free Program.

Each step in this book has a task checklist at the end that provides a listing of the activities in that step. Following is the first of these task checklists.

Task Checklist, Step 1   Notes

Establish and Train the Bully Free Program Team and Develop the Program Time Line

☐ Form a schoolwide Bully Free Program team (or one for each school if the Bully Free Program is being established throughout a system).

- ○ Appoint a team chair and program coordinator.

- ○ Examine desirable team member behaviors prior to selecting the team members.

- ○ Use list of desirable team member behaviors to select team members and appoint a recorder or secretary.

- ○ If systemwide implementation is planned, form the systemwide team made up of the chairs of the schoolwide teams. Ask the superintendent to appoint a chair.

☐ Plan the first team meeting.

- ○ Establish the date, time, and location.

- ○ Order copies of this book for the team members. This book can be ordered from www.bullyfree.com, www.josseybass.com, or another online retailer.

- ○ Make arrangements for refreshments at the first meeting. (Consider possible dietary needs and food allergies.)

☐ Send a cover letter and a copy of this book to all team members. Ask them to examine it prior to the first meeting and to bring it with them to all team meetings.

☐ Conduct the first team meeting.

- ○ Make introductions.

- ○ Discuss the team's charge and mission, roles, responsibilities, and desirable team member behaviors.

☐ At the first meeting, ask team members to examine the example program time line and come prepared at the next meeting to develop such a time line.

(continued on next page)

Task Checklist, Step 1, Cont'd.   Notes

☐ Provide training to team members.

- ○ Determine the method of training.

- ○ Determine the desired date(s).

- ○ Determine the location.

- ○ Identify and secure the trainer (if necessary).

- ○ Determine desired refreshments and how meals will be handled. Remember those who have special dietary needs, including allergies.

- ○ Determine the funding source and request the funds. Secure the funds.

- ○ Secure the resources (technology, tables, chairs, handouts, and so on).

- ○ Make arrangements for refreshments and meals.

Step 2

Provide Bully Free Awareness Training for School Personnel and Volunteers

After members of the Bully Free Program team have been trained, bully free awareness training for all school personnel and volunteers should be provided. You may want to invite me to provide this training. However, you can provide the training yourself or ask selected team members to provide it. I cannot overemphasize the importance of all school personnel and volunteers being knowledgeable about bullying and why it is critical to prevent it, not just stop it. The volunteers who assist with supervision, the school resource officer, bus drivers, teachers, counselors, the librarian, secretaries, cafeteria staff, custodians, administrators, and other personnel should attend this training. The training needs both to inform and to encourage them to feel passionate about preventing and stopping bullying. They need an emotional understanding of the problem. They must hate it when someone is mistreated. Information and passion will drive them to action. Eventually they will be trained to implement the program, so that there is also uniformity in implementation.

For school personnel and volunteers to effectively implement prevention and intervention strategies, they must first understand the nature of bullying, the possible causes of bullying, why it must be prevented and stopped, and why some students are retaliating against those who bully them, harming themselves, or committing suicide.

The objectives of the awareness training will be determined by the needs of trainees. If personnel in your school system or school have already received some antibullying training, use the following suggested agenda to develop an agenda you feel is most appropriate for your school. The supportive material appearing in the appendixes can be used as handouts or used to develop slides. The question format of the agenda also lends itself to small group discussion regarding possible answers to the questions. Therefore, try to have the participants sitting in small groups at tables. After a brief period of discussion, randomly select groups to share their answers. Then present the correct answers through slides or other means.

Suggested Training Agenda for Bully Free Awareness Training

- What is bullying? (see Appendix B)

- What does it look like? (see Appendix B)

- How are males and females similar and different in their bullying behavior? (see Appendix B)

- How often does it occur, and why do students keep it a secret? (see Appendix B)

- When and where does it occur? (see Appendix B)

- Why must bullying be prevented and stopped? (see Appendix B)

- What are the characteristics of bullies, which serve as warning signs? (see Appendix B)

- What are the typical characteristics of victims and potential victims, which serve as warning signs? (see Appendix B)

- What are some typical adult responses to bullying? (see Appendix B)

- What are the major components of the Bully Free Program? (see the summary on the last two pages of Appendix A)

- What bully free materials and resources are available to help prevent and reduce bullying? (Visit www.bullyfree.com, click on "Products," and print the order form as a handout.)

It may take more than one session to cover this agenda. You may prefer to address the topics in a workshop or through a series of faculty and staff meetings. For more information about workshops, visit www.bullyfree.com.

The following task checklist is a detailed listing of the activities involved in implementing this step.

Task Checklist, Step 2

Notes

Provide Bully Free Awareness Training for School Personnel and Volunteers

☐ Discuss the perceived training needs of faculty, staff, and volunteers.

☐ Get permission from the appropriate school officials to organize and implement a bully free awareness training session.

☐ Determine the agenda of the awareness training.

☐ Identify speakers or workshop facilitators, and determine the associated costs.

☐ If desired, develop PowerPoint slides or handouts using the material in Appendixes A and B.

☐ Determine any materials or handouts to be given to the participants.

☐ Determine if there is a need to display Bully Free Program materials and resources at the training sessions.

☐ Determine the number of participants and how they will be invited.

☐ Set the date and time of the training.

☐ Choose and reserve the location and equipment (for example, tables, chairs, screen, laptop, projection device, extension cords, and power strips).

☐ Develop or select an evaluation form to determine the quality and effectiveness of the training.

☐ If there will be refreshments, make the arrangements, taking into account special dietary needs, including food allergies.

☐ Determine the funding source and request the funds. Secure the funds for the training.

☐ Invite the speakers (if consultants are used).

☐ Invite faculty, staff, and volunteers to the training.

☐ Conduct the awareness training.

☐ Ask participants to evaluate training.

Step 3

Provide a Bully Free Awareness Assembly for All Students

Schools frequently have a bully free awareness assembly for all students. My assembly program takes approximately one hour. I usually share my son's story and use movie clips. For example, I show a clip from the movie *Forrest Gump*, where Forrest is bullied on the bus and has rocks thrown at him. I also show a clip from the 1985 movie *Mask*. The main character, Rocky, has a disease that has deformed his skull and face. He doesn't want to go to the new high school because he knows he will be bullied. When he walks up to the school, a student makes fun of him, and other students laugh. I also use props. For example, I hit an apple and talk about how I bruised it. Then I talk about how even verbal bullying bruises people on the inside. I also tell several powerful emotionally charged stories about students I have met who are bullied. These are the kinds of components you can build into your assembly program.

Your assembly program should be based on the questions in the suggested assembly agenda that follows. For your convenience, I have provided the answer to each question (or where to find the answer in this book), as well as speaking points. If you wish, make slides with the following questions, answers, and speaking points.

Suggested Assembly Agenda for a Bully Free Awareness Assembly for All Students

- What is bullying? For the answer, see Appendix B.
- What does bullying look like? For the answer, see Appendix B.

   Note: As you discuss bullying behavior, share stories about students who have been bullied. Do not mention names.

- What kind of memories does our treatment of others create?

   Answer: People who have been mistreated remember it for the rest of their life. When we mistreat others, they have bad memories of us because we have hurt them. But people also remember kindness. Kindness creates good memories of us. We should be concerned about the memories people have of us. When they think of us or hear our name, we should want them to think well of us.

Suggested Assembly Agenda for a Bully Free Awareness Assembly for All Students, Cont'd.

- Where does bullying happen in our school? (Ask students to answer this question.)

  Answer: Everywhere: hallways, stairwells, bathrooms, on buses, in the cafeteria, waiting for the bus, the gym, the locker room, classrooms, the parking lot, and any other place you can think of.

- Why should we treat others the way we wish to be treated?

  Answer: It is the right thing to do. It is also the best way to create a peaceful and safe school.

- Why do we allow others to convince us to mistreat others?

  Answer: We might be afraid they will mistreat us, and we may think we can't tell adults because they might make it worse for us. We also want to be popular and be accepted by those who are mistreating others.

  Note: Emphasize the importance here of students and adults taking a stand together because they have power when they are united against bullying.

- Why should we be careful how we use our words?

  Answer: Words can be more hurtful than physical mistreatment.

  Note: Emphasize the importance of using words to encourage, support, and make others feel good about themselves.

- How do people who are mistreated almost every day feel?

  Answer: Depressed, angry, fearful, anxious, lonely, defective.

- Do you know anyone in our school who is bullied?

  Note: Ask students to close their eyes and raise their hands if they know someone in the school who is bullied.

- Are you bullied?

  Note: Ask students to close their eyes and raise their hands if they are bullied.

- What should be our response when we see bullying?

  Answer: Don't ignore it, and don't laugh. Ask the victim to walk off with you, and if appropriate make an assertive statement on behalf of the victim. (For example, "It makes me angry when you call him that name. He has a real name; his name is John. Call him John." Or, "I don't have to listen to this. This is a waste of my time. I'm out of here.") You should also report the bullying to an adult. This is not tattling or ratting. Reporting is what a good person should do to help someone who is in trouble.

- Why should we seek to make our school bully free?

  Answer: Bullying is very hurtful. It can make a person sick. Bullying also makes our school less peaceful and more violent. Almost all school shootings were caused by bullying. The victims retaliated. Some victims of bullying harm themselves and even commit suicide. (See Appendix B for additional reasons.)

Task Checklist, Step 3

Provide a Bully Free Awareness Assembly for All Students

☐ Get permission from the appropriate school personnel to organize and implement a bully free assembly program.

☐ Put together the agenda of the awareness assembly program (see the suggested assembly agenda).

☐ Determine the speakers and any associated costs.

☐ Decide whether materials should be given to the students. If so, identify them.

☐ Determine if there is a need to display materials (for example, bully free classroom poster, bully free zone poster, and others). If so, plan to display them.

☐ Set a date and time for the assembly, and inform faculty, staff, and volunteers.

☐ Choose and reserve the location and equipment (for example, screen, laptop, projection device, extension cords, power strips).

☐ Determine the funding source for the assembly. Which budget accounts should be tapped if necessary? Request and secure the funds.

☐ Invite the speakers.

☐ Conduct the bully free awareness assembly program.

☐ Ask teachers to discuss with their students the content of the program.

☐ Get feedback from students, school personnel, volunteers, and anyone else who attended regarding the quality and impact of the program.

☐ _____
   _____

☐ _____
   _____

☐ _____
   _____

Notes

Step 4

Provide a Bully Free Awareness Presentation for Parents and the Community

Another important step to take is to provide a bully free awareness presentation to parents and other interested individuals in the community. Because my son was bullied in seventh grade and in high school, I am often asked to make this presentation. I can relate to parents in a special way. The presentation is usually one and a half or two hours in length and addresses the questions listed below. For your convenience, the answer to each question is also provided, as well as other speaking points. If you wish, make slides with the following questions, answers, and speaking points. The material in Appendix B also can be compiled to make a handout for the parents. Another excellent resource for handouts and for planning the presentation is *Protect Your Child from Bullying* (Beane, 2008).

Suggested Presentation Content for Bully Free Awareness Session for Parents

- What is bullying? For the answer, see Appendix B.

- Why must bullying be prevented and stopped? For the answer, see Appendix B.

- Why do some victims harm themselves, retaliate, or commit suicide?

  Answer: They feel that their situation is hopeless and may even get worse. They see no escape from the daily mistreatment. They are deeply hurt, fearful, anxious, and angry. Their anger turns into hate and rage.

- How often does it occur? For the answer, see Appendix B.

- When does it occur? For the answer, see Appendix B.

- How are males and females similar and different in their bullying behavior? For the answer, see Appendix B.

- What are the typical characteristics, the warning signs, of bullies? For the answer, see Appendix B.

- What are the typical characteristics, the warning signs, of victims and potential victims? For the answer, see Appendix B.

(continued on next page)

> ### Suggested Presentation Content for Bully Free Awareness Session for Parents, Cont'd.
>
> - Why don't children tell their parents about their mistreatment at school? For the answer, see Appendix B.
>
> - What can you do at home to give your child a good social and emotional start in school? For the answer, see chapter 4 of *Protect Your Child from Bullying* (Beane, 2008), or search the Internet for suggestions.
>
> - What should you do if you find out that your child is a victim? For the answer, see chapters 6 to 8 of *Protect Your Child from Bullying,* or search the Internet for suggestions.
>
> - What should you do if you find out that your child is a bully? For the answer, see chapter 10 of *Protect Your Child from Bullying,* or search the Internet for suggestions.

A great strategy for getting parents to attend is to host the meetings on the same night that their children are participating in an event (such as a dance) and require that the parents attend the meeting in order for the students to participate. Homework is also often cancelled on that night. If refreshments are to be served, remember those who have special dietary needs, including food allergies.

Consider purchasing a few copies of *Protect Your Child from Bullying* (www.bullyfree.com or www.josseybass.com) as a gift for the first few parents who arrive at the presentation. This is the most comprehensive book available for parents on bullying. In fact, you may want to consider having a class for parents and use this book as a text or ask the parent-teacher organization to have a book study using the book. Educating parents about the topic and providing them with practical guidance are very important.

Sometimes during the parent presentation, some parents want to discuss their own child's mistreatment at school. It is therefore important to let all the parents know at the start of the meeting that this is not the best time or place to address specific situations. Tell them that they and their child deserve more attention than can be given during the presentation and that the school is very interested in meeting with them and helping their child.

Task Checklist, Step 4   Notes

Provide a Bully Free Awareness Presentation for Parents and the Community

☐ Get permission from the appropriate school personnel to organize and conduct a bully free awareness session for parents and others in the community who wish to attend.

☐ Determine the agenda of the awareness presentation (see the suggested presentation content).

☐ Determine the speaker or speakers.

☐ Determine the materials to be given to the parents (if any). Keep in mind that the Bully Free Program includes *Protect Your Child from Bullying* (Beane, 2008) and the student book, *How You Can Be Bully Free* (Beane, 2004a, 2004b).

☐ Determine if there is a need to display materials (for example, bully free classroom poster, Bully Free Zone poster, and books) at the presentation.

☐ Determine the number of participants and how the participants will be invited.

☐ Set a date and time, and inform parents, the community, school personnel, and volunteers.

☐ Choose and reserve the location and equipment (for example, tables, chairs, screen, laptop, projection device, extension cords, power strips).

☐ Develop an evaluation form to determine the quality and effectiveness of the presentation.

☐ Consider if a special event for students could also be held the same night.

☐ If there will be refreshments, make the arrangements. Remember those who have special dietary needs, including food allergies.

☐ Identify the funding source. Request and secure the funds.

☐ Invite the speaker or speakers.

☐ Invite the parents, community, school personnel, and volunteers.

☐ Conduct the awareness presentation.

☐ Obtain feedback from the attendees.

Step 5

Develop a Program Evaluation Plan and Determine the Status of Bullying in the School

Anything worth doing is worth evaluating. A plan should be developed for collecting data and other information that will help determine the impact and effectiveness of the Bully Free Program. The evaluation plan should include ongoing monitoring and assessment of the program, feedback from representatives of all stakeholders, examination of existing pre- and post-data, and administration of presurveys and postsurveys.

I suggest that a Bully Free Program evaluation coordinator be appointed. This person will make sure all of the evaluation strategies are implemented, the data are collected and analyzed, and the reports written and disseminated to the appropriate individuals.

This step involves developing tentative program evaluation plans that should be continually updated as the Bully Free Program team works through the implementation steps. For example, when the team determines which administrative strategies and supervision strategies will be used, the team will need to determine if these plans were implemented and what school personnel, students, and others think about the effectiveness of those activities and strategies. This will be an ongoing task, and the data and feedback should be reviewed throughout the program's implementation and during Step 17.

The evaluation plan should also include pre- and postprogram surveys administered to determine the status of bullying in the school. Also important are ongoing evaluation strategies such as faculty and staff, student, and parent focus meetings to obtain feedback on the effectiveness of the program.

It is important for the team to understand the purpose of the evaluation, the components of the plan, and the various evaluation strategies.

Purpose of the Evaluation Plan

The evaluation plan has three purposes:

1. To provide the school system and community with an impact assessment of the Bully Free Program

2. To provide the systemwide and schoolwide teams with a specific evaluation of the achievement of goals and objectives, as well as to determine whether plans and activities were implemented in the designated order and according to the time frame established

3. To facilitate efforts to improve the Bully Free Program

Evaluation Components

The evaluation plan should make two major determinations: (1) Were the activities, strategies, and curriculum of the Bully Free Program implemented as planned? (2) How effective was the program in meeting program goals and objectives, such as reducing bullying, increasing school attendance, and increasing the percentage of students willing to report bullying?

Evaluating the Program Implementation

From time to time, the Bully Free Program team should determine if the activities, strategies, and curriculum were implemented as planned. If they were not, there is a discrepancy between what was desired and what occurred, and the situation should be remedied and improvement plans implemented. The team may also choose to develop an instrument to evaluate the quality and effectiveness of some of the activities. For example, if a workshop is conducted for school personnel, the team may want the participants to evaluate the workshop.

The effectiveness of the program is affected by how well the program components and elements are implemented. Ongoing evaluation is needed to monitor or assess the degree to which implementation has occurred as planned and specified and to identify areas that need improvement. Such strategies include focus meetings with staff, students, and parents. The evaluation plan should specify the types of meetings to be used, who will be responsible for conducting the meetings, and how the findings will be reported to the Bully Free Program team and other appropriate individuals.

Faculty and Staff Focus Meetings

One implementation evaluation strategy is to conduct faculty and staff focus meetings. Throughout program implementation, some of the scheduled faculty and staff meetings should be considered staff focus meetings to determine the progress of the Bully Free Program and to determine if adjustments need to be made. Questions such as the following could be asked at the meeting:

- What do you consider to be the most successful parts of the Bully Free Program?

- What needs to be changed?

- What factors are keeping people motivated?

- Have there been noticeable differences in the relationships among the students?

- Have perceptions changed among staff, students, and parents with regard to bullying?

- Are additional training opportunities needed to strengthen staff understanding or skills?

- Are additional opportunities needed to strengthen student and parent understanding or skills?

- How can we maintain the momentum of the Bully Free Program?

- Have you noticed any changes in the high-risk areas where bullying takes place?

- Have you noticed an increase in reports of bullying?

- What do you like most about the Bully Free Program?

- What do you like least about the Bully Free Program?

- Is the school doing a better job supervising the bathrooms, the cafeteria, the hallways, and other areas? Where does the school need to do a better job?

- What additional resources do you need?

These questions are only a sampling of those that could be asked during the focus meetings. (For your convenience, these questions are provided in the files located at www.bullyfree.com.)

Student Focus Meetings

Another ongoing evaluation strategy is to hold student focus meetings. These can be conducted by teachers to determine student impressions of the effectiveness of the Bully Free Program and to assess changes in students' opinions about bullying in their school. Following is a sampling of questions that can be asked during the meetings:

- Are you glad your school has a Bully Free Program?

- What is the Bully Free Program slogan?

- What are some of the Bully Free Program rules?

- Do you think the school is doing a good job trying to stop bullying?

- What do you like most about the Bully Free Program?

- Is there something you don't like about the Bully Free Program?

- What should the school do that it is not doing to prevent and stop bullying?

- Do students in your school treat others the way they would want to be treated?

- Is your school doing a better job supervising the bathrooms, the cafeteria, the hallways, and other areas? Where does the school need to do a better job?

Parent Focus Meetings

Meetings throughout the year can be held with parents to discuss their impression of how the program is progressing and address their concerns. These meetings could be scheduled as part of the regular parent-teacher association meetings, or special meetings could be called. The best time for most parents seems to be between 7 PM and 9 PM. Questions generated for the meeting could even be put into a questionnaire and sent home to the parents. Examples of such questions are as follows:

- Do you feel that the Bully Free Program has been effective?
- Have you talked to your child about bullying?
- Is there something the school needs to do better that will help prevent and stop bullying?
- If you reported bullying to the school, was quick and appropriate action taken?
- What do you think the school is doing to prevent bullying that is effective?
- What can your school do to help your child feel safer?

Tracking Reports

One of the goals of the Bully Free Program is to create a "telling environment." In other words, you want students and parents to feel it is safe to tell an adult at school that they or someone else is being bullied. Building such an environment takes time because you are basically changing the culture of the school. You also have to convince students and even some parents that "reporting" is not tattling and is not ratting on someone. The motivation behind tattling and ratting is usually to get someone in trouble. The motivation behind reporting is to help someone who is in trouble. After a period of time, you should see an initial increase in reports of bullying from the students and parents because they trust that you will handle bullying appropriately. When this happens, you have created a "telling environment." However, after the Bully Free Program has been in operation for a while, both student and parent reports of bullying situations should decrease because bullying has decreased. There may also be a decrease in reports if the school has not handled the reports appropriately.

Program Impact Evaluation Strategies

Other impact evaluation strategies allow comparison of pre- and postprogram implementation data comparisons to determine the impact of the program. Strategies for making such comparison are the use of surveys and the examination of existing data.

Bully Free Surveys

Do not develop your own surveys unless you can determine their validity and reliability. *Validity* refers to the appropriateness of the content, which is determined by experts in the field. You want to make sure you are measuring bullying and not something else. *Reliability* refers to the dependability or consistency of the surveys. If you give a survey and administer it again the next week, you should get much of the same results.

Bully Free Systems LLC offers five valid and reliable surveys: Bully Free Survey (for Preschool to Grade 2), Bully Free Survey (for Elementary Students, Grades 3 to 6), Bully Free Survey (for Middle and High School Students, Grades 6 to 12), Bully Free Survey (for School Personnel), and Bully Free Survey (for Parents). If you plan to have Bully Free Systems LLC analyze the data and write a report, changes in the survey must not be made, including renumbering of the survey items, and no other items may be added. Those completing the surveys should be told to skip items that are not relevant for their school. Changes in the surveys require changes in the software used by Bully Free Systems LLC to analyze the data. Therefore, if changes are made in the surveys, additional fees may be assessed.

The survey for elementary students can be used with students in grades 3 to 6 because some elementary schools include grade 6. If your school is a middle school, you should use the survey for middle school (grades 6 to 8). Some schools have used the elementary survey with younger students by reading the items to them. All the surveys are available in Appendix C and may be copied. They are also available at www.bullyfree.com and may be printed and copied. Most schools administer the student survey and the faculty survey, but only a few administer the parent survey. Bubble or scan sheets can be ordered and purchased from Pearson NCS (1-800-347-7704 or 1-800-367-6627, www.pearsonncs.com; the form number for all the surveys is 16504). Of course, bubble sheets are not needed for the survey for students in preschool to second grade. You can administer the surveys, analyze the data, and write a report yourself, or, for a fee, Bully Free Systems LLC will analyze the data and generate a report with charts and graphs. (For more information, contact Bully Free Systems LLC at www.bullyfree.com.)

It is important that those who are completing a survey understand the definition of bullying. Therefore, the survey instructions include a definition. Make sure that the survey administrators read the instructions aloud to younger students. Older students and adults can read the instructions themselves.

When you are making copies of the student surveys, also make copies of the instructions at the front of the surveys (see Appendix C), and give one to each person administering the surveys.

The surveys assess the following areas:

- What bullying looks like and how often it occurs at school
- Where students are bullied in school

- Where students are bullied outside school
- Bullying on buses
- Bullying while walking to and from school
- Who is doing the bullying (one or more students)
- Bystanders' involvement
- How students feel about their safety
- Reporting bullying
- Friends at school
- Adults as models and helpers
- Rules and instruction
- How long bullying has occurred
- How long students have dealt with bullying

Tips for Administering Surveys

It is best to administer the surveys during a time that school life is "normal." Therefore, try to avoid administering them right before or after a break or vacation or during a week when testing is going on. It is also best to administer the pretest and posttest at the same time of year (for example, both in April). Therefore, it is usually not a good idea to administer the pretest in the fall and the posttest in the spring. Another reason to avoid this schedule is that results may be inaccurate. Unfortunately, bullying sometimes increases right before the school year ends. It's as if the bullies want to get one more shot in because they know they will soon be out of school. It is also best not to administer the surveys too early in the school year, when students are on their best behavior. Bullies usually spend the first seven or eight weeks of school looking for easy targets.

Whatever surveys are used, it is important to use the same ones to assess preprogram and postprogram conditions. After the surveys are selected, a plan for administering them, collecting the data, analyzing the data, and reporting the data should be developed.

Cover Letter

A letter could be sent home to parents informing them that the Bully Free Survey will be administered to students at school. The letter should communicate the desire of the school to prevent and stop bullying. Parents are asked to encourage their child to be honest in completing the survey. The letter should also ask the parents to complete and return an attached Bully Free Survey (for Parents).

It is important that parents understand that the surveys are not being administered as a panic response. Their school is not the "bullying capital of the world." The letter should communicate that the school wants to create a caring, peaceful, and safe environment where students can learn and feel that they belong. They should be told that the surveys are anonymously completed at school. The letter should also ask for the support of parents to prevent and stop bullying in the school.

The following example of a letter also appears in the files at www.bullyfree.com.

Sample Cover Letter to Parents

XYZ SCHOOL
Anywhere, USA

Date
Dear Parents/Guardians:

We at _____ [insert school's name] wanted to drop you a note to let you know that we, like you, want all students to have a positive and successful school experience. After all, school is a big part of their lives. We are committed to providing a caring, peaceful, and safe school environment and want all students to have a sense of belonging and to feel accepted at our school. Thanks to the support of parents like you, we can make great strides in this area.

Unfortunately, not all schools in the United States have such positive school environments. Recently you probably have seen a lot on television and in newspapers about bullying. Bullying is persistent mistreatment that can be physical (hitting, tripping, pinching), verbal (name-calling, spreading lies about someone, hurtful teasing), or social (rejection). Sometimes students use technology (cyberbullying) to hurt others. One of our goals is to prevent and stop bullying. Therefore, this year, we will be developing and implementing a Bully Free Program. This is a program that is being used in the United States, and some of its materials are used in several countries. The program teaches students to treat others the way they want to be treated.

To make sure we can make a difference at our school, we need to collect information to determine to what extent bullying exists at our school. Therefore, in the next few weeks, we will be asking students to complete a questionnaire. Since some students are reluctant to tell adults about bullying, please encourage your child to be honest and open when filling out the questionnaire. We will not ask for names on the questionnaires.

We would also like to ask you to complete the attached survey and return it to us within the next two days. Thank you for your cooperation.

We look forward to working with you and your child to make _____ [insert school's name] Bully Free.

Sincerely,

A brief summary of the findings of the surveys should be shared with all stakeholders, including students. In Appendix C, "Interpreting the Survey Data," following the section Instructions for the Teacher (Bully Free Surveys for Students in Grades 3 to 12) will help you interpret the findings of some of the items.

Examining Existing Data

The Bully Free Program team should ask the program evaluation coordinator to make sure someone examines and records data relative to the following areas:

- Parent reports of aggressive occurrences
- Student reports of aggressive occurrences
- Suspensions resulting from aggression or bullying
- Number of reported fights
- Number of detentions resulting from aggression or bullying
- Expulsions resulting from aggression or bullying
- School attendance
- Reported discipline problems
- Academic performance of school

This is only a sampling of existing data areas. The Bully Free Program team should discuss other areas and data to examine. For example, the school may already collect school safety data, and bullying may be an area assessed to some extent. The same areas should be examined again after the program has been implemented for a few months, as indicated in Step 18.

Task Checklist, Step 5

Develop a Program Evaluation Plan and Determine the Status of Bullying in the School

Design a Plan to Conduct Focus Meetings and Record Notes

☐ Decide how and when the faculty and staff, student, and parent focus meetings will be conducted throughout the year and the questions to be asked.

Design the Pre- and Postprogram Evaluation Plan and Collect Baseline Data

☐ Ask someone to coordinate the evaluation effort. This person will be the Bully Free Program evaluation coordinator and work with the Bully Free Program team to design the evaluation plan.

☐ Identify the desired baseline data to be collected.

- ○ When and where students are bullied
- ○ Percentage of students bullied
- ○ Percentage of victimized students who would report bullying to an adult
- ○ Attendance data
- ○ Suspensions resulting from aggressive acts or bullying
- ○ Number of reported fights
- ○ Expulsions resulting from aggressive acts or bullying
- ○ Discipline problems relative to aggression or bullying
- ○ Other: _____
- ○ Other: _____

☐ Identify the sources of existing data and record the data.

- ○ Attendance records
- ○ Number of detentions
- ○ Suspension records
- ○ Expulsion records
- ○ Discipline records
- ○ Number of fights
- ○ Number of student reports of mistreatment
- ○ Other: _____
- ○ Other: _____

Task Checklist, Step 5, Cont'd.   Notes

- ○ Number of parent reports of bullying
- ○ Other: _____

☐ Identify the strategies for collecting, analyzing, and reporting the data.

- ○ Whom do you want to collect information from?
  - • School personnel
  - • Students
  - • Parents
- ○ Will you collect information from all of the individuals in targeted groups or a random sampling?
- ○ Examine, select, or develop surveys to collect baseline data.
- ○ Who will administer the surveys or questionnaires?
- ○ When will the data be collected?
- ○ Who will analyze and summarize the data?
- ○ When will the data be reported, and to whom?

☐ Inform the teachers that they will administer the surveys.

☐ Determine who will make copies of the surveys and distribute them.

☐ Determine who will make copies of the instructions and distribute them to adults administering the student surveys.

☐ Determine who will order the bubble sheets and distribute them.

☐ Determine all of the costs and what accounts will be used. Request and secure the funds.

☐ Make sure all the survey materials have been copied and distributed.

☐ Administer the selected surveys.

☐ _____
_____

☐ _____
_____

☐ _____
_____

Step 6

Develop the Bully Free Program Mission Statement, Objectives, Slogan, and Logo

By this time, the Bully Free Program team will have learned much about bullying and have determined the extent of bullying in the school. They should also have a clear picture of the safe and peaceful school they wish to create. The next step is to develop a bully free mission statement, objectives, slogan, and logo.

Develop the Bully Free Mission Statement

Discussing the following questions will help the team develop the mission statement:

- What would a bully free school look like?
- What must happen for us to have a bully free school?
- What behaviors promote a bully free school?
- What would students do in a bully free school?
- What would school personnel do in a bully free school?
- What would parents do in a bully free school?

The mission statement should be simple and easy to remember and be consistent with the school system's and school's mission, as well as the student code of conduct. There may be a need to revise the school's code of conduct by adding terminology relative to bullying to make it consistent with the mission statement.

The mission statement should communicate to everyone that there is agreement that bullying must be prevented and stopped. It should also help energize people to live out the values that statement communicates. Because bullying is a community problem, not just a school problem, the mission statement could include a statement regarding the community. The Bully Free Program team should develop a rough draft of the mission statement and seek feedback from school personnel, students, and parents before adopting the final statement. They should incorporate all of the appropriate feedback into it and get official approval of the final statement.

Once the bully free mission statement has been approved, it should be posted in a visible location in the school. The following examples of statements may help the team develop its own (these examples also appear in the files located at www.bullyfree.com).

Examples of Bully Free Mission Statements

"Our community and school provide peaceable and caring environments in which students and adults feel psychologically, emotionally, and physically safe. All adults and students model the importance of discipline and responsibility, self-control, kindness, encouragement, empathy, acceptance of differences, support, sensitivity, and respect. Each person strives to promote a sense of belonging and acceptance in others and strives to treat others the way he or she wants to be treated."

"Our school is a place where everyone feels safe and accepted and has a sense of belonging. Bullying will not be tolerated. School personnel, students, parents, and the community will seek to prevent and stop all forms of bullying by being active participants in the Bully Free Program."

Once the statement has been approved, it should be reviewed and communicated frequently. It can be placed on poster boards, on bulletin boards, and in various school publications. The Bully Free Program team, with the principal and other school officials, should determine how and when the mission statement should be communicated and reviewed or revisited throughout each school year.

Develop the Bully Free Program Objectives

The goals of the Bully Free Program have already been established. They are:

- To send a clear message to students, staff, parents, and community members that bullying will not be tolerated.

- To train staff and students and to provide information to parents relative to taking steps to preventing and stopping bullying.

- To establish and enforce rules and policies focusing on bullying.

- To reduce existing bullying situations through administrative and teacher-centered strategies and a comprehensive scope and sequence of age-appropriate lesson plans for each grade level.

- To create safer and more peaceful schools.

- To promote a sense of belonging and acceptance in all students so that they feel connected to their school.

- To involve and empower students as bystanders to prevent and stop bullying.

- To involve parents in the program.

- To involve the community in the program.

- To create a school culture where adults are warm, positive, and trustworthy role models and are viewed as authorities. Adults are clear authorities but caring and respectful in the way they treat students and other adults. These values are communicated verbally and nonverbally.

- To significantly improve adult supervision on school property, especially in high-risk areas.

- To restructure the school culture and social environment in a way that adults and students take action and expect immediate intervention, investigation, and confrontation of students engaged in bullying behavior.

- To implement nonphysical and nonhostile strategies for changing the behavior of students engaged in bullying and follow through with disciplinary actions if the bullying behavior persists.

- To provide intervention for children who are bullied and who bully.

Next the team should develop the Bully Free Program objectives, which measure progress in reaching the listed goals. The objectives should be based on baseline data collected in Step 5 and other information deemed appropriate by the Bully Free Program team.

The Bully Free Program team should examine existing data, such as school attendance data, number of detentions, number of suspensions, number of fights, and so on, and determine what improvements they would like to see in the data. The team chair should capture their thoughts on a flip chart. For example, perhaps the team would like to see the number of detentions reduced by half and school attendance increased. These thoughts should be systematically discussed by the team. Once agreement has been reached regarding the desired program impact, a draft version of the bully free objectives should be written specifying the desired improvements in the data and other information. Therefore, examine the items on the surveys you administered and use the items of concern to develop your objectives.

Following are a few examples of Bully Free Program objectives. Note that many of them correlate with some of the items on the surveys. These are only examples; you will need to develop your own. You may have more or you may have fewer, depending on the data you have collected. The blanks should be filled with actual dates and percentages when these have been determined by the team. These examples also appear in the files located at www.bullyfree.com.

The first draft of the objectives could be presented and discussed at parent meetings, faculty and staff meetings, student council meetings, and a principal's meeting to determine if they are realistic. Take notes regarding everyone's feedback.

Incorporate all the appropriate feedback from the stakeholders into the design and content of the final draft of the bully free objectives. The Bully Free Program team should

Examples of Bully Free Program Objectives

- By _____, 20__, the number of students who say they have been pinched, kicked, tripped, pushed, elbowed, touched, or grabbed in a hurtful or embarrassing way will be reduced from _____ to _____.

- By _____, 20__, the number of students who say they have been called names, teased, made fun of for the way they look or dress, or put down in a hurtful way will be reduced from _____ to _____.

- By _____, 20__, the number of students who say they are bullied in the bathroom will be reduced from _____ to _____.

- By _____, 20__, the number of students who say if they heard or saw someone bullied they would tell an adult will increase from _____ to _____.

- By _____, 20__, there will be a reduction in suspensions as a result of aggressive behavior or bullying from _____ students to _____ students.

- By _____, 20__, school attendance will increase by _____ percent.

- By _____, 20__, there will be a _____ percent increase in academic performance in selected test scores.

- By _____, 20__, the number of students who say they feel safe at school will increase from _____ to _____.

- By _____, 20__, the number of students who say they are ignored, rejected, or lied about, or who have had rumors told about them or had hurtful and mean notes written about them will decrease from _____ to _____.

- By _____, 20__, the number of students who say they are bullied in the hall will decrease from _____ to _____.

- By _____, 20__, the number of students who say that most students try to help other students who are bullied will increase from _____ to _____.

- By _____, 20__, the number of students who say there are some adults at school who bully students will decrease from _____ to _____.

- By _____, 20__, the number of students who feel afraid because they are bullied will decrease from _____ to _____.

- By _____, 20__, the number of students who say they are able to make friends at school will increase from _____ to _____.

- By _____, 20__, the number of students who say they are bullied on the bus going to school will decrease from _____ to _____.

review the feedback of all stakeholders and make changes in the objectives as deemed appropriate. The team then needs to reach consensus on the final objectives.

Seek official approval of the objectives. If necessary, ask the principal and other appropriate school officials to approve them. If you wish, type their names on the sheet listing the objectives, and ask the appropriate individuals to sign on an approval line.

Develop the Bully Free Program Slogan

Next, the Bully Free Program team should develop a slogan: a simple, easy-to-remember, catchy phrase. Here is how to go about it:

- *Work with the team to determine what the slogan should communicate.* For example, you want the slogan to communicate a desire to have a peaceful and safe school where everyone has a sense of belonging. You want it to communicate that everyone has a responsibility in creating and maintaining a bully free school.

- *Develop a draft of the slogan.* Examine with the team what you wish the slogan to communicate, and brainstorm several possibilities. Write all suggestions on a flip chart. Then examine each suggestion, and reach consensus on the best. You may combine two suggestions to develop one slogan.

- *Seek comments on the draft from a sampling of the stakeholders (students, teachers, staff, parents, and volunteers).* The first draft of the slogan may be presented and discussed at parent meetings, faculty and staff meetings, student council meetings, and a principal's meeting to determine its desirability. Keep notes on everyone's comments.

- *Incorporate all of the appropriate feedback in the design and content of the final draft of the slogan.* The Bully Free Program team should review the feedback of all stakeholders and make changes in the slogan as appropriate.

- *Seek official approval of the slogan, post it in a visible location, and duplicate it on banners, bulletin boards, posters, and T-shirts.* If necessary, ask the principal and other appropriate school officials to approve the slogan. If you wish, type their names on a sheet with the slogan, and ask the appropriate individuals to sign on an approval line.

If you wish, a flag or banner can be developed with graphics and the slogan written on it. Examples of slogans appear here. These examples also appear in the files located at www.bullyfree.com.

Develop the Bully Free Logo

The Bully Free Program team needs to determine if it wants the school system or school to have a bully free logo. Logos are often used on banners and T-shirts and remind students and others to help their school be bully free.

Examples of Slogans

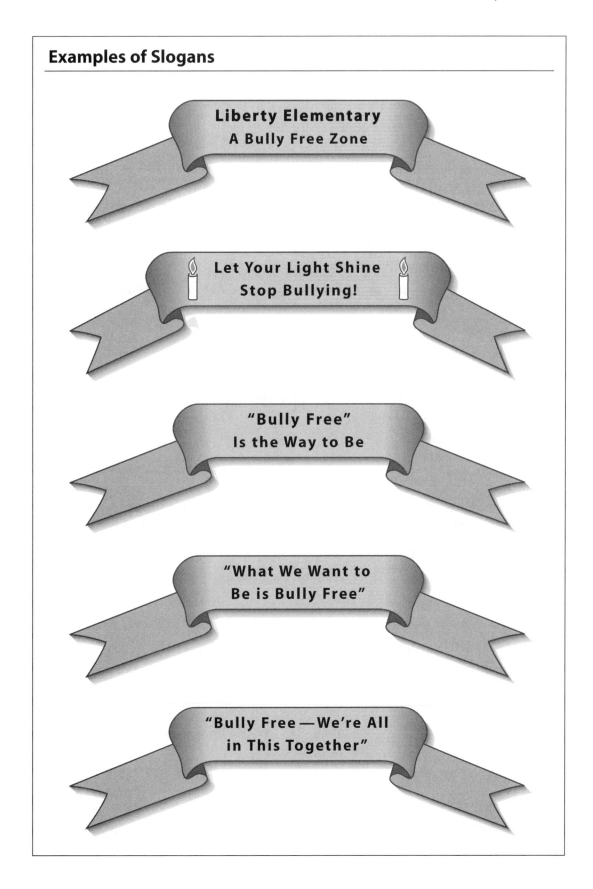

If a logo is desired, the team needs to decide what the logo will communicate and how it will be developed. Two possibilities are to ask a volunteer to develop the logo or hire someone who has expertise in that area. Another is to have a logo contest for students. Kutztown Elementary School in Kutztown, Pennsylvania, conducted such a contest and disseminated the following guidelines.

Anti-bullying Logo Contest

As part of our "anti-bullying program," we invite Kutztown Elementary students in grades K–5 to participate in a logo design contest. The guidelines are as follows:

- The contest will run from January 2 – January 11.
- Logos must be designed (by hand) on the official entry form. Computer-generated designs will not be accepted.
- Drawings must be done in lightly drawn pencil.
- Colored pencil or crayons must be used to color in desired areas.
- The logo must contain the words "Kutztown Cougars."
- Completed logo entries must be submitted to Mrs. Miller in the main office by 3:00 PM on January 11.
- The student's full name, grade level, and teacher's name are to be printed neatly on the back of the poster.
- Only one entry per artist will be accepted.

The winning logo will be used as the official anti-bullying poster for Kutztown Elementary School. It will be displayed in our building as well as in participating businesses in the community.

Good luck, everyone!

Source: Used with permission from Kutztown Elementary School, Kutztown, Pennsylvania.

If the team decides to develop the logo, ask someone to search for examples of anti-bullying logos on the Internet. You can trigger your creativity by examining pictures, words, and logos found on Web sites about bullying. These words and images will help you develop a design. If you wish to use the official Bully Free Program logo, contact Bully Free Systems LLC for permission (for contact information, visit www.bullyfree.com).

Here are some guidelines for developing a logo:

• *Work with the team to determine what the logo should communicate.* You want the logo to communicate a desire to have a peaceful and safe school where everyone has a sense of belonging. You also want it to communicate that everyone has a responsibility in creating and maintaining a bully free school.

- *Develop a draft of the logo.* Examine with the team what you want the logo to communicate, and brainstorm several possible logos. Write all suggestions on a flip chart. Then examine each one and reach consensus on the choice. You may combine two or more suggestions to develop one logo.

- *Seek comments on the draft from a sampling of the stakeholders (students, teachers, staff, volunteers).* The first draft of the logo may be presented and discussed at parent meetings, faculty and staff meetings, student council meetings, and at principal's meetings to determine its desirability. Keep notes regarding everyone's comments.

- *Incorporate all of the appropriate feedback into the design and content of the final draft of the logo.* The Bully Free Program team should review the comments of all stakeholders and make changes in the logo as deemed appropriate.

- *Seek official approval of the logo, and use it on banners, T-shirts, and other places.* If necessary, ask the principal and other appropriate school officials to approve the logo. If you wish, type their names on a sheet with the logo, and ask the appropriate individuals to sign on an approval line.

Task Checklist, Step 6

Develop the Bully Free Mission Statement, Objectives, Slogan, and Logo

Bully Free Mission Statement

☐ Examine the example Bully Free Program mission statements.

☐ Search for other such mission statements on the Internet.

☐ Discuss the following questions:

  ○ What would a bully free school look like?

  ○ What must happen for us to have a bully free school?

  ○ What behaviors promote a bully free school?

  ○ What would students do in a bully free school?

  ○ What would school personnel do in a bully free school?

  ○ What would parents do in a bully free school?

☐ Draft the first version of the mission statement.

☐ Seek comments on the draft from a sampling of the stakeholders (students, teachers, staff, volunteers, key community representatives).

☐ Incorporate all of the appropriate comments into the design and content of the final draft of the mission statement.

☐ Seek official approval of the mission statement.

Bully Free Objectives

☐ Examine the examples of Bully Free Program objectives.

☐ Draft the first version of the Bully Free Program objectives.

☐ Seek comments on the Bully Free Program objectives from a sampling of the stakeholders (students, teachers, staff, volunteers, key community representatives).

☐ Incorporate all of the appropriate feedback into the design and content of the final draft of the Bully Free Program objectives.

☐ Seek official approval of the objectives.

Task Checklist, Step 6, Cont'd.   Notes

Bully Free Slogan

☐ Examine the examples of bully free slogans.

☐ Determine what the slogan should communicate:

    ○ _____

    ○ _____

    ○ _____

    ○ _____

☐ Seek comments on the draft from a sampling of the stakeholders (students, teachers, staff, and volunteers).

☐ Incorporate all of the appropriate feedback into the design and content of the final draft of the slogan.

☐ Seek official approval of the slogan and use it on banners, posters, and T-shirts.

Bully Free Logo

☐ Determine how the bully free logo will be developed.

    ○ Conduct a logo contest.

    ○ Hire someone to develop the logo or seek a skilled volunteer to develop it.

☐ Search for examples of anti-bullying logos on the Internet.

☐ Determine what the logo should communicate.

    ○ _____

    ○ _____

    ○ _____

☐ Obtain a draft of the first version of the logo.

☐ Seek comments on the draft from a sampling of the stakeholders (students, teachers, staff, volunteers).

☐ Incorporate all of the appropriate feedback into the design and content of the final draft of logo.

☐ Seek official approval of the logo, and use it on banners, posters, and T-shirts.

(continued on next page)

Task Checklist, Step 6, Cont'd.   Notes

Other Tasks

☐ Determine the visible locations to post the mission statement, slogan, and logo in every school. All three could appear on the same document.

☐ Determine the cost of framing the mission statement, slogan, and logo and posting them.

☐ Determine the accounts to be used to pay for framing and posting the mission statement, slogan, and logo. Obtain permission to spend the funds.

☐ Devise strategies for sharing and discussing the bully free mission statement, slogan, and logo with students, parents, school personnel, volunteers, and the community. These will be shared at the program's kickoff meeting discussed later in this book.

☐ Post the bully free mission statement, slogan, and logo in the approved visible locations in every school.

☐ At the appropriate time, share and communicate the bully free mission statement, slogan, and logo with students, parents, school personnel, volunteers, and the community.

☐ _____
   _____

☐ _____
   _____

☐ _____
   _____

☐ _____
   _____

☐ _____
   _____

☐ _____
   _____

☐ _____
   _____

Step 7

Implement a Bully Free Curriculum

This step encompasses the implementation of anti-bullying lesson plans, materials, and resources. Effective anti-bullying programs are more than special events (such as assembly programs, Bully Free Week, or presentations for parents and the community). They include a curriculum that helps the school make its anti-bullying program a consistent and systematic way of life in the school.

Bullying is a heart problem, so this kind of effort is extremely important. Therefore, the program should go beyond the "big things" that you do to make a difference and include the "little things" that you can do and say each day to shape the hearts and minds of students. It is not enough to respond to bullying events with problem-solving meetings with students; you must also implement a curriculum that promotes a sense of belonging and acceptance in all students. It is not enough to teach peer mediation and conflict resolution; in fact, these tactics are not usually effective with true aggressive bullies. It is also not enough to teach anger management. There must be a curriculum that prevents what causes the anger. You must seek to prevent interactions that cause anger and conflict. The curriculum should also equip students with the knowledge, skills, and abilities to prevent them from becoming victims and empower them to stop bullying when they are victims or bystanders. And, of course, the curriculum should include elements that lead bullies to change their behavior.

An effective anti-bullying program has a framework, lesson plans, and materials and resources. Such resources are becoming more readily available. For example, the Bully Free Program (www.bullyfree.com) includes age-appropriate kits of materials and resources with lesson plans; books for teachers, counselors, students, and parents; posters, pamphlets; bracelets; and more for every grade level. Each teacher and counselor will need a kit. There is even a school support materials kit that includes books, posters, and PDF files that can be placed on your school's Web site and accessed by teachers, counselors, students, and parents in your school district. You also have permission to print as many copies of these files as you wish. If you wish to implement the Bully Free Program, you should secure these kits of materials and resources (visit www.bullyfree.com).

Lesson Plans

One of the greatest needs of teachers is information-packed, age-appropriate lesson plans that have been tested by other teachers. More and more lesson plans are being made available. For example, the Bully Free Program offers fifteen- to twenty-minute lesson plans for every grade level—preschool, elementary, middle, and high school—and organized in a powerful scope and sequence by grade level. Your school will not have to determine what should be taught at each level. That decision has already been made by experts in bullying and practicing teachers and counselors when the lessons were developed and tested. Some schools have required one lesson each week while others have required two to three lessons each week.

Integration of anti-bullying curriculum in high schools has been a challenge. Some schools have integrated lesson plans into health class or other courses that all students take, such as a teen issues class. This is the least preferred and less effective approach, however. The best approach is to require every teacher to discuss bullying at least once a week during advisor-advisee time. When this approach is used, every teacher is given a set of Bully Free Program lesson plans that extend over fifteen to twenty minutes. Some high schools that require every teacher to spend at least one hour a week on character education have decided to use that time to address bullying.

Classroom Meetings

Classroom meetings are effective in reducing and even preventing bullying, and they also teach students skills such as active listening, problem solving, giving and accepting compliments, negotiation and compromise, respect for different opinions, taking turns, and patience. Such meetings can also be used to reinforce and maintain concepts learned through the Bully Free Program lesson plans. Although review is built into the lesson plans, reviewing this material in classroom meetings can prevent the common practice of covering material and then moving on to new topics. Following is an example of a classroom meeting schedule designed to review topics discussed in the fifth-grade Bully Free Program lesson plans. Only a sampling of the topics is listed in this example.

The classroom meetings include all the students in a class and should be a routine activity. Anti-bullying content from the lesson plans can be reviewed, taught, and discussed during the meetings. Also, the meetings can be used to discuss and seek solutions to certain types of bullying situations. However, the teacher should never discuss a specific bullying situation where the names of victims and bullies are known by the students. When used in elementary and middle schools, the meetings can focus more often on problem solving. When used in high school, they often focus more on reviewing the lesson plans.

When teachers are provided training in using the lesson plans, materials, and resources, they should also be taught how to conduct classroom meetings. The following list of guidelines makes an excellent handout for teachers to discuss at a faculty meeting or during an anti-bullying workshop. (The list is available in a Microsoft Word file located at www.bullyfree.com.)

Schedule for Reviewing Fifth-Grade Bully Free Program Lesson Plans

Teacher: _____

	Lesson Plan Title	Date to Review	Check When Reviewed
Lesson 1	Are We a Welcoming Class?		
Lesson 2	My Favorite Things		
Lesson 3	Create a Class Directory or Scrapbook		
Lesson 4	What Is Bullying?		
Lesson 5	What Does Physical Bullying Look Like?		
Lesson 6	Is Hitting Ever Okay?		
Lesson 7	What Does Verbal Bullying Look Like?		
Lesson 8	Guarding Your Tongue		
Lesson 9	How to Give Compliments		
Lesson 10	Examples of Compliments		
Lesson 11	Practice Giving Compliments		
Lesson 12	How to Accept a Compliment		
Lesson 13	Practice Giving and Receiving Compliments		
Lesson 14	What Does Social Bullying Look Like?		
Lesson 15	What Are Some Myths and Facts About Bullying?		
Lesson 16	Stopping the Bully Machine		
Lesson 17	What Are a Bully Free Classroom and School?		
Lesson 18	What Bully Free Rules Should We Have?		
Lesson 19	What Is a Bully Free Pledge That We Should Sign?		
Lesson 20	Notes-to-the-Teacher Box		
Lesson 21	What Does It Feel Like to Be Bullied?		
Lesson 22	Why Are Some Students Bullies?		
Lesson 23	When and Where Does Bullying Occur in Our School?		
Lesson 24	Behavioral Expectations While Walking to and from School		
Lesson 25	Behavioral Expectations on the Bus		
Lesson 26	Behavioral Expectations in the School's Parking Lot		
Lesson 27	Behavioral Expectations in Front of, Behind, or Between Buildings Before and After School		
Lesson 28	Behavioral Expectations in the Bike Parking Area		
Lesson 29	Behavioral Expectations When Arriving at School, Entering School, and Waiting for School to Start		
Lesson 30	Behavioral Expectations in the Hallways		
Lesson 31	Behavioral Expectations in the Stairwells		
Lesson 32	Behavioral Expectations in the Locker Rooms		
Lesson 33	Behavioral Expectations in the Classroom		

General Guidelines for Conducting Classroom Meetings

- Meetings in kindergarten and first grade typically last fifteen minutes. The amount of time allowed for grades 2 to 4 is fifteen to thirty minutes. Classroom meetings for middle school and high school students may last as long as twenty to forty-five minutes. Teachers can determine the length of the meetings, their frequency, and the best days (once a week) to conduct the meetings.

- During the first meeting, establish ground rules—for example:
  - We raise our hands to get permission to speak.
  - We listen to the person speaking and do not interrupt.
  - We understand that not everyone has to speak.
  - We do not mention names of individuals unless the teacher says it is okay.
  - We do not hurt the feelings of others.

- Time may be used to get to know each other better and plan certain projects.

- Begin by telling students the purpose of the meeting.

- Allocate time to discuss the content of the anti-bullying lesson plans or solve certain types of relational problems. Usually no names are mentioned.

- Time may be allocated for role playing.

- Elementary and middle school students can suggest topics for the meetings by placing their ideas in a suggestion box or a notebook you provide for that purpose.

- Ask elementary and middle school students to sit in a U-shape facing you. This will encourage them to look at you and not each other.

- As students sit down, note good behavior by complimenting the students. Be specific in your praise.

- Encourage discussion by asking open-ended questions. Never ask students to answer a question for which you feel they may not know the answer. In other words, do not embarrass them.

- When appropriate, review major points and concepts halfway through the meeting.

- Ask students to raise their hand if they wish to answer a question.

- When possible, make up an activity or game that uses the content of the Bully Free Program lesson plans. All the students are to be on the same team, not competing with each other. Only call on students who raise their hand.

- Always conduct a review at the end of each meeting.

In addition to reviewing the concepts learned through the selected lesson plans, classroom meetings can be used to explore solutions to bullying situations. When discussing a bullying situation, teachers and students should never mention the names of the involved students. Caution should also be used in presenting a situation where the victim and bully are known by students. The teacher may make up a situation or describe a situation he or she has observed somewhere other than his or her classroom.

The following guidelines (also available at www.bullyfree.com) will help teachers conduct meetings that focus on bullying situations. This list also makes an excellent handout to discuss at a faculty meeting or at an anti-bullying workshop designed to prepare teachers for using the lesson plans, materials, and resources and for conducting classroom meetings.

Guidelines for Conducting Classroom Meetings
Focusing on a Bullying Situation

- Introduce the purpose of the meeting: focusing on solutions to a specific bullying situation (without mentioning names). Also avoid using situations in which students know the involved students. State what the students will learn from the meeting.

- Explain the ground rules for the meeting.

- Describe the bullying situation you have made up. It could be behavior you have observed in the hallway, in the cafeteria, or on the playground. The situation should not involve students in your classroom.

- Let students ask you questions about the situation to clarify information. For example, they may ask you if the bully was bigger and older than the other student or if the mistreated student did something he or she shouldn't have done.

- Help students examine the details of the situation, and review the facts with them.

- Encourage the exploration of different perspectives—those of the victims and the bullies.

- Encourage discussion by asking open-ended questions that will help them develop sensitivity and empathy, and encourage them to treat others the way they would want to be treated. Never ask students to answer a question for which you feel they may not know the answer. In other words, do not embarrass them.

- Help students explore possible solutions and ask them to select and rank the top three or four preferred solutions.

- When appropriate, review major points and concepts halfway through the meeting.

- When possible, use role playing.

- At the end of the lesson, review major points and decisions made during the meeting.

Bulletin Boards, Posters, and Banners

Bulletin boards, posters, and banners can serve as reminders of your school's commitment to be bully free. They can also help change the culture of your school and serve as safety cues (visible things that make students feel safer). Therefore, the team should identify or ask a group of teachers and counselors to identify any anti-bullying bulletin boards, posters, and banners they would like to post in the high-risk areas (bathrooms, hallways, stairs, locker room, cafeteria, gym) of the school. Those not selected could be displayed in the classrooms, the main office, and the counselor's office. Some bulletin boards and posters have even been displayed in the community at the YMCA, doctors' offices, and other places.

Many are available. For example, the Bully Free Program includes *Bully Free Bulletin Boards, Posters, and Banners* (Beane & Beane, 2005) and *Bully Free Bulletin Boards, Posters, and Banners for High School* (Beane & Beane, 2003).

Because student and parent involvement in the program is critical, some schools have asked them to develop the bulletin boards, posters, and banners. Even if you choose this as your strategy, make sure teachers and counselors discuss their content with students.

To prevent redundancy, the team or others may want to develop a schedule for displaying these different materials. The schedule should include the dates that this material is to be displayed; the name of the board, poster, or banner; and where they should be displayed. The following blank schedule form can be used for this purpose. (It is provided as a Microsoft Word file located at www.bullyfree.com.)

Training for School Personnel

The next task is to train teachers to use the lesson plans and related materials and resources as well as conduct classroom meetings. The workshop should be designed so that teachers and their aides have time to examine the lesson plans and materials and make plans for their use.

If the classroom meetings approach is desired for elementary and middle school teachers, discuss how long the meetings should occur and which day of the week they should occur at each grade level. Distribute and discuss both sets of guidelines for conducting classroom meetings, which were set out previously in this chapter. These guidelines can be copied from this book or downloaded at www.bullyfree.com.

Give teachers the materials and resources they need to implement the curriculum, such as the Bully Free Program kits. A list of the materials and resources included in the kits can be found at www.bullyfree.com.

At the workshop, quickly review and discuss some of the bulletin boards, posters, and banners, such as those presented in *Bully Free Bulletin Boards, Posters, and Banners* (Beane & Beane, 2005) or *Bully Free Bulletin Boards, Posters, and Banners for High School* (Beane & Beane, 2003). If the schedule for the display of these was developed, give them a copy.

Bulletin Boards, Posters, and Banners Schedule

Check one: ___ Elementary   ___ Middle School   ___ High School

Dates to Be Displayed	Selected Bulletin Boards, Posters, and Banners	Location to Be Posted

Ask teachers to develop and discuss the other bulletin boards, posters, and banners in their classrooms. Also encourage them to involve students and parents in developing these. Ask teachers to post a bully free classroom poster on a wall in their classrooms. The poster is included in their Bully Free Program materials kit.

Ask the workshop participants to examine the lesson plans for their grade level. Discuss the importance of maintaining a record of the lesson plans used. A record-keeping chart is provided in the Bully Free Program lesson plan books. Indicate that there will be a random checking of the charts to ensure ongoing implementation of the lesson plans. This can be accomplished by asking teachers to make a copy of their charts and turn them in to the main office every three weeks or so.

Task Checklist, Step 7

Notes

Implement a Bully Free Curriculum

☐ Determine the materials and resources needed at each level: preschool, K–8, and high school (see kits at www.bullyfree.com). There are kits for teachers and for counselors and psychologists, and a support kit for each school. See the order form located at www.bullyfree.com.

☐ Determine which accounts will be used to purchase the materials and resources. Request and secure the funds.

☐ Purchase the materials and resources.

☐ Determine how classroom meetings will be used.

    ○ Determine the grade level and frequency of the meetings.

    ○ Determine if the school should establish a consistent day and time for classroom meetings. If so, specify the day and time for each grade level.

    ○ Determine the length of the meetings: _____.

☐ If desired, ask team members or a group of teachers to use *Bully Free Bulletin Boards, Posters, and Banners* (Beane & Beane, 2005) or *Bully Free Bulletin Boards, Posters, and Banners for High School* (Beane & Beane, 2003) and develop a schedule of when and where the bulletin boards, posters, and banners will be posted in the school.

☐ Provide training for school personnel so they can implement the curriculum. At the training, give everyone a copy of the grade-level-appropriate Bully Free Program kit (lesson plans, materials, and resources).

☐ _____

    _____

☐ _____

    _____

☐ _____

    _____

☐ _____

    _____

Step 8

Develop and Implement the Bully Free Program Administrative Strategies Plan and Policies

The administrative leadership's demonstration of an ongoing commitment to the Bully Free Program and desire to maintain the program momentum is critical to achieving positive schoolwide results. For a program to be successfully implemented, there must be effective leadership and collaboration to combat bullying and develop safe and caring environments for students. It is the responsibility of the administration to provide that leadership, support, and encouragement.

Physical and emotional safety require first and foremost a peaceful atmosphere in which students feel secure, comfortable, and happy. Therefore, the school's climate, opportunities, policies, and procedures must be examined, improved, and constantly monitored to ensure the safety of students and their sense of acceptance and belonging. This requires the commitment of the leadership. The school system's leadership can communicate this commitment by using the following strategies. If the principal or assistant principal is not on the Bully Free Program team, the chair of the team should discuss these with him or her.

Leadership Strategies for Demonstrating Commitment to Preventing and Stopping Bullying

- Attending some of the Bully Free Program team meetings

- Offering assistance and resources

- Sharing anti-bullying information found on the Internet and obtained at conferences

- Providing supportive training for faculty, staff, and volunteers

- Providing flexible scheduling for personnel and students when required

- Including bullying on the agenda of all faculty and staff meetings

- Demonstrating awareness of bullying data relative to the school system and school

- Acting as a role model by treating others (faculty, staff, parents, and students) the way he or she wants to be treated

- Providing opportunities for all stakeholders to express concerns and needs

- Voicing appreciation to those seeking to prevent and stop bullying
- Sharing success stories with faculty and staff
- Identifying and eliminating his or her own prejudices, if any exist
- Investigating rumors of bullying
- Prohibiting public comments by students, parents, or colleagues that degrade, condemn, or ridicule others
- Reminding school personnel, volunteers, and students of the importance of their commitment to provide a physically and emotionally safe school environment
- Communicating zero tolerance of bullying
- Avoiding conversations in the hallway with students about their behavioral and personal problems
- Responding appropriately to all bullying situations
- Holding conferences with parents, students, and school personnel and asking them to share their observations and concerns relative to the anti-bullying program and the behavior of students
- Reminding students that administrators will be circulating on school property for the purpose of listening for and watching for bullying, especially during high-traffic times
- Reminding students and personnel that the school has a written supervision plan and that the principal or assistant principal will personally monitor supervision to ensure that high-risk areas are being consistently and effectively supervised
- Scheduling a time with each teacher to observe him or her teaching a Bully Free lesson plan
- Asking teachers, every three weeks, to make a copy of their Bully Free lesson plan charts and turn them in to the principal or assistant principal

Once the Bully Free Program has been launched, additional energy is required to maintain momentum because even the most successful programs lose their edge over time. It is important for the administration to work with the Bully Free Program team to maintain program momentum. This can be accomplished through strategies such as those listed below. The team should place a check mark beside those that it desires to implement during each year and make plans for implementation by assigning individuals certain tasks.

Strategies for Maintaining Momentum

☐ Make sure bullying is on the agenda of all faculty, staff, and parent meetings. Briefly discuss components and elements of the program at these meetings and have "Where are we now?" discussions.

☐ Encourage ongoing parent dialogue on the issue of bullying by including the topic on the agendas of parent meetings and parent-teacher meetings.

☐ Continue to give students or selected classes and parents responsibility for preparing Bully Free Program bulletin boards, posters, and banners to decorate the halls.

☐ Continue to conduct assembly programs around the topic of bullying where teachers or older students role-play inappropriate and appropriate behavior observed by school personnel and volunteers.

☐ Annually host a fine arts contest around a theme of bullying. Possible contest areas are best song, best painting, and best drama or skit.

☐ Ask teachers and counselors to be on a constant search for supportive anti-bullying resource material and guest speakers.

☐ Continue to offer workshops and seminars for school personnel, volunteers, and parents on the prevention of bullying and intervention.

☐ Make sure new school personnel understand the destructiveness of bullying and are familiar with the Bully Free Program.

☐ Provide all stakeholders with periodic program updates throughout the year.

☐ Occasionally ask teachers and staff to share success stories at faculty and staff meetings.

☐ Provide information on bullying in each issue of the school newsletter or devote an entire issue of the newsletter to the school's effort to be bully free. Include students' writing, cartoons, and other artwork to promote bullying prevention.

☐ Provide information on the school's bullying prevention efforts to the parents of all children entering kindergarten and those in other grades who are transferring from other schools.

☐ Ask parents to share success stories at faculty, staff, and parent meetings.

☐ Add bullying prevention books and videos to the parent lending library, and encourage parents to borrow these materials.

☐ Add information about the Bully Free Program on the school's Web site.

☐ Look for opportunities to connect with and learn from other schools that are implementing bullying prevention programs.

☐ Approach public places such as libraries and community centers and seek permission to showcase the bully free work (song lyrics, poems, artwork, and so on) of students.

☐ Show student-produced slide shows or videos at a parent advisory council meeting and school board meetings.

☐ Provide periodic updates on the school's progress toward meeting the program's goals.

☐ Make sure the principal requires teachers to turn in their Bully Free lesson plan record charts.

☐ Make sure the principal has bullying on the agenda of all faculty and staff meetings.

Administrative Strategies Plan

It will take a significant amount of time for the team to select and implement the administrative strategies. These are strategies that mainly require administrative leadership and initiative, such as establishing a hot line and organizing new clubs.

The Bully Free Program is a comprehensive school-community program that encompasses administrative strategies that can be systemwide or schoolwide. Unlike some anti-bullying programs, the Bully Free Program incorporates some optional strategies that allow the school system or school to customize its plans. However, it is important to implement as many of the strategies as feasible.

During this step, the Bully Free Program team selects the administrative strategies to be implemented. It is important to use strategies that focus on the baseline data collected through surveys, prioritized identified needs, and the desired program objectives (for example, to increase the number of students willing to report bullying behavior). The strategies listed in the following Bank of Administrative Strategies are recommended. In addition to anti-bullying strategies, several school safety strategies have been included. Some of them may not be appropriate for your school system or school, so the team should place a check mark beside the desirable ones. The team is also encouraged to brainstorm other strategies. The following bank of strategies also appears in a Microsoft Word file at www.bullyfree.com. To create your plan, you can delete the strategies you do not wish to use.

Several of the administrative strategies help create an environment where students trust that adults will respond appropriately to their reports of bullying—in other words, a "telling environment." This is an environment in which all members recognize that they have responsibilities to the other members in the group; if they are bullied or if they are aware of bullying or any other abuse, they have a duty to tell an adult.

Therefore, it is important for adults to demonstrate that they understand bullying behavior, show that they are committed to stopping it, and are capable of appropriately addressing it.

Bank of Administrative Strategies

☐ Encourage students to anonymously report bullying by asking them to drop a note in a "bully box" or "acceptance box" located in the school (for example, the hall). Some principals ask students where they would like the box placed. Another approach is to ask each teacher and counselor to place a multipurpose box on his or her desk. This box could be used for compliments, encouraging words, complaints, and reports of bullying. Some schools have an e-mail reporting system that can be used by students to make reports regarding bullying, drugs, weapons, and vandalism.

☐ Develop more places for students to belong and feel accepted by increasing the number of clubs and activities. Conduct a survey with students to identify their areas of interest. The following is a listing of clubs and activities offered by some schools:

  ○ *Peers for Peace Club.* This is a club that helps the school be bully free.

  ○ *Peer Mediation Club.* Learn how to mediate and practice peer mediation.

  ○ *Bowling Club.* Students meet with friends to learn about and enjoy bowling. No bowling skills are required for membership. Competition is not allowed.

  ○ *Chess or Board Game Clubs.* Previous knowledge of chess is not necessary. Chess Club alternates every other Friday with Board Game Club.

  ○ *Drama Club.* Students participate in drama, speech, acting, and set design and building.

  ○ *Sign Language Club.* Students gather to learn sign language through various games, activities, and discussions.

  ○ *Knitting Club.* Students learn from experts how to knit.

  ○ *Art Club.* Students meet to learn about art and develop artistic skills.

  ○ *Student Leadership Club.* This is a service organization that participates in fundraisers to help the community.

  ○ *Science Olympiad.* Students learn how to build balsa bridges, trebuchets, and rubber band–powered high-performing indoor airplanes. They also experiment with robots and Rube Goldberg machines. Students have a variety of science-related experiences.

  ○ *Math Squad.* Students meet to increase their skills in math and problem solving.

  ○ *Community Service Club.* Students engage in a variety of community service activities.

- *Baseball Cards Club.* Students who join this club are usually collectors of baseball cards or are interested in becoming collectors.
- *Bible Club.* Students meet to study the Bible.
- *Music Club.* Students meet to learn how to appreciate a variety of music.
- *Comic Book Club.* Students who join this club are usually comic book collectors or interested in becoming collectors.
- *Spanish Club.* Students learn and practice Spanish.
- *Future Teachers Club.* Students learn about teaching while enjoying the company of other students who want to be teachers.
- *SADD Club.* Students against destructive decisions meet to promote sober driving.

☐ Make sure bus drivers, school secretaries, custodians, nurses, and other school personnel understand they have an important role to play in the anti-bullying program and that they should attend the training sessions.

☐ Establish a hot line to encourage students to anonymously report bullying.

☐ Ask teachers to implement strategies that add structure to less structured activities, such as recess and other more or less free times. For example, prior to recess, students could plan a recess activity (see Step 12).

☐ Assign younger and older students to different playground areas and, if possible, different lunch times.

☐ Collaborate with existing agencies to establish a parent education program.

☐ Ask that books, videos, and other materials be purchased and placed in the school and community libraries to promote sensitivity, empathy, and understanding. If possible, these resources should be reviewed by someone knowledgeable about bullying prior to purchasing them to ensure that the materials have appropriate messages.

☐ Establish a policy that prohibits the use of backpacks (unless they are transparent), duffle bags, blankets, and other devices that can conceal weapons.

☐ Establish a policy that prohibits students from wearing clothing, tattoos, or other symbols that degrade others or express intolerance.

☐ Establish a policy regarding the locking of doors in schools.

☐ Provide well-equipped, attractive, and accessible outdoor environments that encourage positive activities.

☐ If any of your students walk to and from school, consider working with the community to establish a "Safe Place" program. Place signs in the windows of approved homes and businesses where students can find refuge when threatened by peers or others.

☐ Encourage maintenance personnel to frequently and systematically search out and remove hurtful graffiti on school property.

☐ Establish a school welcome program for new students by sending letters from students, teachers, and others to new students and their parents welcoming them to the school. Sometimes new students are given gift bags with discount coupons from local businesses, snacks, and a welcoming card signed by the principal and others. Sometimes a student or a team of students serve on a team to welcome new students. They show a video they developed about the school, introduce the student to school personnel and students, and go to parties and sports events with the new student. For example, the Middletown, Pennsylvania, area high school's welcome program has the following elements:

- Each new student receives a bag with a parking permit for those who qualify, a ticket to a nonsports activity, and other valued items.

- The school's designated welcoming student will:

  Guide the student around school and help this person with his or her locker.

  Walk with the student to classes during the first week.

  Eat lunch with the student if they have a corresponding lunch period.

  Provide the student with maps of points of interest in the area if the student is from out of town.

  Introduce the student to any coach or activity director who is appropriate for that student.

☐ Work with community organizations or groups to provide students with opportunities to participate in service projects.

☐ Ask teachers to engage students in projects focusing on areas such as water pollution, air pollution, smoking, drinking and driving, drugs, and cruelty to animals. Such projects create unity among the students. Bullies, when appropriate, could be given leadership roles to play, teaching them that they can have power by doing good deeds.

☐ Establish an elementary and middle school mentoring program using high school students. High school students who were victimized in their early grades can mentor students who are at risk of being victimized or are already being attacked by their peers. Local businesses may support this project by paying the mentors minimum wage. An excellent discussion of how to develop and operate a mentoring program appears in *Bullying in Secondary Schools* (Sullivan, Cleary, & Sullivan, 2005, pp. 199–215).

☐ Ask all school personnel to immediately report and investigate rumors that a student is being mistreated.

☐ Ask the guidance counselors or school psychologists to provide counseling for victimized students.

☐ Ask school counselors and school psychologists to teach victimized students how to deal with stress.

☐ Ask school counselors, school psychologists, and other appropriate individuals to teach assertiveness skills to victims and potential victims.

☐ Establish a committee to review and recommend purchasing or renting videos about the mistreatment of individuals to educate students about the destructive nature of bullying, violence, hatred, prejudice, and biases.

☐ Develop a peer counseling program. This is probably most appropriate in the middle school. Information about such a program can be found on the Internet.

☐ Install video cameras inside and outside the schools in all of the high-risk areas. Make sure your school systematically reviews the recordings to identify problems, rather than only reviewing them when there is a reported problem.

☐ Install a closed circuit television system. One school installed such a system that allows parents and guardians, for a small fee, to observe activities in their school from home through their computers. When students know that their parent or guardian could be watching, it can have a positive impact on their behavior. In a way, parents can serve as external supervisors and can report their observations of inappropriate behavior. This will help your school document certain behaviors and provide justification for increasing supervision in problem areas of the school's property.

☐ Purchase inexpensive disposable cameras for teachers to use to catch students in the act of victimization or for capturing acts of kindness.

☐ Install metal detectors in the school.

☐ Install curved mirrors in strategic locations within each school.

☐ Consider requiring all students to wear uniforms.

☐ Eliminate communal showers by installing partitions or curtains to permit students to shower in private after gym class.

☐ Install doors with locks on bathroom stalls if they have been removed or left off construction plans.

☐ Secure a school resource officer for the school. These officers usually have three main roles and responsibilities: that of law enforcement officer, law-related counsel, and law-related educator. They can also establish meaningful relationships with students and serve as good role models.

☐ Establish a bully stoppers program. This is a program that pays rewards to students who report bullying to the administration once the accuracy of the report has been verified.

☐ Make use of detection dogs to locate drugs and weapons. Victims of bullying sometimes turn to drugs to find relief and sometimes use weapons to equalize the power imbalance between them and the bullies.

☐ Ask teachers to communicate on the first day of school and throughout the rest of the year their intolerance of bullying.

☐ Establish a program that teaches students and school personnel the truth about gangs, hate groups, and cults.

☐ Ask teachers to teach students (and others) to recognize gang clothing colors.

☐ Ask a group of students and parents to work with school personnel to organize and implement a Bully Free Month or Bully Free Week. Activities such as assemblies, guest speakers, door contests, poster contests, and writing contests can be conducted during the week and everyone can wear bully free T-shirts, bully free bracelets, and bully free buttons.

☐ Meet with all the student leaders and encourage them to help you make their school bully free. Train them to use assertiveness skills so that they can help themselves when they are bullied and help others who are bullied. One principal had the student leaders distribute a Bully Free Student Pledge (see Step 14) and ask their peers to sign the pledge.

☐ Eliminate aggressive and competitive games from recess. Fried and Fried (2003, p. 201) report that some schools have implemented this strategy. Children should be able to release energy without the fear of being hurt or of losing. There are other opportunities, even in elementary school, to engage in competitive activities.

☐ Ask all school personnel and volunteers to serve as good role models when interacting with students, parents, and each other.

☐ Consider equipping supervisors with communication devices so they can talk to each other about anything suspicious. This may be helpful as well when two staff members are supervising a large area.

☐ Ask school personnel to identify potential victims of bullying and bullies by being observant and listening to what students say about other students.

☐ Approach local city government officials and ask them to proclaim a Bully Free Week, or similar acknowledgment of the school system's program, as in the two following examples. These examples also appear as files at www.bullyfree.com. If you wish, print the Bully Free Community Representative Pledge (see Step 14) in the local newspaper and ask business owners to sign the pledge and mail it to your school. This pledge appears as a Microsoft Word file at www.bullyfree.com.

Examples of Proclamations of Bully Free Week

Proclamation of April 16–22 as Bully Free Week

Whereas the school shootings in our country, in which students and adults were killed and others have been injured for life, have left an indelible mark on history, there are lessons to be taken from these tragedies and changes to be made to save our children from further horrors of this nature. We must safeguard schools for our children, and, through our recognition of the serious issues that face them each day, offer our children and community a school environment that holds promise and security.

Whereas many organizations, school districts, educators and parents have publicly expressed concern about the bullying of children, we feel it essential to continue to heighten awareness of this serious issue. We hope to make the public aware of the negative effects of bullying and the long-term damage it can cause in our youth. It is time for us to speak out AGAINST bullying and FOR our children.

Our fight against bullying in our schools and community must not, of course, be limited to one week a year. Because bullying is so destructive (causing depression, overwhelming anxiety, poor grades, self-mutilation, and suicide) and in remembrance of the Columbine shootings, Heath High School shootings, and others and as a symbol of our year-round struggle against bullying, we hereby designate the third week of April as Bully Free Week.

Source: Adapted from http://www.bullypolice.org/ProclamationApril16-22.pdf.

Proclamation of October 22–28 as Bully Free Week

Whereas: Bullying is physical, verbal, sexual, or emotional harm or intimidation directed at a person or group of people; and

Whereas: Bullying occurs in homes, neighborhoods, playgrounds, schools, workplaces, and the Internet; and

Whereas: Various researchers have concluded that bullying is the most common form of violence affecting millions of American children and adolescents annually; and

Whereas: Thousands of children and adolescents are victims of bullying; and

Whereas: Victims of bullying are more likely to acquire physical, emotional, and learning problems, and students who are repeatedly bullied often fear such activities as riding the bus, going to school, and using the bathroom; and

Whereas: Children who are bullies are at greater risk of engaging in more serious violent behaviors and attempting suicide; and

Whereas: A large percentage of children who are bullied believe that adult help is infrequent and ineffective.

Now, therefore, I, _____, Mayor of _____, do hereby proclaim the week of October 22–28 as Bully Free Week and encourage parents, schools, recreation programs, religious institutions, and community organizations to engage in a variety of awareness and prevention activities designed to make our communities safer for all children and adolescents.

IN WITNESS WHEREOF, I have hereunto set my hand and caused the Great Seal of the State of _____ to be affixed at this ___ day of _____ in the year of our Lord two thousand and ___.

_____
Signature

Source: Adapted from the State of Minnesota proclamation, http://www.sos.state.mn.us/docs/bullyingpreventionweek.pdf.

Brainstorm other possible strategies and determine whether to include them in the administrative strategies plan. Develop a plan for getting the strategies adopted and approved and a plan for implementing the approved strategies.

Bully Free Policy

Several states have required schools to develop policies for dealing with bullying. If this is the case in your state, your state department of education or state school board association may have recommended a policy. If so, there may be no need for the Bully Free Program team to develop its own policy. If not, your superintendent may wish for the Bully Free Program team or another group to draft such a policy.

It is important that the school system and each school have clear and enforceable bully free policies and procedures to which school personnel, volunteers, parents, students, and the rest of the community can commit. By developing an anti-bullying policy, the Bully Free Program team will help the school create a positive and caring environment where individuals are respected and encouraged to treat others with respect. Such a school climate will help students and school personnel feel socially and emotionally safe, lead to physical safety, and improve academic performances. A bully free school climate will be achieved only if all stakeholders are involved in the development of the policy, if everyone knows what the policy is, if everyone endorses the policy, and if the policy is consistently enforced.

Reach Consensus on a Definition of Bullying

The first step in establishing an anti-bullying policy is to reach an agreement on the definition of *bullying*. The team can develop a definition or adopt one. The definition should always contain the following elements: (1) intent to hurt (physically, socially, psychologically, and emotionally) or frighten, (2) persistent (repeated), (3) direct (physical and verbal) or indirect (social and relational) behavior, and (4) an imbalance of power.

The most accepted definition of bullying has been developed by Olweus (1995). He says bullying occurs when one or more individuals engage in overt, aggressive, hostile, violent, hurtful, and persistent behaviors that are intentional and designed to injure and create fear and distress in one or more persons who seem to be unable to defend themselves and gives the bully some degree of satisfaction. Bullying behaviors range from being overtly teased and intentionally socially isolated to being harassed and assaulted (verbally or physically, or both) by one or more individuals. According to Olweus (1995), bullying is characterized by an imbalance of strength (power and dominance). Therefore, the victim has trouble defending himself or herself and feels helpless. This imbalance of power can be physical or psychological. Small children can bully larger children.

The Bully Free Program uses this definition: *Bullying is a form of overt and aggressive behavior that is intentional, hurtful (physical or psychological), and persistent (repeated). Bullied students are teased, harassed, and assaulted (verbally or physically) by one or more peers and often socially rejected by their peers. There has to be an imbalance of strength (power and dominance).*

Develop the Anti-bullying Policy

Ask your superintendent if the school system has an anti-bullying policy. If not, ask for permission to work on a draft of such a policy. If your school system is implementing the Bully Free Program in several schools, the chairs of each team could be asked to meet to develop this policy for the school system.

If a policy has not been developed, ask your superintendent to contact the state department of education or state school board association for a model anti-bullying policy. You may also find examples of policies on the Internet. The first step to developing a policy is to examine your school system's harassment and intimidation policies and procedures, behavior code books, hazing policies, acceptable use policies (technology), and if necessary, recommend improvements so that they more specifically address bullying. Or perhaps all your team needs to do is develop a position statement that sets out the school system's position on bullying. These policies could be modified to include bullying, or the team may need to develop a new anti-bullying policy. Several states are taking action and requiring school systems to develop policies.

The anti-bullying policy should be consistent with the mission and other policies of the school system and approved by the school system's attorney. An example of a comprehensive policy appears in Appendix D, as well as online at www.bullyfree.com. Note that the policy addresses students and adults in the school, not just students bullying students.

Review Policy Guidelines

The following policy development guidelines have been compiled from existing policies and guides from several states (visit http://www.nde.state.ne.us/safety/). The policy developed by the team should follow as many of the following guidelines as possible.

- If possible, develop a policy that relates to the school system's or school's mission statement. Try to use words from these statements in the anti-bullying policy.

- State a clear rationale for the anti-bullying policy.

- State the school system's or school's definition of appropriate behavior—the opposite of bullying behavior.

- State the school system's or school's definition of bullying.

- State a procedure describing the process for reporting incidents of bullying and the procedures the school will follow in response to the reports of bullying (involving students bullying students, students bullying adults, adults bullying students, and adults bullying adults).

- State the possible consequences of engaging in bullying or falsely reporting another for bullying and the corrective action to be taken.

- State that each school must have the appropriate bully free response plan.

- State that each school must have a written coordinated and monitored supervision plan (see Step 12).

- State that each school must have a student involvement and empowerment plan (see Step 15).

- State that each school must have a parent and community involvement plan (see Step 16).

- State that school personnel and volunteers are to respond to bullying behavior according to the school's bully free response plans and the approved policies and procedures of the school system and school.

- State that each school is to implement a curriculum and activities to prevent and stop bullying.

- State that school personnel, volunteers, students, and parents should report all bullying: students bullying students, students bullying school personnel and volunteers, school personnel and volunteers bullying students, and so on.

- Discuss that parents must be informed about and involved in the bullying situations.

- State that incidents of bullying must be promptly investigated.

- State that those who report bullying are to be protected from retaliation and supported.

- State that school personnel and volunteers are to be notified of the policy.

- State that students are to be notified of the policy.

- State that parents or guardians are to be notified of the policy.

- State that retaliation will not be tolerated. Students, parents, school volunteers, school personnel, and others are not to retaliate because of bullying or because someone has reported bullying.

Address Bullying by School Personnel

Too often I have received reports from teachers, counselors, and principals about school personnel bullying others. The preceding guidelines include a statement about school personnel who bully students and other adults in the school. The example policy (Appendix D) also addresses adults who bully. Such behavior must not be tolerated and must be addressed by the school. Sometimes the adults in our schools are sarcastic, insulting, belittling, overly critical, or hurtful through a variety of behaviors, and their bullying can undermine the effectiveness of the program. These adults are bad role models, and their behavior can discourage students from reporting bullying to them. Therefore, school personnel who bully students, parents, and staff should be confronted by the administration and given a chance to improve. If they do not improve, significant approved negative consequences should be applied, even if they are tenured, belong to a union, or have important connections in the community. Fried and Fried (2003) discovered that one school established a policy where if any staff member observes another staff member bullying a student, he or she is to document the incident and send a memo to the principal. When the principal received a specified number of such memos, he or she had a conversation with the person. Of course, adults bullying adults must also not be tolerated. It is important that the school have policies and procedures that deal with these situations effectively.

Write a Draft and Submit It for Approval

After the team develops the draft policy, the policy should be submitted to the appropriate school officials and bodies for review and approval. Selected school personnel, volunteers, parents, and students should be given an opportunity to critique the draft policy. Feedback from these individuals should be obtained and discussed by the Bully Free Program team and the appropriate revisions made to the policy. Once the policy is finalized, it should be submitted to the appropriate individuals and groups and through the appropriate official school system channels for approval. The approved policy should be communicated to all school personnel, volunteers, parents, students, and others.

Task Checklist, Step 8

Notes

Develop and Implement the Bully Free Administrative Strategies Plan and Policies

☐ Examine and discuss the strategies in the Bank of Administrative Strategies. Check those most desirable.

☐ Brainstorm other possible strategies and determine whether to include them in the administrative strategies plan.

☐ Access the list of strategies at www.bullyfree.com and delete those not checked by the team.

☐ Develop a plan for getting the strategies approved and adopted.

☐ Develop a plan for implementing the approved strategies.

☐ Determine if your school district has an anti-bullying policy. If not, discuss with the principal and superintendent the appropriate channels for developing such a policy and the procedures for getting it approved.

☐ Develop a draft of the policy by following the school district's procedures for developing the policy, and be sure the policy follows the guidelines provided in this book. Be sure to address bullying by school personnel. (Access example policy at www.bullyfree.com.)

☐ Seek input on drafts of the policy.

☐ Seek to have the policy approved.

Selecting Strategies for Maintaining Program Momentum

☐ Ask the team to place a check mark beside the momentum strategies presented in this step that are most desirable to them. Discuss their selections.

☐ Reach consensus on the strategies to be used.

☐ Ask selected members to be responsible for making sure the strategies are approved and implemented.

☐ _____

_____

☐ _____

_____

Step 9

Establish the Bully Free Rules and Behavioral Expectations

Today we have too many students who are impulsive and whose inappropriate behavior is too often ignored or dealt with in a less than effective manner. Unfortunately, sometimes there is a lack of clear rules that specifically address all forms of bullying and behavioral expectations. These circumstances can create a fearful school climate. Students feel safer in schools where clear rules and behavioral expectations are consistently communicated and enforced in a powerful but fair manner. Such an approach not only helps create a peaceful school environment but also assists teachers in their efforts to manage the learning environment and eventually spend more time on instruction.

Establish Bully Free Rules

Students have a right to a safe and peaceful school and classroom, and providing rules with appropriate consequences for violating them is critical. Rules, especially those that deal with how individuals are treated, help schools meet students' physical, psychological, and emotional needs for safety. Most schools already have "traffic rules" and rules that address some student conduct. The Bully Free Program team should examine existing classroom rules and the school's behavior code book and develop or adopt a set of anti-bullying rules that will be posted in every classroom. Not all student behavior code books include language that specifically addresses *all* forms of bullying. Therefore, it is important to provide a set of rules that specifically address all bullying. Some professionals recommend keeping the number of rules to a minimum, such as these four:

- We will not bully others.
- We will seek to help students who are bullied.
- We will seek to include students who are left out.
- We will report to an adult at school and at home when we are bullied or someone else is bullied.

If the team decides to develop a different set of rules, the rules should clearly communicate a zero tolerance for bullying and an expectation of positive behavior. For rules to be effective, they should be:

- Created with student input
- Short and simple
- Easy to understand
- Specific
- Agreed on and accepted by everyone (however, the teacher is the authority figure and ultimately determines the rules)
- Enforceable (they can be enforced consistently and fairly)
- Communicated to and supported by parents, teachers, and staff
- Reviewed periodically and updated when needed

If the team wants to develop its own set of rules, additional examples follow:

Examples of Bully Free Rules

- Bullying is not allowed.
- We don't tease, call names, or put people down.
- We don't hit, shove, kick, or punch.
- If we see someone being bullied, we speak up and stop it (if we can) or go for help right away. It is always right to tell an adult.
- When we do things as a group, we make sure that everyone is included and no one is left out.
- We make new students feel welcome.
- We listen to each other's opinions.
- We treat each other with kindness and respect.
- We respect each other's property and school property.
- We look for the good in others and value differences.

Once the team has drafted the rules, they should present them to the faculty and students and consider their thoughts and comments.

Establishing Consequences

Once the rules have been finalized, the Bully Free Program team should develop a list of consequences. The consequences imposed should be responsible, restorative, and respectful of both the student who has been bullied and the student who bullied. The consequence for the first offense should be less severe than for a second offense. However, a first offense of severe bullying may require that a severe consequence be applied immediately, such as in-school suspension, suspension, or even expulsion. Be sure to follow the policies of the school system and school.

There are two kinds of consequences: negative and positive. The following is a discussion of both, as well as examples.

Negative Consequences

Negative consequences that are administered appropriately can help discourage and eliminate some undesirable behavior in some students. They should be easy for the teacher to use, be unpleasant but not hostile, and be developmentally appropriate for the student's age and personality. When administering negative consequences, it is important to emphasize that it is the behavior you dislike, not the student. It is also a good idea to use negative consequences that are connected to the infraction.

There are basically two types of negative consequences. One is the removal of something valued (for example, attention from peers, privileges). Some of the most familiar are time-out and eating in isolation during lunch. The other type is the use of something negative or unpleasant (such as verbal reprimand, going to lunch last, calling the parents). When using these, keep in mind that positive consequences for appropriate behavior should also be used. These are discussed later in this section.

The following examples of negative consequences have been applied at various grade levels. Your philosophy regarding discipline and the policies of your school will dictate what negative consequences can or should be applied. Also, an effort should be made to identify which consequences have been used with a student in the past and were found to be ineffective and which ones were effective. Other consequences should be added to the following list.

- Give a verbal reprimand and warning.
- Supervise the bully's use of the restroom for one week for misbehavior in restrooms.
- Record the bully's name in a "bully book."
- Place a report in the bully's file, send a letter to the bully's home, and schedule a meeting with the bully's parents.
- Require the bully to apologize to the victim and ask forgiveness (verbally and then in writing).
- Require one of the bully's parents to attend school to monitor his or her behavior for a specified number of days, escorting him or her to and from classes and attending classes.
- Require the bully to read a book about bullying and write a book report.
- Require the bully to watch an age-appropriate video about bullying and answer questions (devised by a teacher or counselor) about it.
- Assign an older student to monitor the bully: the bully cannot go to the playground or around the school without the older student.

- Require the bully to eat lunch in the classroom with the teacher, teacher's aide, or a volunteer supervisor, or require the student to eat lunch in isolation for a specified number of days.

- Require the bully to meet with the counselor or school psychologist once a day for a few days to discuss his or her behavior.

- Require the bully to sit near the teacher's desk.

- Require the bully to record acts of kindness observed during lunch or recess and report the acts to the class.

- Require the bully to call his or her parent at home or work, explain the bullying behavior, apologize, and state what he or she will do to change the behavior. (Note that if the bully may be abused by a parent at home for causing trouble at school, this consequence would not be appropriate.)

- Require the bully to walk to the principal's office with the teacher, teacher's aide, or volunteer supervisor and explain the behavior to the principal, apologize, and state what he or she will do to improve his or her behavior.

- Require the bully to assist a member of staff with special tasks whenever feasible (during recess, before school, or after school).

- Require the bully to write a report about a famous person known for his or her acts of generosity and kindness.

- Keep the bully inside during recess, supervised by someone.

- Require the bully to exercise by walking around the perimeter of the playground during recess.

- Deny the bully access to certain extracurricular activities he or she enjoys for a specified number of days.

- Reduce the bully's recess or free play time by ten or more minutes or prohibit the bully from engaging in a favorite activity.

- Require the bully to have recess alone and in a restricted area for a specified number of days.

- Require the bully to wait three minutes in his or her seat after the rest of the class is dismissed.

- Prohibit the bully from participating in a rewarding activity (art activity, music activity, athletics, clubs, computer time, or something else).

- Require the bully to clean up an outside area of the school.

- Require the bully to do his or her work in a room alone for a day or longer (with adult supervision). Parents must be informed and consent given whenever possible, and school policies and procedures must be followed for such an intervention.

- Require the bully to be the last one to leave school.

- Quietly remove the bully from the assembly, cafeteria, or other areas when he or she is misbehaving.

- Assign the bully a seat away from everyone else.

- Require the bully to go to the end of the lunch line.

- Use positive practice by having the student repeatedly practice the correct behavior.

- Place the bully in detention.

- Place the bully in an in-school suspension (with parents informed and consent given whenever possible), which lasts several hours or up to a day (suspensions more than one day are not usually advisable). During this time, there is no talking or sleeping. The student must stay in his or her seat and work on school assignments. If the student is late or fails to appear, the time period for the suspension can be expanded up to a full day.

- Require the bully to attend a Saturday school. Some school systems hold classes on Saturdays for problem students.

- Require the bully to use the "sit-and-watch time-out" strategy: the bully sits in a corner of the room and watches the classroom activity.

- Have the bully write an accurate description of the misbehavior and sign it.

- Require the bully to use the "interclass time-out" strategy: the student is removed to another classroom and required to work on an academic activity for twenty to thirty minutes. The classroom should be for a grade level at least two grades above the student's grade level.

- Require the bully to research the topic of bullying and write a report about it.

- Require the parents to provide the bully's transportation, if the bullying is occurring on the bus.

- Require the bully to help teachers develop bully free bulletin boards, posters, and banners during recess.

- Have the bully sign a "No Contact Contract" requiring him or her to cease all bullying and to avoid all contact (visual, physical, auditory) with his or her current target or targets. The contract could even specify how far away he or she must stay from the targeted student. If the contract is broken, more significant negative consequences are applied.

- Suspend the bully from school.

- Expel the bully from school.

Positive Consequences

Positive consequences—when administered abundantly, appropriately, sincerely, and consistently—reinforce, encourage, and help change and maintain desired behavior. In fact, positive consequences may be more powerful than negative. These consequences should be easy for the teacher to use; moreover, students should view them as desirable.

The following examples of positive consequences have been applied at various grade levels:

- Verbally and publicly praise the student for his or her good behavior.

- Give the student extra time on a desired activity, such as art, music, or computer time.

- Let the student be first in the lunch line for good behavior.

- Send a note home complimenting the student's change in behavior or call the parents.

- Reward the whole class (perhaps with a popcorn party) for the student's change in attitude and behavior.

- Give the student a leadership opportunity; for example, leading a campaign against animal cruelty or water pollution.

- Initiate positive action and interactions with the bully.

Your philosophy regarding discipline and the policies of your school will dictate what positive consequences should be applied. Other positive consequences should be added to this list. Some teachers ask students to indicate the positive consequences they would like to receive. Sometimes a menu of positive consequences is created and students select the one they desire.

For the enforcement of the rules to occur consistently, the consequences should be standardized and required for every teacher. However, there should be some flexibility to meet individual student needs. After the proposed consequences have been established, faculty comments should be sought, and their ideas may lead to changes in the consequences.

Seeking Input from Students

After the team has formed the rules and associated consequences with faculty input, the rules and consequences should be given to the teachers. The teachers should lead a discussion regarding the rules and consequences with their students.

Although student input is valuable in forming rules and associated consequences, there is no room for compromise on most anti-bullying rules (for example, "We will not bully others.") or consequences. But once the rules and consequences have been determined, teachers should communicate that they need the assistance of students to make them the best they can be and to make sure they are realistic and fair. In fact, the teacher should let students know that they can recommend changes in the proposed rules and consequences. This is, in fact, very important. When students participate in forming the rules and developing the consequences for violating the rules, they are more likely to feel they are being treated fairly, which helps them learn to manage their behaviors. Students are also important in modifying the behavior of children who bully and for encouraging children who are bullied. Both bullies and bullied children who are part of this discussion begin to sense how much the teacher and other students dislike bullying. This can encourage the student who bullies to change and can give hope to the student who is bullied.

Prior to discussing each proposed rule and consequence, students should address the following questions:

- What is bullying?
- What does bullying look like?
- What is the opposite of bullying?
- What kind of classroom do we want to have?
- What can everyone do to make this happen?
- What anti-bullying rules should we have?

With a foundation of information gathered from this discussion with students, the teacher is ready to discuss the proposed rules and their associated consequences.

Discussion of the rules and consequences needs to lead to student ownership of the rules. The discussion might focus on questions such as these:

- What does this rule mean? What do you think about the consequences?
- What would happen if everyone did not obey this rule?
- What would our school be like if everyone obeyed this rule?
- Is it fair for us to expect everyone to obey this rule?
- Are there changes we need to make in this rule?
- Do you agree that we need to have this rule?
- What should be the consequences for disobeying each rule?

After the student discussions and student input has been compiled by the Bully Free Program team, a final draft of the rules and consequences should be approved by the appropriate school personnel.

Then the principal should require every teacher to post the rules in their classrooms. Posting and enforcing the same rules in every classroom helps bring consistency in discipline and, eventually, in behavior. At some point, an effort should also be made to get community organizations like the YMCA, parks and recreation departments, and malls to adopt such rules as well.

Ask the teachers to introduce the rules, discuss their meaning, and provide examples. They may also want to role-play how to obey the rules. Teachers should also occasionally review the rules with students. Initially teachers of young students may want to read (or ask a student to read) the rules each morning for several days. Later, the rules can be read weekly or once a month or so.

Ask the teachers to share the rules and consequences with the parents of their students as well. The parents should be asked to review them with their children.

Administering Consequences

When the final version of rules and consequences is presented to the teachers, it is also important to give teachers the following tips for administering the consequences:

Guidelines for Administering Negative Consequences

- They should be directed toward the inappropriate behavior and not attack the person. The specific undesirable behavior should be specified, and a discussion regarding desirable behavior should occur.

- They should be unpleasant, undesirable, and disagreeable for the student yet fair and respectful.

- If a consequence has to be repeated, a more severe consequence should be applied.

- They should be age appropriate.

- They may include a verbal or a written apology.

- All teachers in the school should apply them consistently.

Guidelines for Administering Positive Consequences

- The specific desired behavior observed should be identified.

- The teacher should be sincere in his or her praise.

- Teachers who see positive behavior should apply the consequences consistently.

- The teacher should use a variety of positive consequences so the student does not get tired of the same consequence.

- After a desired behavior seems to have established itself, positive consequences can be administered on a random schedule rather than every time the behavior is observed. This will help maintain the behavior. The student will keep engaging in the behavior because he or she doesn't know when the positive consequence may be applied.

Ensuring That Teachers and Other Staff Follow Rules

Unfortunately, sometimes teachers and staff members do not follow the rules they have worked so hard to establish. It is critical for the adults to follow the rules and engage in the same behavior expected of students. They need to be good role models and treat students, parents, and other school personnel the way they themselves want to be treated. It is especially important for the school not to tolerate adults who bully.

Establish Behavioral Expectations

The Bully Free Program team should develop and communicate to students and school personnel behavioral expectations for all of the high-risk areas: restrooms, hallways, stairwells, cafeteria, locker rooms, riding the bus, waiting for the bus before school and after school, and others. The preschool, elementary, and middle school Bully Free Program lesson plans address many of these. However, it is also important to post these expected behaviors in high-risk areas and perhaps use one or more assemblies to discuss expectations. As much as possible, the expectations should be stated in positive terms indicating the behavior that is to be expected. The following examples will help you complete this task.

General Behavioral Expectations

- Treat others with dignity and respect using respectful body language, gestures, and words. Be kind, and treat others the way you want to be treated.

- Control your anger, and seek to resolve conflicts peacefully.

- Keep your hands, feet, and objects to yourself.

- Avoid touching the property of others.

- Leave pencils, pens, electronic devices, and other distracting objects in your backpack or pocket until you can lock them in your locker.

- Avoid bumping or pushing people. If you accidentally bump someone, say "Excuse me."

- If you behave badly, accept the consequences for your inappropriate behavior calmly and respectfully.

- Report any bullying, other problems, and dangerous situations to an adult.

- Use an appropriate tone of voice.

- Use polite language: no swearing, no threats, and no verbal abuse.

- When an adult asks you to stop, do so, and listen respectfully.

Walking to and from School

- Treat those who walk with you with respect and dignity. Treat them the way you want to be treated.

- Walk directly to your destination.

- Talk only to people you know. Do not say hello, do not answer questions, and do not give directions to a stranger.

- Report uncomfortable encounters with strangers to an adult.
- Stay on the sidewalk (if there is a sidewalk) except when crossing the street.
- Cross only at designated crossings or corners of streets.

On the Bus

- Obey the bus driver and the bus supervisor or monitor.
- Be responsible for everyone's safety by reporting unsafe items or equipment on the bus and by encouraging everyone to treat each other the way he or she wants to be treated.
- Keep objects and your hands, legs, and feet to yourself (hands in your lap, legs down in front of you and feet flat on the floor, not in the aisle). Don't touch anyone else's body or things.
- Face forward.
- Keep your body and property inside the bus.
- Keep seats open for others. Don't save it for someone in particular.
- Stay seated until the bus driver gives permission to leave your seat.
- Keep track of your belongings.
- Don't litter the bus.
- Walk directly and quietly from the bus to the designated location when instructed to do so.

Bike Parking Area

- Unless you have a bike, do not go to the bike parking area.
- Ride your bike directly to the bike rack, and lock it to the rack.
- Report any attempts to steal your bike to an adult.
- Report any damage to your property to an adult.

Parking Lot

- Obey all traffic laws.
- Appropriately park your car in the designated area.
- Don't litter the parking lot.
- Walk to and immediately enter the school building.
- Report any damage to your property to an adult.

In Front of, Behind, and Between Buildings (Before and After School)

- Refrain from standing near the school building before and after school (except when waiting for a ride) without adult supervision.

Doorways and Entrances

- When entering and exiting doors, use the door on the right.
- Do not linger in doorways.
- Do not linger near the doors.

Arrival Behavior and Commons/Waiting Area (Before School)

- Arrive no earlier than _____ AM, and go immediately to the designated areas in the commons or waiting area. Adult supervision will be provided beginning at _____ AM.
- Follow rules and procedures regarding backpacks, and do not touch anyone else's backpack.
- Keep the area clean by using trash cans.
- Keep track of your belongings.

Hallways

- Take the shortest route to your destination.
- Walk quietly (don't run, don't piggyback) to your destination in an orderly fashion on the right side of the hall, and do not disturb students who may still be working in class. When moving as a class, stay in line order.
- Watch where you are walking.
- Keep your hands off the wall (avoiding displays or decorations).
- Don't litter the hallways.
- Hold the door open for those entering the hallway. Do not slam the door.
- Shut locker doors quietly.
- Have a hall pass while in the hallway during class time.
- Follow the instructions of the hall supervisor.

Stairwells

- Use only the designated stairwells.
- Walk (don't run, don't piggyback) on the right side in an orderly fashion.
- Be the only person using each step on your side of the stairs; do not move onto the same step as the person in front of you.
- Watch where you are walking.
- Put your right hand on the railing.
- Keep your hands off the wall (avoiding displays or decorations).
- If a door is near, hold the door for the person behind you. Do not slam the door.
- Do not stand in stairwells—walk.

Lockers

- Do not block someone's access to his or her locker.
- Do not touch someone who is at his or her locker.
- Open and close lockers quietly.
- Keep your locker clean and neat.
- Hang your coats and book bags on hooks.
- Do not climb into your locker or anyone else's.
- Items requiring refrigeration are not permitted in lockers.
- Lockers are for personal use only. They may not be rented to others or used by others.

Classroom

- When appropriate, hold the door open for others. Do not slam the door.
- Be in your seat before the bell rings.
- Sit in your chair safely.
- Give your full attention to the teacher. Listen, follow instructions, and do your best.
- Use classroom materials and equipment safely and appropriately.
- Raise your hand, and wait to be called on.
- Follow all classroom rules.
- Complete and turn in work on time.
- Return materials to the proper place.

Library

- Quietly enter and exit the library.
- Avoid talking unless an adult gives you permission.
- Take care of books and magazines in the library.
- Return library books on time.

Cafeteria

- When appropriate, hold the door open for others. Do not slam the door.
- Stay in line.
- Take the top tray.
- Refrain from pushing someone's tray out of the way.

- Make menu choices quickly.

- Have your ticket or money ready before reaching the end of the line.

- Pay for your food before you eat it.

- Follow the cashier's procedures.

- Stay in single file until your purchase is complete.

- Look for an empty seat at your assigned table, signified by no food items at that spot and an empty seat. Do not change seats without permission.

- Keep your chair legs on the floor.

- Keep utensils to yourself, your legs in front of you, and your feet on the floor.

- Use appropriate table manners.

- Do not accept food from other students or touch or share another person's food or drink.

- Remain seated unless you are given permission to get up.

- Raise your hand if you need something.

- Keep your eating area neat by cleaning up after yourself.

- Follow the procedures for recycling and waste disposal (put trash in the trash cans).

- Follow the instructions of the cafeteria supervisors.

- Stay in your seat until you are dismissed by an adult.

Bathrooms

- Use designated bathrooms during designated times. When required, obtain a bathroom pass.

- Do not slam the bathroom door.

- Keep your feet off doors and walls.

- Be patient with others, and wait your turn.

- One person per stall.

- Use bathrooms appropriately, and leave them clean.

- Leave stall doors unlocked after use.

- Spend no more than three or four minutes in the bathroom.

- Leave the bathroom as soon as you finish, and return to class promptly.

- Report all messes that need to be cleaned up to an adult.

- Report broken bathroom equipment and misuse of the bathroom to an adult.

Locker Rooms

- Do not slam the door.
- Wipe your feet before entering the gym.
- Sit where instructed.
- Obey the adults.
- Keep the locker room clean.

Playground

- Observe safety rules.
- Remain in the play area designated by the adults unless permission is given by an adult.
- Invite and include all those who want to play.
- Play school-approved games only.
- Race but don't chase.
- Accept the varying knowledge, skills, and abilities of others.
- Exhibit sportsmanship.
- Refrain from "play" wrestling, boxing, and rough play, which can result in injuries.
- Follow game rules.
- Use playground equipment appropriately (for intended purpose) and safely.
- Walk on sidewalks and dirt or grassy areas, not on curbs.
- Take turns on and with equipment.
- Line up quickly after the bell rings.
- Play only in designated areas. Stay away from buildings, bushes, mud, and ditches.
- Stay within view of the playground supervisors.
- Refrain from climbing on trees, fences, or backstops.
- If a ball goes into a street, ask an adult to retrieve it.
- Collect and return playground equipment to the designated area.
- Report broken or unsafe equipment to an adult.
- Report accidents to an adult.

Waiting for the Bus After School

- Report to the bus stop area on time.
- When you are near buses, walk (don't run, and don't piggyback).

- Stay in the area designated by the supervising adults; do not stand or walk between, in front of, or behind buses.
- Follow instructions of the adults who are supervising the area.

Assembly Program Area

- Wait for permission to enter the room.
- With permission, hold the door open for others. Do not slam the door.
- Follow the instructions of adults regarding where to sit. Speak only at appropriate times during the assembly program.
- Stay within your personal space.
- Wait patiently for the program to start.
- When an adult says, "May I have your attention" or steps to the front and raises his or her hand, stop talking, and look at and listen to the adult.
- Listen carefully during the entire assembly.
- Keep your comments and questions focused on the topic.
- Never make fun of what the speaker says, and never boo, whistle, or yell.
- Respect the rights of others to listen.
- When the speaker asks a question, raise your hand to respond. Do not shout the answer unless the speaker asks you to do so. Do not try to be funny by responding with an inappropriate answer.
- Respect the efforts of those speaking or performing, and applaud appropriately to show your appreciation.
- Remain in your seat until instructed by an adult to leave. Leave the room in an orderly manner.

Dismissal

- Remain in your classroom until announcements or the bell signaling dismissal.
- Have all the materials you need before leaving.
- When leaving, adhere to hall, stairwell, and other appropriate behavioral expectations, and walk quietly to your destination.
- Obtain a note from your parents or have them call the school when there are changes in pickup plans.
- Stay in your dismissal area until an adult tells you to leave.
- Walkers must leave the campus immediately and go straight home.
- Students are not to reenter the building.
- Students not leaving by an announced time will be escorted to the office to call parents.

Task Checklist, Step 9

Establish the Bully Free Rules and Behavioral Expectations

☐ Examine examples of rules relative to bullying from other schools. Search the Internet for such rules.

☐ Examine the suggested bully free rules and consequences, and determine their desirability for your school and at what grade levels.

☐ If necessary, develop the rules you wish for teachers to post and implement in their classrooms.

☐ Obtain feedback on the rules and consequences from teachers and students.

☐ Once the rules are approved, make sure they are posted in every classroom.

☐ Examine and modify the examples of behavioral expectations provided, and compare them to those already used by your school.

☐ Finalize the list of behavioral expectations, and obtain feedback from school personnel.

☐ Make plans for having the expectations taught to students.

☐ Consider having behavioral expectations posted in their specific areas.

☐ _____

_____

☐ _____

_____

☐ _____

_____

☐ _____

_____

☐ _____

_____

Step 10

Develop the Discipline Rubrics and Adopt Prosocial (Nonpunitive) Strategies

It is important to have guidelines for disciplining students for bullying behavior. Therefore, a discipline rubric should be established to help your school take consistent disciplinary action when bullying occurs. There should be a rubric that addresses bullying anywhere on school property. You should also encourage your school system's director of transportation to develop an anti-bullying discipline rubric for buses, if one does not already exist.

How to Develop Rubrics

All teachers have a responsibility to hold all students accountable for their behavior, not just students assigned to them. They should be empowered to deal with bullying in their classroom and apply the approved consequences. They should be given permission to call parents or guardians when feasible and when specified in disciplinary action guidelines and to schedule conferences with parents or guardians and other school staff. To assist teachers and other staff members in their efforts, bully free discipline rubrics need to be established.

Prior to developing or adopting the discipline rubrics, the Bully Free Program team needs to examine the school's discipline policy; discipline plan; bus rules; and the school rules, consequences, as well as the behavioral expectations adopted during the completion of Step 9. The behaviors that will be listed in the rubrics will probably be more specific than the rules, but some of the selected consequences may be listed in the rubrics.

The team should also secure the discipline rubrics that have already been developed by their school or district, if any. Examples of other discipline rubrics may be found on the Internet. The team should also examine the school's behavior code book. All of these documents need to be consistent with the bully discipline rubrics. There may also be a need to make changes in the current policies, discipline plans, and code book to ensure that they address all forms of bullying and are consistent with new selected consequences.

Establish an Anti-Bullying School Rubric (Behaviors and Consequences)

The team is now ready to develop the school's discipline rubric and eventually have it approved by the appropriate individuals. The list of behaviors that could make up bullying situations and could be included in a rubric is extensive. They can be physical, emotional or relational, and social. Of course, not all behaviors fit neatly into just one of these categories, and some of them are illegal. Examples of behaviors that could make up a bullying situation are:

Hurtful teasing (intentional)	Name-calling	Pushing
Insulting remarks	Taunting and ridiculing	Throwing objects
Insulting one's family	Demeaning comments	Shoving
Eye rolling	Stealing	Punching
Mean or dirty looks	Damaging property	Hitting
Exclusion (rejection)	Sexual harassment	Kicking
Mean tricks and embarrassment	Racial harassment	Tripping
Slander	Religious harassment	Scratching
Hate notes	Disability harassment	Biting
Starting rumors or gossiping	Sexual orientation harassment	Hair pulling
Threatening or hurtful gesturing	Stalking	Thumping
Staring or leering	Cyberstalking	Setting fires
Writing hurtful graffiti	Cyberbullying	Assaulting with a weapon
Threatening	Intimidation	Public humiliation
	Extortion	Social exclusion
	Spitting	Incitement
		Coercion

The rubric should also include the consequences for engaging in such behaviors. With this in mind, the team should examine the Bully Free Program discipline rubrics appearing in Appendix E. If the team wishes to develop a rubric from scratch, it can use the blank rubric form that also appears in Appendix E. These rubrics and the blank form are also provided as Microsoft Word files at www.bullyfree.com. The examples can be easily modified to create your school's bully free discipline rubric. There are three formats provided in these examples, and your team needs to determine which of the three is most appropriate for your school. They all include behaviors that can make up a bullying situation and examples of consequences. The first example of a rubric requires that your school keep a record of how many times a student has engaged in a certain type of bullying behavior. For this format to work for your school, it must have a system for reporting and tracking the bullying behaviors engaged in by specific students. Many schools have such a system.

Keeping track of which students repeatedly engage in bullying behavior when students have more than one teacher can be difficult. It requires a great deal of communication and discussion regarding individual students. During faculty and staff meetings, school personnel should discuss their observations and concerns about students who may be victims and bullies. This will help identify students who need assistance or intervention plans.

Once a draft of the rubric has been developed, the team may conduct focus meetings with selected students, parents, and school personnel to obtain their feedback. Of course, such meetings could also be held as the team develops the rubric.

Establish an Anti-Bullying Bus Rubric (Behaviors and Consequences)

Buses are high-risk areas for bullying, and what happens to students on the bus to school has a tremendous impact on their behavior at school. Many times, when students arrive they are too upset to start learning. If this is the case at your school, your school system may need an anti-bullying discipline rubric for buses. Your school or system may already have a bus discipline policy and bus rules, but they may not address bullying as fully as they should. Consider asking your school system's director of transportation and one or more drivers selected by the director to develop or improve the existing rules and rubric so that bullying is addressed more specifically. The Bully Free Program team could offer its assistance. Here is an example of a possible anti-bullying bus rubric with a list of behaviors and consequences. This example can be modified to make it consistent with existing bus policies and procedures. Inform your transportation director that Bully Free Systems LLC (www.bullyfree.com) has a complete anti-bullying bus program and provides training for bus drivers. Bully free bus stickers (www.bullyfree.com) are also available and can be placed in a visible location on buses.

Example of Anti-Bullying Bus Rubric

This code classifies unacceptable behavior into three levels for illustration. All consequences are dependent on the severity and frequency of the misbehavior.

Procedures for Reporting

The bus driver will report misconduct occurring on the school bus to the appropriate personnel. A school bus conduct report will be completed and submitted to the bus company operations manager, who will then forward it to the appropriate school principal for action. The principal or designee and the bus company will retain copies of the signed report. Students may also report bullying and other inappropriate behavior. The student should report the behavior to her or his teacher.

(continued on next page)

Example of Anti-Bullying Bus Rubric, Cont'd.

Level 1: Bullying and Other Misbehaviors That Interfere with the Orderly Transportation of Students

Bullying and Other Misbehavior	Consequences
Bullying • Name-calling, teasing, or belittling with the intent to hurt • Refusing to let others sit by him or her • Making mean or nasty gestures or facial expressions • Efforts to embarrass or humiliate someone **Other Behavior** • Talking too loudly • Failure to stay seated • Littering on the bus • Using profanity	The bus driver may address bullying and other misbehavior and report the behavior to the director of transportation. This action may include any of the following: • Issue verbal reprimand and warning to student • Separate victim and bully(ies) • Assign seats • Letter sent to parents or guardians from director of transportation • Conference with director of transportation • Parent conference • Loss of bus privileges for one to three days

Note: The negative consequences for level 1 should be applied consistently. The consequences are progressive in that they get more obtrusive or more negative according to the frequency of the behavior. The more times a behavior is observed, the more severe the consequences are. Consequences greater than those listed above may be applied and will be based on the type of misbehavior, the frequency of the mistreatment, the school's discipline plan, harassment and anti-bullying policies, and relevant board policies. For racial, ethnic, sexual, or other forms of severe harassment, also refer to the school's sexual harassment policy. Negative consequence should be applied with statements regarding inappropriate behavior and the behavior desired. Also, for a time period, the student should receive positive reinforcement for self-control and modeling the desired behavior.

Level 2: More Severe Misbehaviors That Interfere with the Orderly Transportation of Students

Bullying and Other Misbehavior	Consequences
Bullying • Stealing or damaging the property of others • Intimidating or threatening someone • Sending or passing hurtful or embarrassing notes • Physically hurting someone • Making hurtful racial comments • Engaging in unwanted physical content (thumping, pinching, tripping) • Refusal to stop bullying after one request from the bus driver **Other Behavior** • Repeated use of profanity • Repeated offense of littering the bus	The bus driver reports misbehavior on the bus. The principal or designee administers consequences. Illegal behavior must be reported to the police. This action may include any or all of the following: • Conference with principal or designee and parents • Letter sent to parents or guardians from the director of transportation and principal • Assigned seats • Restitution for any property stolen or damaged • Loss of bus privileges for four to five days • Detention • In-school suspension • Suspension from school for up to five days

Note: These negative consequences for level 2 should be applied consistently. The consequences are progressive in that they get more obtrusive or more negative according to the frequency of the behavior. The more times a behavior is observed, the more severe the consequences are. Consequences greater than those listed for level 2 may be applied and will be based on the type of misbehavior, the frequency of the mistreatment, the school's discipline plan, harassment and anti-bullying policies, and relevant board policies. For racial, ethnic, sexual, or other forms of severe harassment, also refer to the school's sexual harassment policy. Negative consequence should be applied with statements regarding inappropriate behavior and the behavior desired. Also, for a time period, the student should receive positive reinforcement for self-control and modeling the desired behavior.

Example of Anti-Bullying Bus Rubric, Cont'd.

Level 3: Behavior That Endangers the Safety of the Driver or Students and Impairs the Driver's Ability to Drive Safely	
Bullying and Other Misbehavior	**Consequences**
Bullying • Refusal to stop bullying after two requests from bus driver **Other Behavior** • Repeated occurrences of levels 1 and 2 behaviors • Refusal to remain seated • Throwing objects, spitting, spit balls • Distracting the driver • Refusal to obey the driver • Fighting, including pushing or wrestling • Lighting matches or lighters • Possession of knives or other dangerous objects • Possession or use of tobacco, alcohol, drugs, or controlled substances	The bus driver reports bullying and other misbehaviors on the bus. The principal or designee administers consequences. At more severe levels, the superintendent or designee may be involved. This action may include the following: • Principal and director of transportation conduct a conference with the parents or guardians. • Loss of bus privileges for six to ten days. • Suspension from school for six to ten days. • Repeated incidents of level 3 behavior may result in a student's being permanently suspended from bus privileges. • Illegal activity will be referred to the police department.

Note: These negative consequences for level 3 should be applied consistently. The consequences are progressive in that they get more obtrusive or more negative according to the frequency of the behavior. The more times a behavior is observed, the more severe the consequences are. Consequences greater than those listed above may be applied and will be based on the type of misbehavior, the frequency of the mistreatment, the school's discipline plan, harassment and anti-bullying policies, and relevant board policies. For racial, ethnic, sexual, or other forms of severe harassment, also refer to the school's sexual harassment policy. Negative consequence should be applied with statements regarding inappropriate behavior and the behavior desired. Also, for a time period, the student should receive positive reinforcement for self-control and modeling the desired behavior.

Source: This rubric was adapted with permission from the Shrewsbury Public Schools Bus Discipline Procedures and Consequences, Shrewsbury, Massachusetts. www.shrewsbury-ma.gov/schools/Central/Transportation/Bus.Discipline.Procedures.htm

Adopt Prosocial Strategies

According to Sullivan, Cleary, and Sullivan, "A climate in which punishment is the response just drives bullying underground" (2005, p. 217). Therefore, in addition to the negative consequences, discipline rubrics, and training already described, training teachers and counselors to use prosocial strategies that are nonpunitive and restorative is important. Examples of such strategies are the no-blame approach, the method of shared concern, the problem-solving circle, and reverse role playing. It would not be practical to describe these in detail in this book, but the strategies are briefly outlined in the next sections. The Bully Free Program team can research these through the Internet, and there are numerous resources that speak directly to these strategies.

Most anti-bullying programs include discipline rubrics because it is a fact of life that inappropriate behavior yields negative consequences. We should not shelter students from this reality. However, it is well understood that positive reinforcement for appropriate behavior can be more powerful than punishment for inappropriate behavior. It is also beneficial to use prosocial (nonpunitive) methods when dealing with inappropriate behavior. Therefore, an effective anti-bullying program should be a blending of all three approaches: negative consequences, positive consequences, and prosocial (nonpunitive) strategies.

Andrew Mellor (2009), director of the Anti-Bullying Network (www.anti-bullying .net), says,

> *It is difficult to argue that serious, intentional, repeated, physical bullying should not be met with the imposition of some sort of sanctions. Indeed physical violence such as this is a crime—and schools are subject to the law of the land. However, this type of bullying is far less common than name-calling and exclusion, although we know from the testimony of victims the hurt which can be caused by being taunted and deliberately isolated.*
>
> *Many parents, pupils and teachers expect "bullies" to be punished, but in many cases punishment will be ineffective or inappropriate—and children cannot be punished for refusing to play with another child. That is why schools are increasingly adopting new reactive strategies such as No Blame (which is now often called the Support Group approach) and the related Shared Concern Method. These strategies allow effective intervention in situations where guilt cannot be proved, or where it is unclear whether what has happened is bullying or a relationship problem.*

No-Blame Approach (Support Group Method)

One prosocial approach the Bully Free Program team should examine is the No-Blame Approach, developed by Barbara Maines and George Robinson (1992). It is a prosocial response to bullying that encourages students to take responsibility for their actions and the consequences of their actions. It is important that some people are critical of approaches that do not also require negative consequences. This approach alone is not enough to stop bullying. The *Support Group Method Training Pack* (Maines & Robinson, 2009) is a training resource. It includes a DVD and facilitator's manual. An excellent summary of this approach appears in *Bullying in Secondary Schools* (Sullivan, Cleary, & Sullivan, 2005) and *School Bullying: Insights and Perspectives* (Smith & Sharp, 1994). An abbreviated version of the steps appear in *The Bully Free Classroom* (Beane, 1999).

It should be noted that the no-blame approach is particularly useful in dealing with group bullying and name-calling. However, it may be an inappropriate response to other types of bullying. It should be applied only with the full agreement of the bullied child and after a professional judgment has been made about whether the bullying children are capable of understanding the hurt they have caused. A small number of children who bully others have serious social, emotional, and behavioral problems. In such cases the no-blame approach could expose the victim to the possibility of even more bullying.

Method of Shared Concern

Another prosocial strategy the Bully Free Program team may want to examine is the method of shared concern. It is a nonpunitive, counseling-based intervention model that was developed by Swedish psychologist Anatol Pikas in the 1980s (Sharp & Smith, 1994). It has since been used successfully in many parts of the world. However, many say this approach alone is not enough to stop bullying, that there should also be consequences. It involves conducting structured interviews with individual bullies, during which they are asked to take responsibility for their actions and commit to more responsible behavior. Interviews are also done with victims and then with groups of bullies and victims together. So, this method can be time consuming, but worth the effort. This method is not designed to teach students how to make friends, or to reveal detailed facts about the bullying situation. It is designed to change the situation by getting children to change their behavior. A summary of this strategy appears in *The Bully Free Classroom* (Beane, 1999). An excellent training tool explaining this method is a DVD and guide developed by Ken Rigby. The training is built around two case studies and can be used for a half-day training session. To order this resource, visit www.readymade.com.

Problem-Solving Circle

Another prosocial strategy to be examined by the Bully Free Program team is the problem-solving circle (Waterhouse, Sippel, Pedrini, & Cawley, 1998). A description of the approach can be found on the Internet. The procedure for this strategy is basically as follows:

- Establish the ground rules (for example, one person talks at a time, no group member speaks out of turn or interrupts, everyone speaks respectfully, there are to be no insults or raised voices and no blaming others).

- All those involved in the incident are brought together and seated in a circle. The group is not left unattended, and no discussion is allowed before the group leader is present and has outlined the rules.

- The leader explains that this group has been called together to solve a problem, not to lay blame. No one is "in trouble." The rules for classroom meetings are mentioned.

- The leader asks the question, "What happened?" and each person adds a piece of the story. It may be necessary to go around the circle several times before the story is clear and each person feels heard.

- Strictly adhere to the rules and acknowledge each contribution in a respectful and nonjudgmental way. One technique is to simply say "Thank you" after each contribution.

- Follow the same procedure for the questions, "What could you have done differently so that this would not have happened?" "What could you do now to make things better?" These questions will be very different for students who are entrenched in a "good person, bad person" frame of reference, so it is very important to solicit an answer from each student as a demonstration that each is willing to move from that stance. This is also a good time to discuss the Golden Rule.

- Tell students you want to challenge them to do what's right. Tell them you have confidence that they will do what is right.

- Schedule a brief follow-up meeting of the group to monitor their individual commitment to "make things better." This could take place from a day to a week later, as appropriate.

Not all children who bully will choose to be cooperative. Require the students to sit and listen. Their lack of cooperation should lead to negative consequences. Consequences imposed should be responsible, restorative, and respectful of both the child who has been bullied and the child who bullied.

Reverse Role Playing

Another approach that may be considered prosocial in nature or purpose by some is the Reverse Role Playing strategy. A description of this approach can also be found on the Internet (Waterhouse et al., 1998). Reverse role playing begins with the student who bullied reenacting his or her part in a bullying episode while a staff member plays the role of the student who was bullied. During the reenactment, the staff member may ask questions to gain clarification about the incident and the role of the student who was bullying. The situation is then reversed with the staff member playing the role of the student who bullied.

While roles are reversed, the student responsible for bullying is encouraged to reconstruct the incident realistically, including details of the time, location, and names of others involved and what they did. Following the role play, the staff member discusses the incident with the student, questioning to determine how the student felt. The meeting should be closed by the staff member's providing a summary of the activity and determining future action for the student (for example, a written apology, commitment to stop bullying, agreement to meet again).

A Reminder

The Bully Free Program encourages the use of prosocial strategies, but endorses the use of negative consequences for inappropriate behavior. It rewards changes in behavior. This is the most accurate representation of the real world.

Task Checklist, Step 10   Notes

Develop the Discipline Rubrics and Adopt Prosocial Strategies

☐ Secure copies of existing school and bus discipline rubrics from your own school or other schools, especially those addressing bullying behaviors.

☐ Print examples of discipline rubrics found on the Internet that address bullying behaviors.

☐ Examine the examples of the discipline rubrics appearing in Appendix E and on the Internet.

☐ Review the rules and consequences and behavioral expectations selected during the completion of Step 9.

☐ Compare the examples with the bully free discipline rubrics provided in this book and in the Microsoft Word files located at www.bullyfree.com.

☐ Develop a draft of a proposed bully free discipline rubric for your school. Examine the school's behavior code book to ensure consistency with the rubric under development. If necessary, recommend changes in the code book to ensure that it completely addresses all forms of bullying.

☐ Conduct focus meetings with selected students, parents, and teachers to obtain their views on the drafted rubric.

☐ Finalize the rubric, and submit it for approval by the appropriate school officials.

☐ Examine the prosocial strategies, determine which ones to adopt, and prepare to train teachers to use them.

☐ Secure copies of the school system's school-bus rules and discipline policy. If there is already a bus rubric, obtain a copy for examination.

☐ Find examples on the Internet of bus discipline rubrics that address bullying.

☐ Examine the example of a bully free bus discipline rubric in this book and in the Microsoft Word file located at www.bullyfree.com.

Task Checklist, Step 10, Cont'd.

Notes

- ☐ Work with the director of transportation to improve the existing policy or existing rubric or to develop a new rubric.

- ☐ Inform your transportation director that Bully Free Systems LLC has an anti-bullying program and trains bus drivers (visit www.bullyfree.com).

- ☐ Examine the example bus rules and consequences and work with the director of transportation to develop bus rules and consequences.

- ☐ _____
  _____

- ☐ _____
  _____

- ☐ _____
  _____

Step 11

Develop the Response Plan

It is critical for your school to develop bully free response plans detailing appropriate responses to bullying situations. The goal of the plans should be to prevent and stop bullying. Because harassment can be a bullying behavior, the team should also review the district's and school's harassment policies and procedures, as well as other discipline-related policies and procedures prior to developing the bully free response plans. A helpful resource in developing the following response plan was *Focus on Bullying: A Prevention Program for Elementary School Communities* (Waterhouse, Sippel, Pedrini, & Cawley, 1998).

Areas to Address

Ideally, schools should have five types of bully free response plans: (1) responding to students who bully students, (2) responding to students who bully school personnel (faculty, staff, and volunteers), (3) responding to school personnel who bully students, (4) responding to school personnel who bully other school personnel, and (5) responding to parents who bully school personnel. All of these should be consistent with the anti-bullying policy developed in Step 8. The bully free response plans should be comprehensive and take into consideration all of the parties involved. They should provide support for the victims and encourage change in the bullies. The first step in developing these plans is to examine existing policies to determine their effectiveness in preventing and stopping bullying in the five areas listed above.

Frequently school personnel deal with situations where they must remind students of school policies, school or classroom rules (behavioral expectations), and the consequences for violating them. Unfortunately even school personnel engage in inappropriate behavior and need to be reminded of policies and consequences for their violation. The response plans bring consistency to responding to bullying that contributes to the effectiveness of the Bully Free Program. Therefore, this is especially important when dealing with bullying.

According to *Focus on Bullying* (Waterhouse et al., 1998), an effective response to student's bullying behaviors has four goals:

- *Encourage communication:* To get adults to serve as models for students by engaging them in discussion about bullying, teaching assertiveness and self-protection strategies, and encouraging students to seek adult assistance

- *Develop empathy:* To teach individuals to recognize and interpret cues that signal others' feelings and needs and to understand the impact of bullying behavior on others

- *Promote accountability:* To help individuals (all students and school personnel) develop the ability to stop and think before they act and take responsibility for their behavior by making reparation for harm they have inflicted on others

- *Enhance prosocial behavior:* To teach, model, and reinforce skills for getting along with others and to promote a sense of belonging and acceptance

Effective response plans must be comprehensive, taking into consideration all parties involved in the bullying incident. They should provide specific support for the victim of bullying, as well as intervention for the individual who was bullying. The plan should also include strategies for responding to individuals who were directly observing the bullying incident. The bully free response plans need to include the following elements:

- Detailed guidelines, procedures, and forms for reporting and responding to incidents of bullying behavior

- Strategies to support, encourage, and help individuals (students and school personnel) who are bullied

- Strategies to respond to individuals who bully in a manner that brings about a change in their behavior

- Strategies to respond to individuals who witness bullying and encourage appropriate behavior

- Restorative interventions to bring together all parties involved in a bullying incident

All members of a school community have a responsibility to challenge poor behavior they observe in students and school personnel. Ignoring it will ensure that it continues and thrives. It is the responsibility of school officials to have clearly described procedures to follow when there are concerns over a student's or a colleague's inappropriate behavior.

All school staff, including volunteer supervisors, should have input into the design of the school's bully free response plans. It is especially important for those who supervise students to be familiar with their responsibilities related to bullying.

The following material is an example of a bully free response plan that focuses on students bullying students. This plan can be modified by the Bully Free Program team with input from all of the appropriate individuals and used in the school. Examples of forms used in this plan are provided in Appendix F. It also appears as a file at www.bullyfree.com. The framework of this example may help you later develop the other four response plans.

The Bully Free Response Plan: Students Bullying Students

This response plan focuses on intervening when students bully students. It is provided to help your school or school district develop a bully free response plan for dealing with students bullying students. You should work with others to modify the plan to match the culture of your school, existing policies and procedures, the administrative leadership styles, existing discipline plans and behavioral codes, as well as local, state, and federal laws.

It is especially critical for adults to respond immediately and consistently to bullying. Because bullying is hurtful and persistent behavior that occurs over time and can have a devastating impact on students, immediate action must be taken. Students need the assistance of adults.

Some bullying situations can be short term and can be stopped rather quickly by an adult who observes the bullying or receives a report. Other bullying situations are more persistent and harmful, requiring the assistance of more than one adult. Responding to some bullying situations may also require the use of more intense interventions and prevention strategies.

Responding to Rumors or Unverified Reports of Bullying

If you receive a report of bullying and are not sure the report is true, avoid accusations. However, be sensitive to what students say about and how they interact with the student who may be mistreated. Keep your eyes and ears open. Also investigate all reports of bullying.

There are only two types of evidence of proof that a student has been bullied: (1) an adult has observed it or has some other proof of bullying, such as a video recording, or (2) the accused admits bullying someone. When these conditions do not exist, bullying has to be treated as a rumor or an unverified report. When rumors or unverified reports of bullying occur, the following steps should be followed by the principal of the school or his or her designee.

Note: Always protect the identity of students who report the bullying. If it was an adult, get the individual's permission before you mention his or her name during the investigation. If video cameras are in the reported area, review the recordings.

Dealing with the First Rumor and Unverified Report

Step 1

Call the parents or guardians of the student who may have been bullied. Say to them,

> *There is a rumor [or report] that your child is being mistreated. Unfortunately, we do not have proof of the mistreatment. But we try to investigate all rumors and reports of mistreatment, because we care and do not tolerate any mistreatment. There is a school policy against bullying, and there are significant consequences for the behavior. Why don't you have a conversation with your child and determine if there is any truth in the rumor [or report]. Do not interrogate your child but find out if the mistreatment is occurring. Be sure to write down what your child tells you, and let me know what you discover. We have found it best if we don't get too excited or try to figure out who to blame. It is also best not to ask your child why he is being mistreated. Most of the time students do not know. If it appears that your child is mistreated, ask him to keep a record of his mistreatment, recording who is mistreating him, who is following along with it, who observed it, what happened, as well as when and where the mistreatment occurs. Tell your child to keep his teacher and me informed. We will try to take care of things at school.*

If appropriate, ask the alleged victim's parents not to call the parents of the alleged bully. The Bullying Situation Report in Appendix F may be completed if you think it is important to record elements of the rumor. Check "Suspected bullying situation" on the report form, and briefly summarize your response. Also record the date and time and the name of the parent you talked to. Write a brief summary regarding your telephone conversation with the parent or guardian.

(continued on next page)

The Bully Free Response Plan: Students Bullying Students, Cont'd.

Step 2

Call the parents or guardians of the alleged bully. Say to them:

> There is a rumor [or report] that your child may be mistreating someone. We do not have any evidence that the rumor [or report] is true, but we are obligated to let parents know about it and do what we can to discover the facts. Your child deserves that from us. We always investigate because we care about our students, and we don't want anyone to be mistreated. There is a school policy against bullying, and there are significant consequences for the behavior. We also do not want anyone to be treated unfairly or accused unfairly of mistreating others. We are not accusing your child; we are just giving you a chance to talk to your child, and we will do all that we can to find out the facts. Why don't you have a conversation with your child and determine if the rumor [or report] is true. Please do not interrogate your child, but find out what, if anything, may be happening. Write down what your child tells you, and let me know what you discover. We will try to take care of things at school while you talk to your child.

Step 3

Communicate with the teachers. Talk with all of the teachers of the students who may be involved in a bullying situation. Ask them not to mention the names of or confront the students allegedly involved, but to heighten their awareness and supervisory efforts to the possibility of mistreatment. Ask them to increase their supervision of the students who may be involved and seek to monitor areas where the bullying may be occurring. Ask the teachers to remind all students of the school's anti-bullying policy and the consequences for bullying.

Dealing with the Second Rumor or Unverified Report

When a second rumor or unverified report of bullying is received involving all or some of the same students, the principal should take the following steps:

Step 1

Privately interview the student who may be a victim of bullying. Before you ask questions, explain the rumors and reports you have received. You could start your statements with: "Some students have reported that . . ." or "An adult has reported that . . ." Explain that you are concerned because this is the second time you have heard of the possible mistreatment. Explain that you are obligated to investigate all rumors and reports and that you want everyone to be treated fairly. Explain that you and the school will not tolerate bullying. When it is age appropriate, ask the student to complete the Bully Free Statement Sheet—Reported Victim (see Appendix F). Ask the student to write down only the facts. Young students may require assistance. However, make sure only the student's words are recorded. Ask the student to sign and date the form. Keep in mind that the student may refuse to fill out the sheet for a variety of reasons. For example, the student may be fearful of retaliation or may have not been completely truthful. If the student refuses to write a statement, make a record of the refusal.

Step 2

Privately interview the student, or each of the students, who may be engaging in the bullying. Interview each one separately, and schedule the interview so that there is not time for them to talk to each other before you interview all of them. Do not appear judgmental, and do not seek blame. Use a firm yet gentle and respectful tone of voice throughout the interviews. Maintain a comfortable level of eye contact. Before you ask questions, explain the rumors and reports you have received, and explain that you are obligated to investigate all rumors and reports and that

The Bully Free Response Plan: Students Bullying Students, Cont'd.

you want everyone to be treated fairly. You could start your statements with: "Some students have reported that . . ." or "An adult has reported that . . ." Explain that you are concerned because this is the second time you have heard of the possible mistreatment. Explain that you and the school will not tolerate bullying. Remind them of the school's anti-bullying policy (including cyberbullying and cell phone policies) and the consequences for such behavior.

Explain the school's anti-bullying policy and the significant consequences for bullying others. Then ask the student to complete the Bully Free Statement Sheet—Accused (see Appendix F). Ask the student to write down only the facts, admitting or denying the mistreatment. Young students may require assistance. However, make sure only the student's words are recorded. Ask the student to sign and date the form. Keep in mind that the student may refuse to fill out the sheet for a variety of reasons. For example, sometimes the student may not have been completely truthful. If the student refuses to write a statement, make a record of the refusal.

Step 3

Prepare to talk to the parents or guardians of the alleged victim by reading his or her completed statement sheet. Call the parents and explain that you are concerned because this is the second time you have heard about the possible mistreatment. Explain that you feel it is time to step up efforts to discover the facts. Ask them again to talk to their child and to write down what they are told. Also explain that you have interviewed all of the students who may be involved. Schedule a time for the victim's parents to come in and talk to you about the comments of the students and what you have discovered. Ask them not to bring any children to the meeting.

Step 4

Prepare to talk to the parents of the alleged bully by reading the completed statement sheet, and call the parents as soon as possible. Explain to them that you are concerned because this is the second time you have heard about the possible mistreatment. Explain that you feel it is time to step up efforts to discover the facts. Ask them to talk with their child again. If the rumors or reports appear to be true, explain that you have interviewed all of the students who may be involved and you feel it is best that they come in and talk to you. Schedule a time to meet with them. If the situation appears to involve more than one bully, have a separate meeting with each set of parents. Ask them not to bring any children to the meeting. Explain that you realize they have more authority over their child than you do, but you are responsible for making sure students follow the school's rules and behavior codes. Also explain that it is your job to investigate all rumors and reports of mistreatment and to do all you can to make sure all students are treated appropriately, including their child.

Most parents are cooperative. However, if a parent is disrespectful, explain to him or her that children deserve adults who can cooperate and work together. Explain that you called the meeting and you have the authority to end the meeting. Tell the parent that you would prefer not to end the meeting, but you will.

Responding to Bullying Events

This section includes a discussion of general responsibilities as well as specific responsibilities of adults who observe and respond to bullying. Although specific responsibilities are listed, each school should assign certain responsibilities to school personnel. For example, some schools may prefer that the school counselor or psychologist rather than a teacher gather information by interviewing students.

(continued on next page)

The Bully Free Response Plan: Students Bullying Students, Cont'd.

General Responsibilities of Adults Responding to Bullying

- Investigate all rumors and reports of bullying.
- Follow the established school discipline plans, policies, and procedures.
- Try to make each situation a teachable moment. Always tell the student the behavior expected.
- Respond immediately and consistently to bullying.
- Maintain open communication lines with victims, bullies, followers, and bystanders, as well as parents.
- Immediately respond to rumors, reports, and observations of bullying.

Specific Responsibilities of Adults Responding to Bullying

When there is potential for a fight or an actual fight, walk toward the students with authority. Quickly scan the situation to determine what is happening and who is involved. Also determine if weapons are being used. Just the presence of an adult can stop the fight. Call the students by name with a forceful voice, and tell them to stop. Never step between two students who are physically fighting. Make a mental note of onlookers, and ask them to leave the area and tell them you may talk to them later. Send a student for help. After the fight, document what happened, and report it to the appropriate school personnel. If there is an obvious victim, provide emotional support.

When bullying is observed, the following steps should be taken.

Step 1

- Immediately confront and deal with the bully. Call the student by name and, in a demanding voice, tell him or her to stop.
- Move closer to the bully and, if appropriate and safe, step between the victim and bully to block eye contact between them. Never step between two students who are physically fighting.
- Maintain occasional eye contact with the bully. Sometimes it's best not to give constant eye contact. Some bullies may find constant eye contact threatening and may feel a need to defend themselves in the presence of other students.
- In a firm but quiet and matter-of-fact voice, let the bully know you saw or heard him or her mistreating the individual. Command the bully to stop. Make sure you specify the inappropriate behavior to be stopped and the behavior you desire. "Bobby, I heard you make fun of Billy's ears, and I want you to stop calling him 'Elephant' and call him by his name: Billy."
- When commanding a bully to stop, do not shout from a distance unless injuries are possible.
- Do not ask a question, for example, "Bobby, would you please stop?"
- At this time, do not ask the students to explain what is happening.
- When a student has been threatening, he or she should be immediately taken to the principal's office.

When approaching a bullying situation, there may be times that you may choose to take a less assertive approach. In these situations, consider making the following adaptations of statements developed by Lajoie, McLellan, and Seddon (1997):

"Looks like some nasty things are happening to _____ that are against the rules."

"Hey, I just heard something that is really inappropriate and will not be tolerated."

"You know that is against our rules."

"Come here, _____. I need to talk to you for at minute."

"Be careful that feelings are not being hurt here."

"Hey, this looks [or sounds] like bullying to me. You know our school rules."

The Bully Free Response Plan: Students Bullying Students, Cont'd.

If the bully does not stop, stay between the two and maintain eye contact with the bully. State that bullying violates school policy (state the behavioral code being violated) and state the associated approved negative consequences. Communicate the seriousness of the behavior. If the bully stops, compliment him or her. Make it clear that it is the behavior that you dislike. Explain that it will not be tolerated. In addition:

- Do not send the victim and bully away unless it is determined to be appropriate or necessary.

- Do not ask the victim or bully in front of other students to explain what happened.

- Record or log the event in a notebook or other ways approved by the school. This information must be kept in a secure location.

Step 2

If you are the student's teacher or homeroom teacher, you may immediately apply the negative consequences you are allowed to apply, as specified in the school anti-bullying policy and bully free discipline rubrics.

- Respond according to the severity and frequency of bullying behavior. For example, the consequence for the first offense should be less severe (perhaps time-out or loss of privileges, such as lunch in the cafeteria or free time on the computer) than it would be for a second offense. Of course, some behaviors result in more severe consequences.

- Be consistent with the application of all negative or reductive consequences.

- Resist the temptation to apply what might be considered minimal negative consequences for bullying behaviors that may appear "less severe." The degree of severity depends on the nature, experience, and needs of the student being bullied and a host of other variables. What you or others may consider mild bullying may have a devastating impact on some victims. For example, social rejection and name-calling can be just as hurtful as being hit with a fist. In fact, the hurt may be deeper and last longer. The negative consequences should also be coupled with what the bully needs to learn in order to get along with others and treat others the way he or she wants to be treated. While it is extremely important to stop and prevent bullying, the ultimate goal of any form of intervention is behavior change in the bully and provocative victims (those who engage in behavior that provokes others to mistreat them). Since helping a bully often requires a change of attitude and heart, as well as thinking, it takes time.

- Students in grades 3 through 8 who bully should be asked to complete the following Inappropriate Behavior Card. Blank cards are kept by teachers and other supervisors.

Inappropriate Behavior Card

Student's Name (Print): _____ Date:_____

Time: _____ Location: _____

Supervising Adult (Print Name): _____

Accurately and specifically write what you did to whom:

Student's Signature: _____

(continued on next page)

The Bully Free Response Plan: Students Bullying Students, Cont'd.

- Give the completed card to the student's teacher or homeroom teacher and explain what has been observed.
- If the victim is in the same class as the bully, ask the teacher to provide emotional support for the victim by actively listening and giving the student hope that the bullying will stop.
- Ask the teacher or homeroom teacher to tell the bully that such behavior will not be tolerated and that the adults in the school will be watching how he or she treats others.
- Ask the teacher or homeroom teacher to increase supervision of the victim and bully.
- The teacher or homeroom teacher may apply the approved consequences based on the behavior and the number of cards that have been received. For example, the bully may be required to carry out a restitution plan, replacing damaged or destroyed property. Once the teacher or homeroom teacher receives three cards on a child, the Bullying Situation Report (see Appendix F) will be completed by the teacher or homeroom teacher and sent to the school counselor and the principal, who will follow up with the information from the report. All Bully Situation Reports should be kept in a secured single file or notebook in a central location, such as the principal's office.

Step 3

Privately provide emotional support for the victim:

- Let the victim know that you are thankful to know about the bullying because you know how hurtful it is.
- Explain that you and other adults in the school will not tolerate this behavior.
- Explain that appropriate action will be taken to bring it to an end.
- Explain the importance of telling an adult.
- Tell the student that you will maintain contact with him or her to see how things are going.
- Set a time that the student will report to you about his or her day. Eventually, this could be once a week, and so forth.
- Do not promise you will not tell anyone else. Tell the student that dealing with the situation may take the assistance of others.

Step 4

Speak to the bystanders before they leave the bullying scene:

- At this time, do not ask them to describe what they saw.
- Use a firm, calm, and matter-of-fact voice to let them know you saw their response to the bullying.
- If their response was appropriate, compliment them.
- If their response was inappropriate, explain what they could have done differently and what you expect them to do the next time they see someone bullied.

Step 5 (Optional)

If the behavior warrants and if determined appropriate by your school, contact the parents or require the victim and the bully to tell their parents or guardians.

In some cases, it may be best not to notify the parents or guardians of the student who bullies, especially when parents are known to be abusive. Before calling the parents, discuss the situation with the appropriate school personnel.

When the parents are contacted, tell them that additional information will be gathered and that they will be contacted soon to discuss the situation. If the student refuses to tell or call the parents, tell the student you will make the call.

The Bully Free Response Plan: Students Bullying Students, Cont'd.

Step 6 (Optional)

Meet with the parents:

- Some bullying situations may require a meeting with the victim's parents and a separate meeting with the bully's parents. It is usually not wise to have both sets of parents in the same meeting.
- Prior to each meeting, gather information about the situation. Of course, it is possible that some of the intervention and prevention strategies have been implemented prior to the parent meeting. Also discuss anything you have done to keep the child safe.
- Prior to the meeting, discuss plans for the meeting with the appropriate school personnel. Seek their guidance for the meeting.
- At the meeting, discuss the school's view of the problem and the need for intervention. Discuss the strategies (for example, negative consequences and prosocial strategies) that have already been implemented and whether these have been effective. Be sure to allow time for parents to voice their concerns and for you to answer their questions.
- Provide the parents with a plan they can implement at home. The plan may include resources and activities to meet the needs of their child, as well as to stop and prevent the bullying. An excellent resource to give parents of victims and bullies is *Protect Your Child from Bullying* (Beane, 2008); a book for victims is *How You Can Be Bully Free* (Beane, 2004a and 2004b).
- At the end of the meeting, tell the parents you will keep them informed, and ask them to keep you informed as well.

The following steps can be time-consuming, but they are important and should be taken when it is deemed necessary. It may be necessary for more than one adult to conduct the interviews; for example, the counselor, school psychologist, and assistant principal.

Step 7

Gather information from the victim, bully, followers, and bystanders (witnesses):

> *Immediately and privately interview the victim, and develop a safety plan for him or her. Sometimes the school counselor or school psychologist conducts this interview.*

- Find and schedule a private location for the interview, one without windows, so other students cannot see you with the student.
- If appropriate, ask a colleague to observe the meeting and help you record information.
- If the student doesn't know you, introduce yourself, and tell him or her your position at the school.
- Be sensitive to the stress level of the victim.
- Encourage the victim to express his or her emotions.
- Provide encouragement and emotional support for the victim.
   - Say no one deserves to be bullied.
   - Be an active listener.
   - Give the victim hope that the bullying will end.
   - Voice pleasure that the victim (or someone else) told you or someone about the bullying.
- Do not make the victim feel he or she is being interrogated, but ask the following questions and record the answers. Mention that you would like to hear what happened from his or her point of view.

   "Who was involved?"

   "What was said and done by the bully and others?"

(continued on next page)

The Bully Free Response Plan: Students Bullying Students, Cont'd.

"What happened or usually happens immediately before the bullying occurs?"

"Who were the bystanders, and what did they say and do?"

"Did you or anyone else get physically hurt?"

"Did your property or anyone else's property get damaged or stolen? If so, please explain."

"When does the bullying occur?"

"Where does it happen?"

"Was there adult supervision? If so, who was it?"

"What happened or usually happens after the bullying?"

"Who has been told about the bullying, and what have they done (if anything)?"

"How long has this been occurring?"

- Be careful about asking the student why he or she is being bullied. If you ask this question too soon, the student may not share everything with you or may not tell the truth. And sometimes the victim does not know why he or she is bullied.

- If video cameras are in the area where the bullying occurred, review the recordings. It is important to have the facts about what has happened. Sometimes students leave out critical information that affects your understanding of the incident.

- At the end of the meeting, develop a safety plan for the victim:

  - Explore ways to avoid bullies. Note that ignoring does not usually work.

  - If appropriate, teach the victim a few assertiveness tips (see *The Bully Free Classroom*, Beane, 1999).

  - Seek to increase supervision of the bully.

  - Ask the victim to report to you (daily or weekly) regarding the effectiveness of the safety plan. Maintain contact and open communication lines with the victim.

  - Ask the victim to immediately report when he or she is bullied or sees others bullied.

- After a few days, meet to assess the effectiveness of the safety plan you developed with the victim. Whenever possible, spend time with him or her, but do not smother the student with your attention.

Interview the bystanders (witnesses) separately and privately.

- Find and schedule a private location for the interviews, one without windows, so that others cannot see you and the student.

- If the bystanders do not know you, introduce yourself, and tell them your position at the school.

- If they witnessed what happened, they must complete the Bullying Witness Statement Form (Appendix F). Of course, the child's age and abilities will dictate the appropriateness of asking him or her to complete the form.

- Ask the following questions. As you listen to their answers, do not appear judgmental. Use a firm yet gentle and respectful tone of voice throughout the interviews. Maintain a comfortable level of eye contact. Be mindful that some bystanders may be followers of the bully or encouragers of the mistreatment.

"What happened?"

"Did you or anyone else get physically hurt?"

"Did anyone's property get damaged or stolen? If so, please explain."

"How do you feel about what you saw?"

The Bully Free Response Plan: Students Bullying Students, Cont'd.

"Why would this be called bullying?"

"How would you feel if you were treated the same way?"

"How do you think the student felt?" (Describe to the followers and bystanders the impact you feel the bullying is having on the victim.)

"Did you feel a need to encourage or discourage the mistreatment? Why do you think you felt this way? What did you do? Did your actions encourage or discourage the bullying?"

"How do you feel now about what happened? What could you do differently next time?"

"What can you do to help the student feel a sense of belonging and acceptance?"

"What can you do to encourage others not to mistreat their peers?"

- Facilitate a problem-solving session with the followers and bystanders to discover ways they can help the victim and stop the bullying. Encourage them to carry out their plans or ideas and to tell an adult when they see someone mistreated. Explain that they will be "reporting," not "ratting." When they report, they are trying to help someone in trouble.

- Schedule a meeting with all the followers and bystanders in a week to assess their follow-through with their plans to help the victim.

Privately interview the bully and followers rapidly one after another.

- If appropriate, ask another adult to observe the interviews and help record information.

- If a student does not know you, introduce yourself and say what your position is at the school.

- Let each student know why you are interviewing him or her. Say that you want to find out what happened and to discover ways to help the victim have a sense of belonging and acceptance.

- Do not appear judgmental. Use a firm yet gentle and respectful tone of voice throughout the interviews. Maintain a comfortable level of eye contact.

- Communicate the seriousness of the bullying behavior and the code of behavior that it violates.

- Do not accept comments such as, "It was all in fun." or "He brings it on himself." You cannot accept these as excuses. Make it clear that no one deserves to be bullied. Keep in mind that most students who bully will minimize or deny wrongdoing. Bullies often lie and get defensive, even antisocial.

- Ask the following questions:

"What did you do that has required that you meet with me?"

"Did anyone's property get damaged or stolen? If so, please explain."

"Why did you mistreat him or her?"

"What was wrong with what you did?"

"What did you want?"

"Did you get what you wanted? If not, why not?"

"What could you have done differently?"

"Will you be able to make a better behavior choice next time?"

"What will you do to make sure this doesn't happen again?"

(continued on next page)

The Bully Free Response Plan: Students Bullying Students, Cont'd.

- During the interviews, make sure you communicate the following:
  - ○ You know they are engaging in bullying (state the specific behavior).
  - ○ Bullying is against school policy (state the possible consequences).
  - ○ The bullying must stop immediately.
  - ○ School personnel will be keeping an eye on this student.
  - ○ When appropriate, parents will be notified and kept informed.
  - ○ There will be follow-up meetings with everyone involved. At first, schedule the meetings every week.
  - ○ There will be serious consequences for retaliation.

Step 8

Seek information about the bully, followers, and victim from other school personnel and school volunteers. Make sure it is not hearsay. If appropriate and deemed necessary, develop intervention plans for the victim and bully. Responding to bullying is more than interviewing and applying consequences. It also involves developing an intervention plan to help the victim and to help the bully change his or her behavior. Developing such a plan may involve one or more school personnel and may include parents or guardians. The following are suggested steps to developing intervention plans.

- Complete the Bully Free Intervention Questionnaire (see Appendix F) and the Bully Free Intervention Plan Form for the victim (see Appendix F).
  - ○ Make sure accurate information has been collected thus far.
  - ○ Assess the needs of the victim by reviewing the completed Bully Free Intervention Questionnaire and studying the student's school records. It will take time to find answers to all of the questions, but do not let unanswered questions prevent you from implementing a few strategies to help the victim. Of course, other strategies may be used to assess his or her needs. The Bully Free Intervention Questionnaire will trigger your thoughts about the student and drive you to discover more about the student and serve as a guide in determining how to help him or her secure a sense of belonging and acceptance and to cope with the bullying.
  - ○ Determine when and how the parents need to be involved in development of an intervention plan. You may want to develop a preliminary plan before asking for their input.
  - ○ Complete the Bully Free Intervention Plan Form (see Appendix F). As you answer some of the questions on the Bully Free Intervention Questionnaire, it is important to write down what needs to be done to help the victim. For example, the victim may need activities or counseling to enhance self-esteem or improve social skills. Or he or she may need to have certain behaviors modified that contribute to the mistreatment. The victim may also need to learn assertiveness skills. After the plan is developed and implemented, schedule a time to review the effectiveness of the plan.
  - ○ Encourage school personnel to support the victim and monitor his or her interactions with others. However, make sure your discussions are professional, respectful of confidentiality, and conducted in private.
  - ○ Ask the victim to name an adult in the school to report to. At first, the reporting could occur on a daily basis, then weekly, and then monthly.

The Bully Free Response Plan: Students Bullying Students, Cont'd.

When you feel it is appropriate, recommend that the victim receive counseling, and refer the student to the guidance counselor or school psychologist. Once the victim has met with you and intervention and prevention strategies have been implemented, support the victim and encourage him or her to apply the selected strategies. Build the victim's confidence that he or she can cope with future bullying events if they occur and that the school will act appropriately to stop and prevent the bullying.

- Complete the Bully Free Intervention Questionnaire and the Bully Free Intervention Plan Form for the bully.
  - Make sure accurate information has been collected thus far.
  - Assess the needs of the bully by reviewing the Bully Free Intervention Questionnaire and studying the student's school records. It will take time to find answers to all of the questions, but do not let unanswered questions prevent you from implementing a few strategies to help the bully. Of course, other strategies may be used to assess his or her needs. The questionnaire will trigger your thoughts about the student and drive you to discover more about him or her and serve as a guide in determining how to help the bully change.
  - Determine when and how the parents need to be involved in developing an intervention plan. You may want to prepare a preliminary plan before asking for their input.
  - Complete the Bully Free Intervention Plan Form (see Appendix F). As you answer some of the questions on the questionnaire, write down on the intervention form what needs to be done to help the bully. For example, the bully may need activities or counseling to boost his or her self-esteem, negative consequences may need to be applied, and a behavioral contract may need to be written. After the plan is developed and implemented, schedule a time to review the effectiveness of the plan.
  - Encourage school personnel to reinforce the bully for appropriate behavior and monitor his or her interaction with others. However, make sure your discussions are professional, respectful of confidentiality, and private.
  - Ask the bully to name an adult in the school to report to. At first, the reporting could occur on a daily basis, then weekly, and then monthly.

If it appears that the bully will continue mistreating others unless he or she receives counseling, refer the student to the guidance counselor or school psychologist. Once the bully has met with you and the planned intervention and strategies have been implemented, encourage him or her to apply the selected strategies. Build the bully's confidence that he or she can change, but say that there will be significant consequences if there is no change.

Responsibilities of the Supportive Personnel

In order to help victims cope with their feelings and the bullying, other adults may need to be involved. This is especially true of efforts to change the behavior of bullies. More intense prevention and intervention strategies may be needed that require the involvement of support personnel.

Some of the specific steps that may be taken by supportive school personnel are:

- Step 1: Read and study the Bullying Situation Report completed by the adult who first responded to the bullying.
- Step 2: Privately and separately interview the victim, bully, and bystanders and cross-check information documented in the Bullying Situation Report. Ask the same questions asked earlier by the adult initially responding to the bullying.

(continued on next page)

The Bully Free Response Plan: Students Bullying Students, Cont'd.

- Step 3: Keep the parents of the victim and the bully informed, and seek their cooperation in designing an appropriate plan of action. Modify or develop a new Bully Free Intervention Plan for the victim and bully.

- Step 4: Determine what additional negative or reductive consequences (see Step 9) should be applied. Apply consequences for the bullies that are supported by school board policies and local, state, and federal laws. The consequences imposed should be responsible, restorative, and respectful of both the student who has been bullied and the student who bullied.

- Step 5: Determine if additional preventive strategies need to be used and what those should be.

- Step 6: Maintain open communication and contact with the victim, bully, and bystanders. Frequently meet with them to discuss progress toward improvement of the bullying situation. When accepting and supportive behavior is observed, reward them with positive consequences.

Responsibilities of the Administration

When a behavior has been determined to be of such a magnitude that it needs administrative interventions or when all efforts of the teachers and supportive personnel have failed, the principal or his or her designee will work with all parties to stop and prevent the bullying. The administration may determine that more severe consequences need to be applied. An outside agency, such as the police, may even be used. In fact, some threats must be reported to the police.

Task Checklist, Step 11

Develop the Response Plan

Notes

☐ If your school system or school has approved an anti-bullying policy, review it prior to developing the response plan to ensure consistency with the response plan the team will develop. Also review the harassment policy.

☐ Review and examine the example Bully Free Response Plan presented here and the forms presented in Appendix F. This plan also appears as a Microsoft Word file at www.bullyfree.com.

☐ Modify the example response plan (students bullying students) to match the culture, policies and procedures, and codes of your school system and schools.

  ○ Outline the responsibilities of the adults responding. See Appendix E.

  ○ Detail a list of behaviors that warrant an administrative response.

  ○ Detail guidelines and procedures to support students who are bullied.

  ○ Detail guidelines and procedures for responding to students who bully students.

  ○ Present a draft of the response plan to all of the appropriate school personnel, students (if age appropriate), and selected parents. Solicit their feedback. This may be accomplished through a series of meetings.

  ○ If necessary, present input from parents and students to school personnel.

  ○ Discuss the final draft of the response plan with the appropriate school officials and groups in the school system or district.

  ○ Once the plan is implemented, solicit feedback from school personnel (faculty, staff, and volunteers), parents, and students regarding their experience with the response plans.

  ○ Review the feedback and revise the response plan as needed.

(continued on next page)

Task Checklist, Step 11, Cont'd.   Notes

☐ Determine the need to develop the four other response plans and follow the above process where appropriate: (1) responding to students who bully school personnel (faculty, staff, and volunteers), (2) responding to school personnel who bully students, (3) responding to school personnel who bully other school personnel, and (4) responding to parents who bully school personnel and volunteers.

☐ _____
_____

☐ _____
_____

☐ _____
_____

Step 12

Identify the High-Risk Locations and Times and Develop and Implement a Coordinated and Monitored Supervision Plan and Schedule, as Well as a Reporting and Information Exchange System

This is one of the most important steps in implementing the program. Bullying happens in schools as much as it does because we have allowed it to happen where there is no adult supervision, not enough adult supervision, and poor supervision. And where there is a lack of structure, students are free to roam and interact without supervision. Another problem has been the lack of recording and reporting by supervisors who observe behaviors that could make up a bullying situation. The Bully Free Program addresses all of these issues.

Identifying High-Risk Areas and Times

The Bully Free Program offers a variety of strategies for identifying areas and times on school property that are high risk. There are several strategies that can be used, including observation reports from supervisors, examination of records, map marking and photograph labeling, and review of survey data. Of course, the strategies used to identify high-risk locations should be age appropriate.

Observation Reports

It is sometimes obvious where students are mistreated, such as the back door of the school, in restrooms, on the playground, or on buses. Therefore, one way to discover the high-risk areas is to simply ask teachers, students, and staff to tell you where those areas are. They could respond to a questionnaire or be asked to provide a list of high-risk areas.

Examination of Records

Another strategy for identifying high-risk areas is the examination of school records such as discipline reports. Look for areas where bullying incidents are often reported.

Map Marking and Photograph Labeling

Sharp and Smith (1994) offer the following suggestions for identifying high-risk locations with young children:

- Supply the pupils with maps of the school property, inside and out, and ask them to highlight or color the places where students are mistreated or where they feel unsafe. Areas described as unsafe by more than half the pupils should be viewed as high risk.

- Take photographs of different locations in and around the school. Stick them on the wall or on poster board so that pupils can see them clearly (level with their line of vision). Underneath each photograph, pin two envelopes, one with a happy face and one with an unhappy face. Each pupil is asked to place a token in the happy or unhappy envelope to indicate how she or he feels about each location. Count up the tokens in each envelope. Locations that have been identified as "unhappy" places by more pupils could be high-risk locations.

Review of Survey Data

Most bullying surveys ask students to indicate when and where they are being bullied. Examining the survey data may help the team identify the high-risk areas and times.

To complete the above tasks, the Bully Free Program team should determine what resources are needed to collect the information. The methods used to identify the high-risk areas and times will dictate the resources needed. For example, map marking requires photocopies of the school's floor plan and surrounding property.

The team should determine who will collect the information. Someone on the team should be asked to collect the data and compile a written report for the team. The principal and the chair of the team should facilitate the efforts of this team member. The program evaluation coordinator can discuss the results of the surveys relative to high-risk areas and times.

The team also needs to determine when the data are to be collected. Identifying high-risk areas and times in the school is critical to a successful anti-bullying program. Therefore, all school personnel should assist in this effort. When time for this task seems to be an issue, some schools have required teachers to use adviser-advisee time to collect information through the map marking method or by asking students where they see bullying most often in the school and recording their comments.

Finally, the team should determine when a report on the identified high-risk areas will be submitted to the team. Establishing a deadline will encourage the collection and analysis of the data in a timely manner. The report should be submitted to the team and discussed at one of its meetings.

Supervision

Building excellence in supervision requires common sense, planning, sufficient resources, adherence to policies and procedures, and accountability. Sometimes bullying happens because there is no adult supervision, not enough supervision, or poor supervision. Passive supervision involves adults not taking their supervision responsibilities seriously. For example, they may chat with teachers or students instead of observing the area they have been assigned. I have been involved in five lawsuits concerning bullying, and one of the main issues was the absence of and quality of supervision provided by the teachers. Some courts may view "passive supervision" as "negligent supervision." Perhaps we have reached a time that middle school and high school students should not be left alone unsupervised. It is important for the Bully Free Program team to communicate the importance of adequate and quality supervision by the adults, and for adults to be held accountable for the quality of their supervision.

The following issues and realities seem to bear on supervision:

- School personnel may mistakenly think bullying is not a problem in their school because they are unaware of much of it.

- School personnel may not see that it is their responsibility to supervise high-risk areas. If they belong to a teachers' union, there may be times that the school can't require them to supervise (during lunch, outside when students are waiting for the bus) unless they are paid for providing this service. In my opinion, this is not a good policy.

- The school may be understaffed.

- The school district has a policy, written or unwritten, that volunteers will not be used as supervisors.

- The school can't afford video cameras or curved mirrors.

- The school can't afford to hire additional supervisors.

- School personnel do not take their supervisory roles seriously. They don't realize there have been and will continue to be lawsuits regarding poor supervision.

- School personnel aren't trained to provide quality supervision.

Supervisors, volunteers, and school personnel must provide quality supervision and implement the policies and procedures (discipline rubric, response plan). Most school systems have a policy that school personnel are to hold students accountable for their behavior.

Develop and Implement a Supervision Plan and Schedule

Bullying often happens in areas where there is poor adult supervision, a lack of adult supervision, or no adult supervision (such as in stairwells, locker rooms, or bathrooms), and during unstructured times (such as waiting for the bus, waiting for school to start, in the parking lot or cafeteria, or on the playground).

Therefore, the development of a written plan to improve supervision and add structure is critical. The plan should list the high-risk locations and times and the plan for supervising these areas and, when appropriate, the strategies to be used to add structure. An example supervision plan form follows later in this chapter to assist you in this effort. It is also provided as a file located at www.bullyfree.com.

Work with the team to determine the roles staff should play in supervision. This role is not just a matter of policy. It is also a matter of professionalism and fulfilling their responsibility to help create and maintain a peaceful and safe school.

Determine if volunteers will be used to provide supervision. Check with the central office personnel to determine if the school or school system has policies regarding the use of volunteers as supervisors. Even when there are not policies, some administrators prefer that volunteers not be used. Before you seek permission to explore the use of volunteers, have a clear idea of where and how they will be used. For example, will they be used on playgrounds, stairwells, on buses, in locker rooms, in bathrooms, or somewhere else? Make sure you can clearly communicate the rationale for using volunteers. The data from the survey, map marking, and other strategies could support your rationale.

Determine who will supervise the supervisors. Ultimately it is the principal's responsibility to make sure staff appropriately fulfill their roles as supervisors. Therefore, the principal and the assistant principal should routinely circulate in the building to check the presence and quality of supervision in the high-risk areas. Faculty and staff should be confronted by the principal and assistant principal when they are not applying the basic supervision principles as directed. When a teacher is sued for passive or negligent supervision, often the assistant principal and principal are also sued.

Determine how the importance of increased supervision and quality will be communicated to all school personnel and volunteers. Not only should faculty and staff be taught and given the basic supervision principles listed in this step, but supervision should be a topic that is frequently on the agenda of faculty and staff meetings. This is also a good time for the principal to express concerns based on his or her observations.

The Bully Free Program team or the principal should develop a written supervision schedule for faculty, staff, and volunteers. The schedule can be a separate document and not included in the supervision plan. It should be a written document listing all areas to be supervised, the assigned supervisor, and the times this person will be supervising the area. It is the principal's responsibility to ensure that personnel and volunteers are providing quality supervision of their areas as scheduled.

Once the plan is developed, it is important to let students know that there is a plan and that the adults they see in specific areas will be intently listening for and watching for bullying. They should also be told that when bullying occurs, it will not be tolerated and that there will be a response from the supervisor and perhaps others.

Supervision Strategies

Supervision Provided by Staff and Volunteers

The most effective deterrent to bullying is adult authority and supervision, especially in high-risk areas and during high-risk times. The visible increase in adult supervision will communicate to students that the school is serious about preventing and stopping bullying and that any form of bullying behavior (direct and indirect) will not be tolerated. In order to increase supervision, consider using trained volunteer supervisors and requiring all school personnel to assist in the supervision of high-risk areas.

I have been in some schools where teachers were not required to supervise high-risk areas. This is a mistake. If you haven't already, consider requiring school personnel to supervise specific high-risk areas. One principal stopped bullying in the boys' bathroom by scheduling the male teachers who taught nearest the bathroom to step into the bathroom between classes to provide supervision. Quality supervision may not be possible by just standing outside the bathroom door.

For increased supervision to be an effective deterrent, supervisors must make appropriate responses, including seriously considering all reports of bullying and monitoring the interactions of specific students. Therefore, it is important for all supervisors, paid and volunteer, to have anti-bullying awareness training. They should also be trained and empowered to use the response plan discussed in Step 11. Students will feel comfortable talking to adults about problems they experience if they know that the problem will be acknowledged, understood, and addressed by trained individuals. Volunteer supervisors who ignore bullying or respond inappropriately after being given a chance to improve should not be retained.

Supervisors are often required to intervene immediately in some of the most difficult student behaviors. Ideally, they are trained in the skills of de-escalation, intervening in fights, active listening, detecting bullying, intervening in bullying events, and supporting students who are bullied. They should also be taught basic supervision principles. The following basic supervision principles should be used as a handout when training supervisors. Clearly communicate that everyone is expected to apply these principles. During one school visit, I noticed a teacher leaning against the door frame of another colleague's office and interacting with his colleague while attempting to supervise the hall. This is not quality supervision.

Basic Supervision Principles

The following principles also appear as a Microsoft Word file at www.bullyfree.com. It should be given to and discussed with all supervisors.

- Know the school rules, and know how to respond to bullying when it is observed.

- Supervision is a full-time responsibility that requires understanding, good judgment, being a good example, being impartial, and an absence of discrimination. Therefore, fulfill your role as a supervisor throughout the day by seeking to hear and see bullying wherever you are and everywhere you go.

- Rumors, reports, and observations of threats and weapons must be immediately reported to the administration so that the students can be immediately interviewed.

- Never ignore bullying. Do not let any inappropriate behavior, regardless of severity, go uncorrected, but try to respond in an unemotional manner. Enforce all behavioral expectations. Immediately correct and, while using a professional tone of voice, state the desired behavior and follow the school's approved Bully Free Response Plan. Younger students could be asked to state the rule being violated and the desired behavior.

- When talking to individual students, position yourself so you can keep visually scanning the area with a glance.

- Keep a clipboard or note pad and a pen with you at all times to log observations and events relative to bullying that concern you, or use the approved reporting systems designed by the school (for example, the Inappropriate Behavior Card). Make sure you record the names of students involved. Report this information to the teachers of those students. Review your log on a regular basis to identify patterns of behavior indicating bullying. Report your concern and even your suspicions about specific students (those bullied and those bullying) during faculty and staff meetings, and encourage others to intensify their observation and supervision of these students when in their areas. Persistent mistreatment should be reported by completing the Bullying Incidence Report Form.

- When outdoors with bright sunny conditions, wear sunglasses.

- When you feel that a student is in a bullying situation and is repeatedly being mistreated, fill out the Bully Free Situation Report (available from the Bully Free Program team).

- Step into the hallway and visually scan the halls and other areas between classes. Be purposeful about scanning the area. Be focused, and pay attention to nonverbal signals of trouble.

- Intentionally monitor the behavior of those who bully others and those who are often targets of bullying.

- Maintain a heightened awareness for suspicious activity, including an intense gathering of students, increased whispering, and suspicious packages.

- Maintain a heightened awareness of angry facial expressions, gestures, eye shifting, whispering, increased movement of individuals indicating agitation, veins protruding, eyes squinting, fists formed, arms waving, and intentional ignoring of individuals seeking to enter a group, for example.

- When necessary, remind students of the school's behavioral expectations for your area, as well as the school's behavior code and possible consequences.

- Do not stand in one area, and do not sit down. Keep moving around within your assigned area. If you have a large area, keep students guessing where you are by taking different travel patterns.

- If you are supervising a large area, stay longer in the problem areas. If necessary, stay close to students who are bullies or often targets of bullying.

- When assigned to supervise an area during a specific time period, try to be a few minutes early.

- Do not leave your assigned area until it is time to do so.

- Do not let other adults or students distract you from your supervisory responsibilities. If someone engages you in a conversation, stand to the side of the individual rather than standing directly in front of him or her with your back to the area.

- Do not threaten or use sarcasm.

- Do not argue with students.

- Do not touch an agitated or angry student.

- Maintain a positive atmosphere by smiling at students and making positive comments, but visually scanning the area. Seek to make more positive than negative comments. Greet students as they enter your area. Try to be a friendly but professional adult presence.

- When deemed appropriate, ask students to engage in "positive practice." This requires students to demonstrate the correct behavior: the opposite of what they were doing wrong.

- When deemed appropriate, use "restitution": cleaning up a mess, for example.

- Sincerely praise students who treat others the way they want to be treated or engage in other appropriate behavior.

- When necessary, send a student for other adult help.

- When there is potential for a fight or an actual fight, walk toward the students with authority. Quickly review the situation to determine what is happening and who is involved. Also determine if weapons are being used. Just the presence of an adult can stop the aggression. Call the students by name and, in a demanding voice, tell them to stop. Never step between two students who are physically fighting. Make a mental note of onlookers, and ask them to leave the area. You may need to talk to them later. Send a student for other adult help. After the fight, document what happened, and report it to the appropriate school personnel. Provide emotional support to the victim.

- When there are minor injuries, administer the appropriate first aid on site if allowed by the school. If not, send the student to the nurse for treatment. If necessary, send another student with the student.

- When there are serious injuries that require the student to remain still, if allowed, administer the appropriate first aid, remain with the student, and ensure the administration is informed.

- Report to the office any potential hazards or equipment malfunction. Take the appropriate action to keep your area safe.

- Report hurtful graffiti, and seek to have it immediately removed.

Walking School Bus

Sometimes students are bullied while they walk to and from school, so it may be necessary to provide supervision for them. The "walking school bus" is an idea suggested by David Engwicht of Australia in the early 1990s. The Canadian Go for Green program picked up the idea and has promoted it, and some school districts in the United States now use this simple strategy.

A parent or other volunteer is assigned to walk a certain route and collect students at specified locations along the way, and drop them off on the way home. The benefits are many: students are part of a large, visible, and supervised group; students learn pedestrian safety skills while getting regular exercise; car traffic around the school is reduced; and the supervising adults become eyes on the streets and can help identify unsafe areas along the route.

Electronics and Other Hardware

Electronic devices in high-risk areas can enhance supervision efforts. Video cameras are often installed on buses, in hallways, and other high-risk areas. Some schools have installed cameras on playgrounds and parking lots, as well as in hidden areas, such as between buildings. Curved mirrors may also be mounted in strategic locations. If video cameras are used, they should be routinely checked to make sure they are working. The tapes should also be routinely reviewed to identify problems. It's not enough to examine the recordings only when a problem is reported. Someone should be assigned by the principal to examine the recordings routinely.

As mentioned in Step 8, one school installed a closed circuit television system that allows parents and guardians to observe activities in their school from home through their computers. Parents pay a small fee for this service at home. When students know that their parent or guardian could be watching, it can have a positive impact on their behavior. It also adds another dimension of supervision in the school. Parents and guardians report their observations of inappropriate behavior.

Adding Structure to Unstructured Times

There are a number of ways to add structure to unstructured times—for example:

- Designate areas outside the school building where students must remain while waiting for the bus, and ask personnel to supervise these areas.

- Make sure all schools require students to use hallway passes.

- Make sure all school personnel are consistently applying consequences for tardiness.

- Have assigned seats on the bus. Since high school students often mistreat middle school students, one school required high school students to sit in the rear, elementary students in the middle, and middle school students toward the front of the bus.

- On the bus, require the girls to sit on one side and the boys on the other side.

- Have required seating in the cafeteria. One school used a software program that randomly assigned numbers and tables to students.

- Designate areas in the commons area where students must stand while waiting for school to start.

- Ask teachers to require students to plan recess activities prior to recess that include everyone.

- Structure arrival and dismissal time for students riding in cars. The following is one example of an elementary school's arrival and dismissal plan for students riding in cars.

Arrival and Dismissal Plan for Students Riding in Cars

The drop-off and pick-up location for cars will be the fire zone area by the side of the building between the front entrance and the recess yard. Parking in the lot during arrival and dismissal will be permitted only for parents who must escort their child due to emergency circumstances. At no time are students allowed to linger in the halls, entryways, exits, bathrooms, or elsewhere.

Arrival Procedures for Cars

Parents who are dropping their child off will enter the parking lot, drive around counterclockwise, and loop back to the front of the school to enter the car line.

- Parents may drop off their child once they are beyond the "Student Drop-Off" sign and in the fire zone area. Letting students exit a vehicle before this point is not safe and therefore not permitted.
- Two staff members will be on duty to assist students who are being dropped off.
- Students will enter the front of the building after exiting the vehicle.
- Drop-offs will commence at 8:45 as it is likely to be 8:50 before students enter their classroom.
- Two staff members on duty will motion when it is time to begin dropping off students.
- Parents who are dropping off must remain in their vehicles at all times.
- Once students have safely exited all vehicles in the drop-off location, the vehicles may exit the fire zone.
- When all vehicles have left the fire zone, the next set of cars will be directed to move up, and so on until all students have been dropped off.
- Parents are not permitted to pass another vehicle while children are attempting to exit.

Dismissal Procedures to Cars

Parents will follow the same driving procedure for entering the parking lot for picking up students in the afternoon.

- Car rider students will be dismissed at 3:40 from the front entrance of the building and will wait on the sidewalk by the flower garden.
- Two staff members will be on duty to assist students who are being picked up.
- Two staff members will supervise each child to his or her car once all vehicles in the pick-up location have completely stopped.
- Parents may pick up once they are beyond the stop sign and in the fire zone area. Letting students enter a vehicle before this point is not permitted.
- Parents who are picking up must remain in their vehicles at all times.
- Parents are not permitted to pass another vehicle while children are attempting to enter a vehicle.
- When all vehicles have left the fire zone, the next set of cars will be directed to move up, and so on until all students have been dismissed.
- If a student is not present when his or her parent arrives, the parent will be asked to pull into a parking spot to wait.

- Teach appropriate and enjoyable playground games.

- Provide supervised activities for rainy days. Fried and Fried (2003) suggest a strategy that takes this a step further. They report that the PTA at Brooks Elementary School in Windsor, California, set up an alternate recess program. Every Friday students can play board games and other activities (knitting, arts and crafts) inside for students who wish to take a break from the playground. The parents help supervise the alternate recess.

- If there are storage or maintenance sheds and buildings on the playground, ask the custodian to spray-paint a line on the grass in front of them indicating they are off-limits. Students are not to cross the painted lines.

- Fried and Fried (2003) report the use of "Safety Zones." A flag and other markers are placed in a certain area of the playground to declare it a safety zone. An adult is always available at the safety zone for any students who feel that they need protection. The existence of such an area communicates the school's commitment to have a bully free playground.

- Structure the dismissal time for students riding buses. The following is one example of a K–12 school's dismissal plan for students riding buses.

Dismissal Plan for Students Riding Buses

- At no time are students allowed to linger in the halls, entryways, exits, bathrooms, or other areas.

- K–1 staff will escort the Bus 1 students downstairs and out to buses at 3:05. All other students will remain in their classrooms with staff.

- At 3:10, the bell will ring, and staff will escort Bus 1 students grades 2–3 and grades 4–5 downstairs and out to the buses. All of the Bus 2 students will remain in their rooms with staff.

- At 3:10, the bell will ring, and all grades 6–12 students will be dismissed from class, and staff will escort them to the buses. The Bus 1 students will go to their bus, and the Bus 2 students will go to the designated gathering space. At the same time, an announcement will be made for staff to bring elementary students riding Bus 2 downstairs and outside to the buses. Staff will remain outside at the bus loading area and supervise students until all buses pull out.

- Students who are being picked up by parents will be supervised in the movement room. Students going to the Wee Care day care will be picked up in the movement room.

- Students are not allowed to leave the school and then return; for example, they are not allowed to run up the escalators and get a drink and come back to the school or buses.

Supportive Supervision Strategies

The following strategies can be employed to lessen the number of bullying incidents and enhance supervision efforts. Some of the strategies appear in the example supervision plan provided in this step. Brainstorm with your team to identify other strategies. You can also search the Internet for information.

- Where necessary, provide supervisors with cellular communication devices, mobile phones, or walkie-talkies.

- Minimize the number of class changes because crowded hallways are a prime location for bullying.

- Stagger recess times of older and younger students.

- Divide the playground, with one side designated for younger students and the other side designated for older students.

- Start a playground buddies program. Such programs usually pair older and younger students. Developers of such programs say students usually feel safer on the playground when they see the familiar face of their playground buddy and are friends with older students. For more information, search the Internet using the keywords *playground buddy programs*.

- Train students to serve as playground conflict managers (Fried and Fried, 2003). This is a program developed in California that trained elementary students to help with their classmates' conflicts on the playground.

- Make bully free table tents (signs) to stand on each cafeteria table. The tent could include a message, such as the school's anti-bullying slogan, "Bully Free Is the Way to Be," or "We Are a Bully Free School." The tent could also include your school's bully free rules.

- Consider establishing a bully free section of the cafeteria. The only students allowed to eat in that section are those who sign a pledge not to bully others in the cafeteria and to adhere to the behavioral expectations for the cafeteria. As students agree to sign, they may eat in that area. If a student mistreats someone, he or she is removed from that eating area for three days. Make an effort to get students who seem to be leaders to sign the pledge.

- Form a student leadership club where older students are trained to be playground leaders. They can help younger children with group games and other activities.

- Post Bully Free Zone posters in all of the high-risk areas.

- Post a bully free classroom poster in each classroom.

- Use spray paint to draw lines on the grass, or use other marking devices, such as orange plastic cones, to indicate areas on the playground that are off-limits, such as behind maintenance buildings.

- Ask two students in each grade to be secret reporters of bullying as well as reporters of students who performed an act of kindness. They can drop anonymous notes in a box located in each teacher's room. The box could be a multipurpose box used for reporting a variety of observations and even thoughts about ways to improve the school.

- Some researchers have discovered that traditional games like skipping rope, hopscotch, and other noncompetitive games can reduce bullying on playgrounds.

Adam Hawkins and colleagues of Brandon, Canada, instituted a playground pass system that has been effective. I refer to this adaptation of it here as the "Bully Free Ticket." A student who is known to bully others on the playground is given a Bully Free Ticket (see the illustration) to take to the playground. This student is required to show the pass to the adult supervisor and get the adult's signature. This signals the supervisor to be alert and observant of this student's behavior. During the entire recess period, the student must be observed by the supervisor as engaging in appropriate behavior. If the adult approves of the student's behavior, the adult signs the ticket again, which the student returns to his or her teacher. If the supervising adult has not signed the pass twice, the student loses one or more recess periods and must walk around the perimeter of the playground during this time period.

Bully Free Ticket

Name of Student: _____ Date: _____

Teacher: _____

First Signature of Supervisor: _____

Second Signature of Supervisor: _____

Rewarding Anti-Bullying Behavior

In addition to responding appropriately to bullying incidents, supervisors play a powerful role in encouraging appropriate behavior. Supervisors should be taught to reinforce and reward desirable behaviors. For example, when they see young students being kind to others, they can give them a "Golden Rule Reward" card (see illustration). The student gives the card to his or her teacher, who places the card in a jar. At the end of the week, the teacher can select a card to see who receives a small, inexpensive prize.

Golden Rule Reward

This Student Was Observed Obeying the Golden Rule!

Name of Student: _____ Date: _____

Signature of Supervisor: _____

Write the Formal Supervision Plan

Use the supervision plan example that follows to develop your own supervision plan. This example and blank form are available as files at www.bullyfree.com. After the team has developed its own plan, obtain feedback regarding the plan from various stakeholders, and incorporate any changes. Then get approval of the final plan from school officials.

Example of Supervision Plan

School: XYZ Elementary

Date: April 4, 2010

High-Risk Areas and High-Risk Times	Supervision Strategy (Including Supportive Strategies)
Gym before school; waiting for school to start	Video cameras will be installed in the gym and the tapes reviewed at least weekly to identify problems. Before school starts, students will have assigned seating (sections of the bleachers) by grade level and will not be permitted to roam. They are not allowed to walk on the court floor or visit other sections. They must also keep their bottoms on the seats. Students will be taught by their teachers the behavioral expectations while in the gym. The supervisors of this area will be informed of potential problems of students so that they can be watched more carefully. A Bully Free Zone poster will be posted in a prominent location in the gym.
Bathrooms	Selected teachers will be scheduled to supervise inside the bathrooms nearest to their rooms between classes and other critical times. Students will be taught by their teachers the behavioral expectations for that area. The supervisors of this area will be informed of potential problems of students so that they can be watched more carefully. A Bully Free Zone poster will be posted in a prominent location in the bathrooms. Students are to be escorted to the bathroom by the teacher or teacher's assistant. The bathroom supervisor will make sure students do not linger in the bathrooms.
Hallways	Selected teachers will be assigned a specific section of the hallway nearest their classrooms unless a different area is assigned by the principal. Video cameras will be installed in hallways and the tapes reviewed at least weekly to identify problems. Curved mirrors will be installed in the appropriate locations. Students will be taught by their teachers the behavioral expectations while in the hallways. The school counselor will walk and assist with supervision in the hallways before school starts, between classes, and after school. The supervisors of this area will be informed of potential problems of students so that they can be watched more carefully. A Bully Free Zone poster will be posted in a prominent location in the hallways. Students are required to use hall passes. All the classes for eighth grades will be on the third floor, classes for the seventh grades will be on the second floor, and classes for the sixth grades will be on the first floor. Students are not allowed to travel the hallway of unassigned halls. Students are to be escorted in the hallway by the teacher or teacher's assistant.

Example of Supervision Plan, Cont'd.

High-Risk Areas and High-Risk Times	Supervision Strategy (Including Supportive Strategies)
Locker room	Instructors are expected to stay in the locker rooms until students have exited. An adult volunteer will be asked to supervise the gym area until all students have left the area. Once the students have left the locker room, the instructor is expected to help the other adult supervise the gym area. Students will be taught by their teachers the behavioral expectations while in the locker room and gym area. The supervisors of this area will be informed of potential problems of students so that they can be watched more carefully. A Bully Free Zone poster will be posted in a prominent location in all locker rooms.
Cafeteria	At least two trained volunteers will be used to supervise the cafeteria. Students are randomly assigned tables every week and are not permitted to save seats and will not be sitting with the same people every week. Video cameras will be installed and the recordings reviewed at least weekly to identify problems. Students will be taught by their teachers the behavioral expectations while in the cafeteria. Bully Free Zone posters will be posted and visible from each table. Bully free table tents (with our bully free slogan on them) will be placed on each table. Students are not allowed to bring backpacks or book bags to the cafeteria. To leave the lunch room before the period ends, a student must raise his or her hand and receive a pass. Also, a student may not leave his or her eating area until it is clean. At the end of the lunch period when the bell rings, students will be dismissed by rows of tables. Staff have the right to move students to the rear or front of the lunch line. A "bully free section" of the cafeteria will be established. The only students allowed to sit in that section are those who sign a pledge not to bully others in the cafeteria and to adhere to the behavioral expectations for the cafeteria. As students agree to sign the pledge, they may eat in that area. If a student mistreats someone, he or she is removed from that area for three days.
Recess/playground	At least three trained volunteers will be used to supervise the playground. Each week, students will be assigned areas. For example, grades 1–3 will use a certain area and grades 4–5 a different area. Video cameras will be installed and the recordings reviewed at least weekly to identify problems. A student leadership club will be formed where older students are trained to be playground leaders. They will help younger children with group games (for example, managing equipment and refereeing) and other activities. The custodian will spray-paint on the grass near the maintenance sheds and buildings indicating areas that are off limits. Students are not to cross the painted lines. Students will be taught by their teachers the behavioral expectations while on the playgrounds. The supervisors of this area will be informed of potential problems of students or individual students who bully so that they can be watched more carefully. Teachers will ask selected students to serve as secret reporters and such an assignment will be rotated among the students. The "Bully Free Ticket" will be used by each teacher and the "Golden Rule Reward" will be used by the playground supervisors. Recess times for older and younger students will be staggered. Students are not allowed to reenter the building without permission and must immediately go to an area supervised by an adult. When the weather is extremely cold or wet, students will remain in the

(continued on next page)

Example of Supervision Plan, Cont'd.

High-Risk Areas and High-Risk Times	Supervision Strategy (Including Supportive Strategies)
	cafeteria or gym. We will make this announcement prior to the start of the lunch periods. Board games will be available for students' use in the cafeteria. Students are responsible for the setup and cleanup of all games. The games are stored in the main office closet. An assigned staff member will come to the office to get the games.
Waiting for the bus after school	Students will have designated areas to stand and wait for their bus. They will be taught by their teachers the behavioral expectations while waiting for the bus. The supervisors of this area will be informed of potential problem students so that they can be watched more carefully. The school counselor will help supervise this area.
Stairwells	Selected teachers and other selected school personnel will be scheduled to supervise specific stairwells: one person at the top and one at the bottom of each stairwell. Video cameras will be installed in stairwells and the tapes reviewed at least weekly to identify problems. Students will be taught by their teachers the behavioral expectations while walking in the stairwells. The supervisors of this area will be informed of potential problem students so that they can be watched more carefully. A Bully Free Zone poster will be posted and visible while on the stairwells. When possible, the school counselor will walk and supervise the stairwells before, during, and after school.
Doors	A staff member or volunteer will supervise each entrance and exit and the immediate area before school and after school.

Visually Changing the Atmosphere of the School

A strategy for creating a sense of peace and safety in the school is to increase the number of visual safety cues in the school and on school property. When students see these visual cues, they are reminded of the anti-bullying rules of the school, the behavioral expectations, and the consequences for bullying. They are also reminded of their responsibility to help maintain peaceful and safe areas. Visual cues can be the increase in the number of adults supervising the area, the observance of the quality supervision and intervention of adults, and posted rules and posted clear behavioral expectations. They can also include bully free bulletin boards, posters, and banners (available at www.bullyfree.com). Bully free classroom posters should be posted in every classroom, and Bully Free Zone posters should be posted in all of the high-risk areas in visible locations. These will contribute to your efforts to provide quality supervision and encourage students to behave appropriately. Excellent resources for bulletin board, poster, and banner ideas are *Bully Free Classroom Bulletin Boards, Posters, and Banners* (Beane & Beane, 2005) and *Bully Free Classroom Bulletin Boards, Posters, and Banners for High School* (Beane & Beane, 2003). These books are included in the bully free kits of materials for teachers.

Reporting and Information Exchange System

Because your team has already developed policies and a response plan, it is probably clear how observations and reports of bullying are to be recorded and reported. It is important that there is a continuing sharing of information and concerns among school personnel. One way to ensure good information exchange is to always have bullying on the agenda of faculty and staff meetings, with time allocated to discuss anti-bullying issues in general and concerns about specific students. The counselor's and principal's doors must always be open to hear expressed concerns. The principal should also ask for reports from the Bully Free Program team, which should be given at faculty and staff meetings.

Task Checklist, Step 12

Identify High-Risk Locations and Times and
Develop and Implement a Coordinated
and Monitored Supervision Plan and a
Reporting and Information Exchange System

Identify High-Risk Locations and Times for Bullying

☐ Determine who will coordinate the effort to identify the high-risk areas.

☐ Identify and select strategies for identifying high-risk locations.

- ○ Observation reporting

- ○ Examination of records

- ○ Map marking

- ○ Photograph labeling

- ○ Examination of survey data

☐ Determine the resources needed to collect the information.

☐ Determine who will collect the data.

☐ Determine when the data are to be collected.

☐ Determine when a report on high-risk areas will be submitted to the team.

☐ Establish a plan for training future new supervisors.

☐ _____

_____

☐ _____

_____

☐ _____

_____

☐ _____

_____

☐ _____

_____

Task Checklist, Step 12, Cont'd.   Notes

Develop and Implement a Coordinated and Monitored Supervision Plan

- ☐ Review the high-risk locations and high-risk times.
- ☐ Determine the roles faculty and staff should play in supervision.
- ☐ Determine if volunteers will be used to provide supervision.
- ☐ Determine who will train the supervisors to use the bully free response plans.
- ☐ Determine who will supervise the volunteer supervisors.
- ☐ Determine how the importance of increased and quality supervision will be communicated to all school personnel and volunteers.
- ☐ Establish the supervision schedule for faculty, staff, and volunteers.
- ☐ Review and decide on supervision strategies.
- ☐ Determine the technology (for example, video cameras, disposable cameras, curved mirrors) that needs to be purchased to support supervisory efforts. Make a recommendation to the principal.
- ☐ Write the formal supervision plan.
- ☐ Obtain input and feedback regarding the supervision plan from various stakeholders and school officials.
- ☐ Seek the approval of the plan from school officials.
- ☐ Implement the bully free supervision plan and schedule.
- ☐ Post Bully Free Zone posters in high-risk areas.
- ☐ Post bully free classroom posters in all classrooms.

Develop a Reporting and Information Exchange System

- ☐ Make sure bullying is always on the agenda of faculty and staff meetings and time has been allocated for discussing issues and concerns about students.
- ☐ Make sure school personnel are prompted to bring their concerns about students to the meeting.
- ☐ Present a report from the Bully Free Program team at faculty and staff meetings.

Step 13

Train School Personnel, Volunteers, and Other Key Individuals to Adhere to Policies, Procedures, Discipline Rubrics, Prosocial Strategies, and Response Plans

The next step is to equip all school personnel, volunteers, and other appropriate individuals with the knowledge and skills to adhere to the bully free policies, procedures, discipline rubrics, prosocial strategies, and response plans.

- *Discuss the perceived training needs of all school personnel.* It may be that you have already provided some training for faculty, staff, and volunteers relative to the new policies and procedures, discipline rubrics, and response plans. If not, provide that training now. It may be that you have had so many discussions with them during the development of the policies and procedures and discipline rubrics that all you need to do at this point is to provide training on implementing the response plan, including the prosocial strategies.

- *Get permission from the appropriate school personnel to organize and implement the training sessions.* Meet with the professional development coordinator of your school district and other school officials to determine the best time for the training. If only certain days have been set aside and those dates do not fit in the Bully Free Program time line, consider using a series of faculty and staff meetings to do the training. When possible, you can still use the regularly scheduled professional development days that have been set aside to reinforce some of the things learned.

- *Determine the agenda of the training sessions.* Once you have determined the training needs and the time frame in which the training is going to occur, you can develop an agenda (one is provided later in this chapter). Be sure to allow time for questions and answers and expressions of concerns.

- *Determine who will conduct the training.* By this time the Bully Free Program team will be so familiar with all of the documents that have been developed, they can conduct the training. Determine who on the team will be most effective in presenting the material. Of course, all of the team members should be present to help answer questions and address concerns.

- *Determine the materials to be given to the participants.* You may need to make copies of the approved policies and procedures, the final draft of the discipline rubrics, and the approved response plan. You may also want to give them a handout detailing the steps to the adopted prosocial strategies discussed in Step 10.

- *Determine if there is a need for displays at the training sessions.* Examples are posters and banners displaying the slogan and logo. If you wish, you can display summaries of the survey data, the program goals, and some of the Bully Free Program materials and resources. You could also display a bully free classroom poster and a Bully Free Zone poster.

- *Determine the number of participants and how the participants will be invited.* Since all faculty and staff in your building should attend the training, the number of participants will be easy to determine. This of course determines the number of handouts you will need. It is probably best for your principal and/or professional development coordinator to schedule the training. Of course, you may want to discuss with your principal the possibility of using a series of faculty and staff meetings after school.

- *Determine a date and time.* Check the school system's calendar and school's calendar, and avoid as many conflicting programs as possible. Work with your principal to ensure that band directors, athletic personnel, speech and debate coaches, and others involved in special programs will be available for the entire training. Try to avoid having a training session the day before holidays or at other times when personnel are dismissed from school for a significant length of time.

- *Determine and reserve the location and equipment (tables, chairs, screen, laptop, projection device, extension cords, power strips, and so on).* Well in advance of the workshop, make room and equipment reservations, and determine if there are any equipment repair needs. Two days before the training, make sure you still have the reservation and that all of the equipment will be available. One day before the training, make sure all of the handouts have been copied. At least one hour before the training, make sure the room arrangement is appropriate for the training and that all of the equipment, supplies, and handouts are in hand. Make sure all of the equipment is working.

- *Use an evaluation form to evaluate the training.* If you are conducting the training during a series of faculty and staff meetings, you may not want to take the time to ask everyone to complete an evaluation form. But if you are conducting a three- to six-hour training program, it is always a good idea to ask participants to evaluate the workshop. Your school system or school may have a form used for such an evaluation. The feedback from the participants may help you plan and design future training.

- *Determine the need for refreshments, and make the arrangements.* Even if you are meeting for just one hour, it is always thoughtful to have refreshments available. Be sure to take into consideration those who have special dietary needs, including food allergies.

- *Determine the funding source for the training; request and secure the funds.* Your main expense may be copying the handouts and the refreshment. Determine which accounts to use and the appropriate procedures for these expenditures.

The agenda for the training session(s) could include the following and other items as the team deems appropriate.

Training Agenda: Adhering to Policies, Procedures, Discipline Rubrics, Prosocial Strategies, and Response Plans

- What is our definition of bullying? (a review)
- What does it look like? (a review)
- What are our bully free mission statement, objectives, and slogan?
- What is the school system's and school's bully free policy?
- What are the bully free discipline rubrics, and how can we use them?
- What are the bully free bus rules and consequences?
- What prosocial strategies have been adopted?
- What is the school's bully free response plan?
- What does the response plan require of everyone?
  - Investigate all rumors and unverified reports of bullying.
  - Investigate all reports of bullying.
  - Intervene immediately in observed bullying situations.
  - Be sure you know how you should respond.

Task Checklist, Step 13

Train School Personnel, Volunteers, and Other Key Individuals to Adhere to Policies, Procedures, Discipline Rubrics, Prosocial Strategies, and Response Plans

Notes

☐ Discuss the perceived training needs of faculty, staff, and volunteers.

☐ Get permission from the appropriate school personnel to organize and implement a training session to prepare school personnel, volunteers, and other key personnel to adhere to the new policies, procedures, and response plans.

☐ Determine the agenda of the training session(s).

☐ Determine who will provide the training, and contact them.

☐ Determine the materials to be given to the participants.

☐ Determine if there is a need for displays at the training sessions.

☐ Determine the number of participants and how the participants will be invited.

☐ Determine a date and time for the training.

☐ Determine and reserve the location and equipment (tables, chairs, screen, laptop, projection device, extension cords, power strips, and so forth).

☐ Develop or use an existing evaluation form to determine the quality and effectiveness of the training.

☐ Determine the need for refreshments, and make the arrangements. Remember those who have special dietary needs, including food allergies.

☐ Determine the funding source for the expenses. Request and secure the funds.

☐ Invite the participants.

☐ Conduct and evaluate the training.

☐ _____

☐ _____

Step 14

Conduct a Meeting with Adults and an Assembly Program for Students to Increase Awareness and Involvement

Although the Bully Free Program team is responsible for initiating and guiding the program, full commitment from all personnel, volunteers, parents, and students is essential to bring the program to life. Therefore, it's good to have additional meetings for adults and students to increase their involvement in the school's efforts to be bully free, and to increase awareness that there is bullying in the school and that the team has been working to implement a plan of action. Step 14 is designed to help your team conduct such important meetings. When the adults and students hear about the team's effort to launch the program, the importance of the program and the commitment of the school and school system will ring loud and clear.

Meeting with Adults

By this time, the Bully Free Program team has already made awareness presentations to school personnel, students, parents, and community representatives. It is now time to increase awareness and encourage involvement. Hold another meeting with faculty, staff, volunteers, parents, and key community representatives. This should be an information-sharing meeting, not a training session. The following tips will help you conduct the meeting:

- Ask your principal to welcome everyone and introduce other school officials and the Bully Free Program team. If students are presenting or role playing at the meeting, be sure to introduce them.
- Communicate the purpose of the meeting: to discuss the efforts of the school to prevent and stop bullying and to review why such an effort is important.
- Explain that neither specific bullying incidents nor the individuals involved will be discussed. Ask the attendees to respect this in their discussions and avoid references to specific situations or students. Explain that there is a lot of material that needs to be covered and that time will not permit discussion of specific cases. However, make it clear that the school invites and encourages reports of bullying.
- Present the school's definition of bullying, and discuss key words in the definition. This will help those attending understand the criteria used to determine when a child is in a bullying situation.

- Talk briefly about why the school decided to initiate a bullying prevention program and briefly address the question: "Why must bullying be prevented and stopped?" This will be a review for those who attended the awareness session.

- Outline the steps the school has undertaken and will undertake in implementing the Bully Free Program. Mention the bully free policy, and present the bully free mission statement and bully free slogan. Ask the faculty, staff, and volunteers attending the meeting to sign the faculty, staff, and volunteer pledge and the community representatives to sign the community representative pledge (see the examples at the end of this step). Tell the parents a parent pledge (an example is provided at the end of this step) will be sent to them through their children, and they will be asked to sign the pledge and keep it in their home. Ask them to review it with their children. Tell the parents that students will be asked to sign a student pledge (see the grade-appropriate examples at the end of this step) during an assembly program and will be asked to share this with their parents. All of these pledges are available as files at www.bullyfree.com. Also tell the parents that they will receive through their child the bully free brochure for parents, *Together We Can Be Bully Free: A Mini-Guide for Parents* (Beane, 2004c), and that their child will also be given the Bully Free brochure, *Together We Can Be Bully Free: A Mini-Guide for Students* (2004d, 2004e). Ask the parents to discuss these materials with their children.

- Present a brief overview of the major components of the Bully Free Program:
  - Data will be collected. You may want to share some of the baseline data already collected.
  - High-risk areas have been identified.
  - A bully free supervision plan and schedule has been developed for the high-risk areas.
  - Personnel have been trained to respond to bullying when they see it.
  - A parent and community involvement and education plan will be developed. Emphasize the importance of parent and community involvement.
  - A student organization, Peers for Peace—Bully Free Club, may be established and that the students will spearhead a campaign against bullying. In a high school, the student council is very involved in a campaign against bullying.
  - A student involvement and empowerment plan will be developed. Emphasize the importance of student involvement and empowerment.
  - Bully free kits with materials and resources will be used in the program. (You may want to display them at the meeting.)

- Mention that a bully free administrative strategies plan has been developed. You may want to give a few examples of strategies selected by the team.

- Explain how the Bully Free Program curriculum will be implemented—for example, through class meetings, lesson plans, or adviser-advisee meetings.

- Allow time for questions and answers. Listen to the attendees' concerns. Bullying is an emotional topic, and discussion may rekindle memories of bullying at school.

After this meeting, additional meetings can be held to address issues and concerns. A suggested agenda for the meeting with adults follows. This agenda also appears online at www.bullyfree.com.

Suggested Agenda for Meeting with Faculty, Staff, Volunteers, Key Community Representatives, and Parents

Welcome and Introduction

- Introductions
  - School officials
  - Bully Free Program team
  - Student role playing
- Purpose of meeting
- Ground rules for meeting

What Is Bullying? (a review)

Why Bullying Must Be Prevented and Stopped (a review)

Our Bully Free Program

- Bully free policy
- Bully free mission statement
- Bully free slogan and logo
- Bully free pledges for faculty, staff, and volunteers
- Bully free pledge for community representatives
- Bully free pledge for parents
- Bully free pledge for students
- Brief overview of major components
  - Data collection
  - Identification of high-risk areas and times
  - Supervision plan and schedule
  - Response plans
  - Parent and community involvement and education plan
  - Student involvement and empowerment plan
  - Peers for Peace—Bully Free Club (student club) or student council campaign
  - Bully free kits (materials and resources)
  - Administrative strategies plan
  - Classroom meetings and lesson plans

Questions and Answers

Student Assembly Program

By now teachers have been teaching the bully free lesson plans and conducting classroom meetings and perhaps have asked students to help develop bully free bulletin boards, posters, and banners. The students have also seen the bully free classroom poster and the Bully Free Zone poster displayed on school property. Now it is time for them to hear more about the school's efforts. A school assembly program is an effective way to unveil other components of the Bully Free Program to students. The assembly is also a natural vehicle for involving students in the program. Therefore, ask some of your student leaders to assist in planning the meeting. Their contributions to the program will help ensure that the message is communicated to the student body in a meaningful way. You could ask them to make a banner with the bully free logo and slogan written on it and develop other such items for display at the assembly. You could also ask students to role-play a bullying situation and the appropriate way for the victim and bystanders to respond.

A suggested agenda for this meeting follows. (This agenda also appears in the files located at www.bullyfree.com.) It is similar to the agenda of the adult awareness meeting. The goal is to establish the students' confidence that there are strategies to address bullying and the adults know how to help them in ways that will not make it worse for them. Underpinning this is the need to gain the trust of pupils so that they will

---

Suggested Agenda for Assembly Program for Students

Welcome and Introductions
- Introductions
  - School officials
  - Bully Free Program team
- Purpose of meeting

What Is Bullying? (Role Play by Students)

Why Bullying Must Be Prevented and Stopped (a review)

Our Bully Free Program
- Bully free policy (only mention major components)
- Bully free mission statement (read this)
- Bully free slogan and logo (read slogan and display logo)
- Bully free pledges for faculty, staff, volunteers, community representatives, and students (mention these)
- High-risk areas identified (indicate awareness of areas)
- Increased supervision
- Response plans in place (explain what the plan is)
- Peers for Peace—Bully Free Club or student council involvement

The Role Students Must Play—Reporting Is Not Tattling
- Take a stand against bullying
- Sign bully free pledge

Questions and Answers

report when they are mistreated or they see someone else being mistreated. They need to realize that there are available support structures that will help them and that the school takes bullying seriously. They must also understand the value of a "telling" environment and report bullying; reporting is not tattling.

At this assembly for students, ask them to sign the bully free pledge for students (see the age-appropriate examples at the end of this step). Ask students to take a stand against bullying. Make sure you find out which students are absent and ask them to sign the pledge when they return to school. As mentioned earlier in this book, one principal asked all the student leaders of her school to distribute the pledges and personally ask students to sign the pledge. Of course, you can give the pledges to teachers, who can ask students in the class to sign the pledge. Teachers can collect the pledges or let students keep them.

Bully Free Faculty, Staff, and Volunteers Pledge

We, the school personnel and volunteers of _____ school, say . . .

AT THIS SCHOOL, WE BELIEVE . . .

WE SHOULD BE . . .

BULLY FREE!

Bullying is when one individual (or group) seeks to repeatedly dominate, control, and hurt or frighten another person. Bullying can be pushing, shoving, hitting, spitting on someone, as well as name-calling, picking on, making fun of, laughing at, or excluding someone, and many other behaviors. Bullying causes pain and stress for victims and is never justified or excusable. We believe no one deserves to be bullied. We believe everyone should feel that they belong and are accepted in our school.

By signing this pledge, we the faculty, staff, and volunteers of _____ school agree to:

- Participate in activities to help us learn more about bullying—how to prevent it and how to respond to it.
- Communicate to students that bullying will not be tolerated.
- Post bully free rules in the appropriate locations, and seek to consistently apply approved consequences.
- Enforce behavioral expectations in all areas of school property.
- Respond consistently to the best of our ability to bullying incidents according to the bully free discipline rubrics, response plan, and policies.
- Investigate all rumors and reports of bullying.
- Educate students about bullying as deemed appropriate by our school.
- Teach students about all forms of bullying, including cyberbullying and less obvious forms like gossiping, eye-rolling, lying about someone, and social rejection.
- Discuss proactive anti-bullying strategies with students that empower bystanders, such as having lunch with a student who has been socially rejected, and using assertiveness skills to defend those who are bullied.
- Encourage and support students who are bullied, refusing to laugh or join in on the bullying.
- Seek to help bullies change. Provide emotional support to students who are victims and bystanders.

Bully Free Faculty, Staff, and Volunteers Pledge, Cont'd.

- Seek to provide a peaceful and caring atmosphere where students feel safe reporting incidents of bullying, and instill confidence that bullying will be dealt with and not ignored.
- Seek to treat everyone involved in a bullying situation fairly and help them learn better strategies.
- Seek to be caring, active, alert, and involved in each student's life.
- Serve as a role model for students and others.
- Provide quality supervision in my assigned areas and be observant in high-risk areas.
- Take appropriate action in school when I see adults mistreat students.
- Take appropriate action in school when I see adults mistreat adults.

Signed by: _____

Print name: _____

Date: _____

Source: Adapted with permission from Rick Spurling, March 27, 2004.

Bully Free Community Representative Pledge

I, a community representative and supporter of _____ school, say . . .

MY COMMUNITY SHOULD BE BULLY FREE!

Bullying is when one individual (or group) seeks to repeatedly dominate, control, and hurt or frighten another person. Bullying can be pushing, shoving, hitting, spitting on someone, as well as name-calling, picking on, making fun of, laughing at, or excluding someone, and many other behaviors. Bullying causes pain and stress for victims and is never justified or excusable. We believe no one deserves to be bullied. We believe everyone should feel that they belong and are accepted in our schools.

Bullying behavior is not welcome in our community.

By signing this pledge, I agree to:

- Work with other community representatives to provide community environments that are bully free—safe, caring, and peaceful, and where people seek to treat others the way they want to be treated.
- Work in partnership with the school to encourage positive behavior, valuing differences, and promoting sensitivity to others. I will work with them to create safe, peaceful, and caring environments.
- Discuss regularly with children their feelings about school, friendships, and relationships and to have a positive impact on their lives.
- Inform the appropriate individuals when I observe bullying or receive a report that students are bullied.
- Serve as a role model to students and adults in the community.
- Take appropriate action when I see someone (adults or children) mistreated.

Signed by: _____

Print name: _____

Date: _____

Source: Adapted with permission from Rick Spurling, March 27, 2004.

Bully Free Parent Pledge

Bullying is when one individual (or group) seeks to repeatedly dominate, control, and hurt or frighten another person. Bullying can be pushing, shoving, hitting, spitting on someone, as well as name-calling, picking on, making fun of, laughing at, or excluding someone, and many other behaviors. Bullying causes pain and stress for victims and is never justified or excusable. We believe no one deserves to be bullied. We believe everyone should feel that they belong and are accepted in our school.

I will work with my child's school and the community to provide environments that are bully free—safe, caring, and peaceful, and where people seek to treat others the way they want to be treated.

By signing this pledge, I, the parent of a student, agree to:

- Keep my child and myself informed and aware of school bullying policies.
- Work in partnership with the school to encourage positive behavior, valuing differences and promoting sensitivity to others. I will work with them to create a safe, peaceful, and caring school.
- Discuss regularly with my child his or her feelings about school, friendships, and relationships and seek to be involved in and have a positive impact on my child's life.
- Inform school personnel of changes in my child's behavior or circumstances at home that may change his or her behavior at school.
- Alert the appropriate school personnel when I observe or receive reports of bullying.
- Serve as a role model for my child and others.

Signed by: _____

Print name: _____

Date: _____

Source: Adapted with permission from Rick Spurling, March 27, 2004.

Bully Free Student Pledge for Kindergarten to Grade 5

AT THIS SCHOOL, WE BELIEVE . . .

WE SHOULD BE . . .

BULLY FREE!

By signing this pledge, I agree to:

1. Be kind to others and not hurt their feelings, body, or things.
2. Help students who are bullied.
3. Tell an adult at school when I am bullied.
4. Tell an adult at school when I see someone bullied.
5. Refuse to ignore bullying, refuse to laugh at bullying or join in on the bullying.

Student's name: _____

Date: _____

Source: Adapted with permission from Rick Spurling, March 27, 2004.

Bully Free Student Pledge for Grades 6 to 12

AT THIS SCHOOL, WE BELIEVE . . .
WE SHOULD BE . . .
BULLY FREE!

Bullying is when one individual (or group) seeks to repeatedly dominate, control, and hurt or frighten another person. Bullying can be pushing, shoving, hitting, spitting on someone, as well as name-calling, picking on, making fun of, laughing at, or excluding someone, and many other behaviors. Bullying causes pain and stress for victims and is never justified or excusable. We believe no one deserves to be bullied. We believe everyone should feel that they belong and are accepted in our school.

By signing this pledge, I agree to:

1. Value differences and treat others with respect.

2. Refuse to ignore, laugh, or join in when someone is being bullied.

3. Adhere to the school's anti-bullying.

4. Report bullying immediately to a teacher, guidance counselor, principal, or another adult at school.

5. Support and encourage students who have been or are being bullied.

6. Participate fully and contribute to class discussions dealing with bullying.

7. Be a good role model for other students and support them if bullying occurs.

8. Encourage teachers to discuss bullying issues.

Signed by: _____

Print name: _____

Date: _____

Source: Adapted with permission from Rick Spurling, March 27, 2004.

Task Checklist, Step 14

Conduct a Meeting with Adults and an
Assembly Program for Students to Increase
Awareness and Involvement

Meeting with Adults

☐ Secure permission to conduct the meeting for adults from
the appropriate school officials.

☐ Establish the date, time, and location of the meeting.

☐ Determine the agenda of the meeting.

☐ Determine who will facilitate the meeting.

☐ Determine who will address each agenda item.

☐ Determine if refreshments are to be served, and make the
necessary assignments and arrangements.

☐ Determine how expenses will be paid.

☐ Determine who will mail the invitations and publicize the
event.

☐ Determine the handouts for the meeting, and make
arrangements for copying and delivering them to the
meeting site. Determine if some of the handouts need to
be in a different language.

☐ Determine the need for an interpreter or someone skillful
in signing.

☐ Make arrangements to have a sign-in sheet, name tags, and
handouts at the reception table.

☐ Determine the equipment (for example, tables, chairs, laptop
computer, projection device, extension cords, power strip, flip
charts) needed for the meeting, and make arrangements for
the equipment to be at the meeting site.

☐ Review the effectiveness of the meeting with the team. Make
note of the team members' observations, and discuss the
comments of the participants. This information will help you
improve the next meeting.

☐ If appropriate, arrange for translators.

☐ Conduct the meeting.

Task Checklist, Step 14, Cont'd.   Notes

Student Assembly Program

☐ Determine the agenda of the student assembly program.

☐ Select students to do the role playing.

☐ Ask someone to guide the students' practice of the role-playing scenes.

☐ Determine who will inform the teachers and students of the assembly program.

☐ Determine the time, date, and location for the assembly program.

☐ Determine if the students will sign the student pledge at the assembly program or later in class.

☐ Determine the handouts for the assembly program, and make arrangements for copying and delivering them to the assembly program site.

☐ Determine the materials to be displayed. Ask selected students and teachers to develop banners or posters to display at the assembly program.

☐ Determine the equipment (for example, tables, chairs, laptop computer, projection device, extension cord, power strip, flip charts) needed for the assembly program and make arrangements for the equipment to be at the assembly program site.

☐ Conduct the assembly program.

☐ _____
  _____

☐ _____
  _____

☐ _____
  _____

Step 15

Develop and Implement a Student Involvement and Empowerment Plan

Students should be involved in the planning and implementation of the Bully Free Program and empowered to effectively intervene in bullying situations when adults are not around. The students need to feel that the program is as much theirs as it is the school's.

To accomplish this, the team should work together to develop a student involvement and empowerment plan, an important step for these reasons:

- Students can make a valued contribution to the Bully Free Program by helping change the attitudes and behavior of their peers.

- Because most bullying occurs where there is no or little adult supervision, students must be empowered to intervene in an appropriate manner.

- Efforts to involve and empower students build their confidence and trust in the school's ability to prevent and stop bullying, which helps create a telling environment. They are more willing to report bullying events.

- Student involvement helps create a positive peer culture and encourages students to treat others the way they would want to be treated.

- To feel connected to the schoolwide Bully Free Program, students need to be involved in activities within and outside the classroom.

The Bully Free Program offers a variety of strategies for involving and empowering students. In this step, you will examine a list of strategies, and select those that are most desirable for your school. You will then brainstorm with the Bully Free Program team to develop other strategies. The team can also research strategies on the Internet. Additional tips for bystanders appear in *How You Can Be Bully Free: For Students* (Beane, 2004a, 2004b). Both are available at www.bullyfree.com. If your school purchased the bully free school support materials kit, it received a license to put this book as a PDF on the school's Web site. Copies of this book can also be printed for the students in your school.

Following is a bank of student involvement and empowerment strategies. (This bank appears as a Microsoft Word file at www.bullyfree.com.) Select the preferred strategies and develop the student involvement and empowerment plan. Brainstorm with the Bully Free Program team to identify more strategies, and add them to your list. Discuss each strategy, and check those that the team feels are most feasible and desirable. Then finalize the list of strategies to be used. The plan can be created by deleting from the Microsoft Word file the strategies not to be implemented. The team may choose to implement only a few strategies the first year of the program and gradually introduce others.

Student Involvement and Empowerment Strategies Plan

☐ Train bystanders in supportive strategies and assertiveness skills so that they can encourage and defend victims of bullying. The bully free lesson plans address these empowering techniques.

☐ Review the student representation on the Bully Free Program team. If the selected students have been unable to attend, talk to them, and perhaps their parents, and determine if other students need to serve on the team.

☐ Involve students in the development of surveys.

☐ Develop a Peers for Peace—Bully Free Club (see the booklet "Establishing a Peers for Peace—Bully Free Club," Beane, 2005b, www.bullyfree.com). High schools can ask their student council to spearhead the campaign (see "Bully Free Handbook for Student Councils," Beane, 2005a).

☐ Ask students to sign the bully free student pledge at the assembly program for students, or as detailed in Step 14.

☐ Conduct a fine arts contest around the bully free slogan or a theme. The contest categories could be (1) best posters, (2) best songs written, (3) best poems, and (4) best drama or skits.

☐ Give students opportunities to anonymously report bullying events. Students could drop notes in a bully free box located in the school hallway or a multi-purpose box located in every classroom. If placed in the classrooms, the box could be referred to as the "notes to the teacher box." Students could use the box for compliments, complaints, encouraging words to someone, or reports of bullying. Having such boxes reinforces the school system's desire to have a telling environment where individuals report bullying. Also, an e-mail reporting system could be established on the school's Web site for reporting bullying, drugs, weapons, and vandalism.

☐ Invite students to speak at faculty meetings (especially at the meeting for adults), parent meetings, and other meetings.

☐ Invite students to role-play at anti-bullying assembly programs, faculty and staff meetings, and other appropriate gatherings.

☐ Invite students to participate in anti-bullying awareness activities conducted in the community with various community organizations.

☐ Have teachers ask students to assist them in developing anti-bullying bulletin boards, posters, and banners. Suggested resources for this activity are the book *Bully Free Bulletin Boards, Posters, and Banners* (Beane & Beane, 2005) and *Bully Free Bulletin Boards, Posters, and Banners for High School* (Beane & Beane, 2003).

☐ Conduct a classroom door decoration contest focusing on bullying. Have students design and decorate the doors under the guidance of their teacher. Ask members of the community who do not have relatives in the school to serve as judges.

☐ Have T-shirts printed with "Peers for Peace—Bully Free," "Bully Free Is the Way to Be," or the school's anti-bullying slogan. Ask a civic organization to purchase the T-shirts for your students. Occasionally ask students and school personnel to wear them. The T-shirts could also include the bully free logo, using iron-on transfer paper or rubber stamps.

☐ Conduct a bully free T-shirt contest to determine the best bully free T-shirt design. Select a few students to serve as the judges.

☐ Teach students, as well as the faculty and staff, the bully free handshake, a way for two students to indicate that they are in agreement that bullying should be prevented and stopped—that is, to be bully free. The handshake is made by making the symbol for love by folding the middle and ring fingers down into the palm leaving the thumb, index finger and little finger straight. Then, you proceed to "shake hands" by touching the back of the hands together.

☐ Teach the following bully free cheer to older students, as well as faculty, staff, and volunteers.

Empowered Bystanders Are Bully Free
Immanuel Reeve Lamb and Allan Lane Beane

> Together we stand,
> and never will we part,
> we will think for ourselves,
> not letting others control our hearts,
> peace is what we'll strive for,
> we'll do the best we can,
> to make bullying no more,
> we want all to understand.
> We aim to be Bully Free,
> for we know in our hearts,
> Bully Free is the way to be,
> so let's make a new start!

☐ Ask students to submit anti-bullying articles and stories for the school newsletter, school newspaper, and local newspapers.

☐ Distribute bully free bracelets. These bracelets can be worn by anyone in the school who is committed to helping the school be bully free. (These bracelets can be ordered at www.bullyfree.com.) If your school purchased the Bully Free Program kits, teachers already have twenty-five bracelets. Faculty and staff especially should wear the bracelets during a specified period of time or all year. Faculty, staff, and students should encourage all students to make a commitment to preventing and stopping bullying and encourage them to wear the bracelets.

☐ Have students design bully free buttons. This could also be a contest.

☐ Form "bully courts" in which bullies are "tried" and "sentenced" by their peers. Half of the court's members are elected by the bully's classmates, and half are appointed by the teacher. The teacher serves as chairperson to ensure fair play. "Sentences" have included banning bullies from school trips and other class activities for a time period and having bullies perform service-related tasks such as tidying classrooms. Bully courts might be more appropriate for older students than younger students. If you want to examine the related research and explore the possibility for your classroom, search the Internet using the keywords *bully courts*.

☐ Train peer listeners: students who volunteer to be available to listen to students who are victimized. They do not give advice. They need to respect confidentiality and must be good role models. An adult must also supervise them.

☐ Ask students to suggest ways to create more places for students to find a sense of belonging. For example, what additional clubs and student organizations would they like to see in the school? (See Step 8 for ideas.)

☐ Ask a group of students and parents to work with school personnel to organize and implement a Bully Free Month or Bully Free Week. Activities (for example, an assembly, guest speakers, door contests, poster contests, writing contests) can be conducted during the week, and everyone can wear bully free T-shirts, bully free bracelets, and bully free buttons. Prior to this time, teach the bully free cheer and handshake to all students and school personnel. (See Step 8 for more details.)

☐ Ask a select group of students to work with the school to establish a welcome program for new students. Ask local businesses to sponsor the program by providing discounts, coupons, and gifts for new students. Ask local video production specialists to donate their time and expertise to help develop a video to show new students and their parents. This is also a community involvement strategy.

☐ Ask students to help organize a No Name-Calling Week. For more information about this week, visit www.nonamecallingweek.org.

☐ Ask students to help organize a No Gossiping Week.

Task Checklist, Step 15

Notes

Develop and Implement a Student Involvement and Empowerment Plan

☐ Discuss the value and importance of involving and empowering students.

☐ Brainstorm additional strategies, and record them.

☐ Search the Internet for additional ideas.

☐ Ask school personnel to submit ideas to the team.

☐ Discuss each of the strategies for involving and empowering students.

☐ Select the preferred strategies.

☐ Write the student involvement and empowerment plan.

☐ Seek approval of the plan from the appropriate school officials if necessary.

☐ Implement the plan.

☐ _____

_____

☐ _____

_____

☐ _____

_____

☐ _____

_____

☐ _____

_____

☐ _____

_____

Step 16

Develop and Implement Parent and Community Involvement and Education Plans

The parent and community involvement and education plans are key components in the Bully Free Program. This involvement and education starts with parents and community representation, on an as-needed basis, on the Bully Free Program team. Input from these representatives should also be sought at various stages of the Bully Free Program. Their sustained involvement and education can have a tremendous impact on the success of the program, home-school relationships, and school-community relations and safety, as well as influences on school climate, student academic achievement, and student behavior.

Parent involvement is an important component of the bully free lesson plans. Much of the "homework" requires interaction with parents and guardians. They are not placed into a formal teaching role with their children but have meaningful interaction with their children regarding bullying. This has been an important way to educate parents and to build their support of the school's efforts to be bully free.

Select the preferred strategies from the following list of parent involvement and empowerment strategies, and develop the parent involvement and empowerment plan. (These strategies appear as a Microsoft Word file at www.bullyfree.com.) Brainstorm with the Bully Free Program team to identify additional strategies, and add them to the list. Discuss each strategy, and check those the team considers most feasible and desirable. Then settle on the final list of strategies to be used. The plan can be created by going to the Microsoft Word file on the Web site and simply deleting the strategies that are not to be implemented or copying and pasting the preferred strategy into Microsoft Word. The team may choose to implement only a few strategies the first year of the program and gradually introduce other strategies.

Parent Involvement and Education Strategies Plan

☐ Send a letter to parents listing the anti-bullying rules that will be used in all environments: classrooms, buses, cafeteria, playground, and hallways, for example.

☐ Distribute the bully free parent pledge by sending it home with every student.

☐ Make sure parents are represented on the Bully Free Program team, when appropriate, and on any related committees. If the parents selected have been unable to attend the meetings, discuss their situation with them and seek to appoint other parents.

☐ Ask available parents to supervise high-risk areas during high-risk times and perhaps more often. Be sure they are trained and are empowered with authority to respond to bullying events they observe.

☐ Make sure teachers are requiring the homework included in some of the bully free lesson plans.

☐ Ask a group of students and parents to work with school personnel to organize and implement a Bully Free Month or Bully Free Week. Activities (assembly, guest speakers, door contests, poster contests, writing contests, and others) can be conducted during the week, and everyone can wear bully free T-shirts, bracelets, and buttons. Prior to this time, make sure the elementary and middle school teachers have taught the bully free cheer (see Step 15) to all students and school personnel. Ask the parents to discuss the cheer with their children.

☐ Survey parents for their concerns about bullying issues and their ideas for the school anti-bullying program.

☐ Invite parents to presentations and workshops focusing on bullying.

☐ Organize a study group or series of meetings for interested parents and school staff to discuss relevant articles, books, and videos on bullying. This group could also be used to critique resource materials prior to their use in the schools.

☐ When a student bullies someone, ask the parent to attend classes with the child.

☐ Encourage informal discussions on bullying issues between classroom teachers and parents.

☐ Pay the expenses of the parent-teacher association president to attend a regional or state conference that focuses on bullying.

☐ Ask parents who are available to supervise a "safe room" for victims. This is a room that victims can go to when there is a bullying event and time is needed to talk to the bully. The parent can supervise the room and engage the student in activities and provide emotional support to him or her.

☐ Conduct a parent interest and occupations survey that asks them to note their hobbies, knowledge, skills, and abilities. This will help identify parents who can present on various topics or assist with activities. Asking the parent of a victim to demonstrate a skill at school could also net some social prestige for a victim.

☐ Ask a group of parents to assist in making bully free bulletin boards, posters, and banners. Suggested resources for this activity are the two *Bully Free Bulletin Boards, Posters, and Banners* books (Beane & Beane, 2003, 2005, available at www.bullyfree.com).

☐ Ask a group of parents to help the parent-teacher organization and school organize a series of presentations about bullying that could be made at meetings. The meetings should be no longer than an hour and should include refreshments and handouts. Remember those who have special dietary needs, including food allergies. Content addressing the following possible topics (and many others) for the presentations appears in the book *Protect Your Child from Bullying* (Beane, 2008), available at www.bullyfree.com and www.josseybass.com. In addition, I frequently speak to parents. Visit the Bully Free Program Web site for a description of my presentations. Possible topics for the presentations are:

- What can parents do to give their child a good start at school?
- How should parents conduct family meetings to develop empathy and sensitivity?
- What is bullying, and what does it look like?
- How are girls and boys different regarding bullying?
- Why must bullying be prevented and stopped?
- What are the school's bully free policies, rules, and response plans?
- What should you do when your child bullies others?
- What should you do when other students bully your child?
- What should you do when school personnel bully your child?
- What should you do about electronic bullying?
- What can you do to help the school be bully free?
- What bully free resources are available to help parents?
- What does the school's Bully Free Program include?

☐ An alternative to parent-teacher organization presentations is for the schoolwide Bully Free Program team to sponsor a series of one-hour presentations and invite all parents to attend. A strategy for getting parents to attend is to host the meeting the same night that their children are participating in an event (perhaps a dance) and require that their parents attend the meeting in order for the students to participate. Other incentives are to (1) cancel homework for that night, (2) declare that students of parents who attend will not have to wear the school uniform that day or could wear a cap to school the next day, and (3) cancel sports events that night.

☐ Make the book *Protect Your Child from Bullying* (Beane, 2008) accessible for parents of victims and bullies. You may want the parents to use this book for a book study.

- If your school ordered the bully free school support materials kit, it received a license to place the fact sheets "Helpful Tips for Parents" (as PDF files) on the school's Web site. The school may also make as many copies of the fact sheets as desired for parents of students, especially parents of victims and bullies.

☐ Consider purchasing sets of the *Together We Can Be Bully Free* mini-guides for parents at www.bullyfree.com.

☐ Teach assertiveness skills to a group of parents of victims, and ask them to help teach these skills to their children.

☐ Include a series of short articles addressing these activities in the school newspaper and newsletters that are sent to parents.

☐ Ask parents to help organize a No Name-Calling Week.

☐ Ask parents to help organize a No Gossiping Week.

☐ Keep parents informed about the efforts of the school to be bully free.

Following is a listing of sample community involvement and education strategies. (This also appears in the files located at www.bullyfree.com.) Brainstorm with the team to identify additional strategies, and put them on the list. Discuss each of the strategies and check those the team feels are most feasible and desirable. The Bully Free Program team should discuss these and decide which strategies are most appropriate to implement. The team may choose to implement only a few strategies the first year of the program and gradually introduce others.

Community Involvement and Education Strategies Plan

☐ Ask the local newspaper to run a series of informative articles about bullying.

☐ Ask local civic organizations to sponsor a series of community seminars on bullying. I am often asked to make community presentations.

☐ Ask community youth program directors such as Girl Scout and Boy Scout leaders, youth ministers, and YMCA directors to attend the appropriate anti-bullying training sessions offered at the school for school personnel and volunteers.

☐ Ask local faith-based organizations to have a Golden Rule Week or School Safety Week (or month) that focuses on bullying.

☐ Ask local faith-based organizations to host a series of seminars on bullying for members, especially parents and children.

☐ Ask for volunteers from the community to help supervise high-risk areas (the hallway, playground, bus, and cafeteria, for example). Make sure they are trained and empowered with authority to respond to bullying according to policies and procedures.

☐ Work with the appropriate business representatives, program directors, and city and county officials to identify high-risk areas in the community and implement strategies for more adequately supervising and monitoring these areas.

☐ Ask the directors of youth programs in the community to address bullying and establish policies and procedures for reporting it. Ask them to train their personnel to respond appropriately to bullying. They could attend some of the training provided by the school or district as well.

☐ With the permission of appropriate school officials, ask local businesses to have a donation display in their stores labeled "Help Us Stop School Violence" to fund the Bully Free Program.

☐ Ask service organizations (for example, Habitat for Humanity or homeless shelter programs) in the community to collaborate with the schools to provide students (especially victims and bullies) opportunities to help others.

☐ Train a group of community volunteers to mentor victims of bullying.

☐ Ask selected community representatives to serve as judges in a school arts contest focusing on bullying. The contest categories could be (1) best posters, (2) best songs written, (3) best poems, and (4) best drama/skits.

☐ Conduct a classroom doors decoration contest focusing on bullying. Require students to design and decorate the doors under the guidance of their teachers. Ask members of the community who do not have relatives in the school to serve as judges.

☐ With the appropriate school officials' permission, ask local civic organizations to raise funds to support the Bully Free Program. You may even ask a local country club to host a golf tournament to raise funds.

☐ Ask local clothing stores to sponsor a style show at school for males and females, providing clothing for the students to wear, makeup, and other help. Make sure victims of bullying are included and have the opportunity to dress up.

☐ Establish a welcome program for new students. Ask local businesses to sponsor the program by providing discounts, coupons, and gifts for the new students. Ask local video production specialists to donate their time and expertise to help develop a video to show new students and their parents.

☐ Ask local organizations that work with youth or provide activities for youth to sponsor a Bully Free Month at their establishments. For example, one YMCA placed banners and posters about bullying in its building and sponsored other activities.

☐ Ask community representatives to help organize a No Name-Calling Week.

☐ Ask community representatives to help organize a No Gossiping Week.

☐ Ask local businesses and organizations to provide financial support.

☐ Ask local businesses and organizations to provide material support or free services (posters, flip charts, awards, T-shirts, printing, photography, and so on).

☐ With the approval of parents, ask trusted individuals in the community to serve as mentors or buddies to students in need of such a relationship.

Task Checklist, Step 16   Notes

Develop and Implement Parent and Community Involvement and Education Plans

☐ Examine the list of parent involvement and education strategies.

☐ Brainstorm ideas for additional strategies, and record them.

☐ Decide which parent involvement and education strategies will be used.

☐ Examine the list of community involvement and education strategies.

☐ Brainstorm with the team ideas for additional community involvement and education strategies and record them.

☐ Decide which community involvement and education strategies will be used.

☐ Decide whether to purchase copies of *Protect Your Child from Bullying* (Beane, 2008) for dissemination to parents of victims and bullies. Ask the PTA to use this book as a book study.

If a series of presentations is to be given to parents and others in the community:

☐ Decide the topics to be addressed.

☐ Identify who will address the topics.

☐ Prepare handouts and overheads or slides (if the speaker desires). Determine if handouts in other languages need to be provided.

☐ Determine the need for an interpreter or someone skillful in signing.

☐ Confirm the date, time, and location of the presentation.

☐ Confirm the room arrangement (how many chairs and tables, the setup, and so on).

☐ Reserve equipment (a screen, projector, and other items).

☐ Arrange logistics including child care and translators.

Task Checklist, Step 16, Cont'd.   Notes

☐ Arrange for refreshments, and consider those who have special dietary needs, including food allergies.

☐ Determine the need for displays and the content of displays.

☐ Determine who will moderate the meeting.

☐ Determine who will serve as the meeting recorder (records comments made at the meeting).

☐ Determine how the presentations will be advertised and who will be responsible for the advertisements and publicity.

Step 17

Review and Confirm the Implementation and Completion of Program Components and Activities

At this point, you should be several months into the program, so the team needs to review the work that has been completed thus far. It is important for the team to determine what plans have been fully implemented, those that need more attention, and the plans that have failed to get implemented. The team should review Steps 2 to 16, and make a list of all the strategies, initiatives, and activities they said would be implemented and determine whether they have been. If necessary or deemed appropriate, a small questionnaire could be given to each teacher to determine the degree to which they have carried out their responsibilities. Each team member could also be charged with the responsibility of determining the degree to which certain things have been implemented.

This is also an excellent time to conduct another focus meeting with faculty and staff, students, and parents. Use the same focus questions discussed in Step 5. Get permission to conduct the faculty and staff focus meeting at a regularly scheduled meeting. Ask the president of the parent-teacher organization to give you a few minutes at the next meeting to conduct the parent focus meeting. The student focus meeting could occur during a student council meeting. If your school does not have a student council, consider asking each teacher to conduct a focus meeting with their students. Or you could have a special assembly program to get feedback from students.

Ask the program evaluation coordinator to collect feedback from all of the groups and compile a report that addresses the questions and indicate whether the feedback was from faculty, staff, parents, or students.

Work with the team to generate a list of items that were not implemented. Try to determine why they have not been done and whether they should be pursued. Then develop a list of improvements that need to be made in the program. Seek to make these changes and to have them approved by the appropriate school personnel.

Task Checklist, Step 17

Review and Confirm the Implementation and Completion of Program Components and Activities

☐ Ask the Bully Free Program evaluation coordinator to facilitate efforts to collect progress data and to submit a report to the team. Determine when the progress data will be reported to the team.

☐ As a team, review Steps 2 to 16 and determine if selected strategies, initiatives, and activities have been implemented as planned. The following checklist items will help you.

☐ Make sure all school personnel have been trained as planned and have received the bully free materials and resources.

☐ Make sure bully free rules have been posted in the appropriate classrooms, sent home to parents, and reviewed with students.

☐ Make sure the discipline rubrics are established and used.

☐ Make sure behavioral expectations for the high-risk areas have been developed and communicated to students and school personnel.

☐ Make sure all personnel, volunteers, parents, and students have been made aware of the new bully free policies, mission statement, goals, slogan, and logo.

☐ Make sure the bully free mission statement, slogan, and logo have been posted in the selected locations.

☐ Make sure the team developed the bully free response plans, the appropriate individuals have been trained to use the plans, and the procedures are being used appropriately.

☐ Make sure the bully free supervision plan and schedule, developed during Step 12, has been implemented. Make sure the supervisors have been trained, and new supervisors are trained.

☐ Make sure Bully Free Zone posters have been posted in the high-risk areas.

☐ Make sure bully free classroom posters have been placed in all classrooms.

Task Checklist, Step 17, Cont'd.   Notes

- ☐ Make sure the bully free curriculum (lesson plans, classroom meetings, and kits of materials) have been implemented.

- ☐ Make sure the bully free administrative strategies plan has been developed and implemented as planned in Step 8.

- ☐ Make sure the student involvement and empowerment plan has been developed and implemented as planned in Step 15.

- ☐ Make sure all students have signed the bully free pledge.

- ☐ Make sure all school personnel have signed the bully free pledge.

- ☐ Make sure the bully free pledge for parents has been sent home with every student.

- ☐ Make sure selected key community representatives have signed the bully free pledge for community representatives.

- ☐ _____

  _____

- ☐ _____

  _____

- ☐ _____

  _____

Step 18

Readminister the Survey Instruments, Analyze Pre- and Post-Data, and Make Improvements

Now it is time to collect the postprogram data and compare them to the baseline data collected during Step 5 and throughout the year through surveys, focus meetings, and other strategies. This is accomplished by administering the surveys again, reexamining existing data (on attendance and suspensions and expulsions resulting from bullying, for example), and examining reports (parent reports of bullying, student reports of bullying, and so on) and the notes of various focus meetings.

Readminister the Surveys

By this time, the Bully Free Program has probably been implemented for about twelve or thirteen months, so it is time to administer the surveys again. After readministering the surveys, analyze and compare the data with the baseline survey data collected before the program was implemented to determine what improvements have been made and where improvement still needs to be seen. It is best to administer the surveys during a time that school life is "normal." Therefore, try to avoid administering them right before or after a break or vacation. It is also best to administer the pretest and posttest at the same time of year (for example, each April). Therefore, it is usually not a good idea to administer the pretest in the fall and the posttest in the spring. It is also a good idea not to administer the questionnaires too early in the school year when students are on their best behavior. Also avoid asking students to complete the surveys during the last two weeks of the year.

It is very important to note that during the first year, it is not uncommon for the evaluation data to indicate an increase in reported bullying (Olweus, 1995). Reports of bullying increase as awareness of the problem increases and as students observe the actions of the school in supporting students who are bullied. As students gain confidence and trust adults to respond to the situations appropriately, they are more willing to report bullying, so more bullying may be initially reported. But then the incidence of bullying should decrease, and therefore reports of bullying should decrease. Sometimes this decrease in bullying and reports happens rapidly in a school.

It varies from school to school. Keep in mind that the program will definitely decrease bullying in your school if it is implemented systematically as recommended in this book. By the end of the second year, you should see a greater reduction in bullying.

Reexamine Data

Next reexamine data and compare them to data gathered before the program was implemented (as discussed in Step 5)—for example:

- Reports of aggressive occurrences
- Suspensions resulting from aggression or bullying
- Expulsions resulting from aggression or bullying
- School attendance
- Reported discipline problems
- Academic performance of school
- Number of reported fights

Examine Bullying Reports and Notes Taken During Focus Meetings

Examine changes in the frequency and nature of the bullying reports from parents and students. Also examine and compare notes taken over time during the staff focus meetings, parent focus meetings, and student focus meetings.

Do Not Relax

If the evaluation shows that the Bully Free Program is successful, *do not relax*. Bullying is a problem that must be supervised and monitored on an ongoing basis. There should also be a constant effort to identify other effective strategies and resources.

Write an evaluation report that summarizes all the findings. The program evaluation coordinator should write an evaluation report and submit it to the team. At some point, you may want to submit it to the appropriate school officials. The report should include a list of the program goals listed in Step 6 and the objectives developed in this step, and indicate whether each was met. Pre- and posttest data relative to each goal should also be included. If your team did not write objectives, the report should at least include these data relative to the survey and the preexisting data collected at the beginning of the program. It would also be helpful to school officials if the report included a brief summary regarding the effectiveness of the program, highlighting areas of improvement and areas that still need work. This report will be helpful in supporting any requests for additional funds for the program.

Work with the team to generate a list of objectives that were not measured. Try to determine why they have not been addressed, and seek to correct the problem. Then develop a list of changes that need to be made in the program. Seek to make these changes and have them approved by the appropriate school personnel.

With the permission of the appropriate school officials, discuss the report with school personnel, parents, students, and other appropriate individuals. Develop a brief handout and PowerPoint presentation summarizing the evaluation and effectiveness of the program. Then schedule a time to present the data to school personnel, parents, and others. This could be done during a faculty and staff meeting and during parent-teacher organization meetings. Or you could present the data at the celebration event, the next, and final, step. Depending on the age of students, you may want to share the findings with them during an assembly program or at a celebration party or open house. Also, make sure you express gratitude to faculty, staff, parents, and students for their assistance in making the school bully free.

Task Checklist, Step 18

Notes

Readminister the Survey Instruments, Analyze Pre- and Post-Data, and Make Improvements

☐ Administer the Bully Free Survey (for School Personnel). Analyze and compare the data to the baseline data.

☐ Administer the Bully Free Survey (for Students). Analyze and compare the data to the baseline data. There are separate surveys for each level: preschool, elementary, middle school, and high school students.

☐ Administer the Bully Free Survey (for Parents). Analyze and compare the data to the baseline data.

☐ Compare the existing data on attendance and suspensions, for example, with the baseline data collected earlier.

☐ Examine the notes from staff focus meetings collected over time, and look for improvements and concerns.

☐ Examine the notes from parent focus meetings collected over time, and look for improvements and concerns.

☐ Examine the notes from student focus meetings collected over time, and look for improvements and concerns.

☐ Write an evaluation report that summarizes the findings.

☐ Generate a list of strategies and activities that have failed to be implemented. Determine why they have not been done. Seek to get them implemented or justify why the team plans not to use them next year.

☐ With the permission of the appropriate school officials, discuss the report with school personnel, parents, students, and other appropriate individuals.

☐ _____
_____

☐ _____
_____

☐ _____
_____

Step 19

Celebrate Success and Plan for Next Year

When you see bullying prevented and reduced or even stopped, you will feel like celebrating, and you should. Make public the program's success through newspapers, newsletters, and other avenues. Be sure to involve stakeholders in celebrating the program's success, including the school system's board of education. You may even want to have a celebration open house at your school.

Invite the public to hear about the program and see the bully free bulletin boards, posters, banners, and other displays in the school. Display students' artwork related to bullying, and have students role-play inappropriate and appropriate behavior, perform skits, or present videotapes they have created. You could also share pre- and post-data as evidence of success. In addition to the celebration, you may want to make a presentation to the school system's board of education or trustees.

Certainly celebrate, but do not relax. Maintain the program's momentum by planning for next year's continuation of the program. The Bully Free Program never ends. It's a way of living.

Task Checklist, Step 19

Notes

Celebrate Success and Plan for Next Year

☐ Obtain permission from the appropriate school officials to have the celebration.

☐ Ask someone to coordinate the event.

☐ Form a committee to work with the event coordinator.

☐ Determine if the celebration should be an open house celebration or a special event, such as a banquet.

☐ Determine if refreshments will be served or a dinner. Remember those with special dietary needs, including food allergies.

☐ Determine the agenda and the speakers, what data will be presented, and how students will be involved (for example, role playing or developing a video or personal testimonies).

☐ Determine what handouts should be given to the attendees. Determine if handouts need to be in a different language.

☐ Determine who should be invited.

☐ Determine the need for interpreters or someone skillful in signing.

☐ Set the date and time.

☐ Assign someone to acquire and send the invitations.

☐ Determine the displays to be exhibited.

☐ Determine the desired room arrangements, displays, and decorations.

☐ Choose a place to hold the event.

☐ Reserve the facilities, tables, chairs, and equipment: laptop, screen, sound system, tables for displays, and so forth.

☐ Celebrate!

☐ After the celebration, meet with the Bully Free Program team and plan for next year.

☐ _____

_____

☐ _____

_____

Appendix A

Description of the Bully Free Program

The materials in this appendix are available in the files located at www.bullyfree.com. The last two pages can be used as a handout for workshops. After entering the Web site, click on "Click here to access our training resources." Then click on "Resources for Bully Free Program Committee." Type *bfp1* when you are asked your user name and *bullyfree* when you are asked your password.

Description of the Bully Free Program

This document reviews the philosophy, targets, structure, and effective elements and components of the Bully Free Program. This program is the most comprehensive schoolwide (and systemwide) anti-bullying program being adopted by schools and districts around the world. It is a research-based program that includes administrative strategies, teacher strategies, lesson plans for each grade level (preschool through high school), classroom meetings, student involvement, and bystander empowerment. The program also includes parent involvement, community involvement, and all of the elements and components that must be present in effective anti-bullying programs.

What Are the Goals of the Bully Free Program?

The goals of the program are:

- To send a clear message to students, staff, parents, and community members that bullying will not be tolerated.

- To train staff and students and to provide information to parents relative to taking steps to preventing and stopping bullying.

- To establish and enforce rules and policies focusing on bullying.

- To reduce existing bullying situations through administrative and teacher-centered strategies and a comprehensive scope and sequence of age-appropriate lesson plans for each grade level.

- To create safer and more peaceful schools.

- To promote a sense of belonging and acceptance in all students so that they feel connected to their school.

- To involve and empower students as bystanders to prevent and stop bullying.

- To involve parents in the program.

- To involve the community in the program.

- To create a school culture where adults are warm, positive, and trustworthy role models and viewed as authorities. Adults are clear authorities but caring and respectful in the way they treat students and other adults.

- To significantly improve adult supervision on school property, especially in high-risk areas.

- To restructure the school culture and social environment in a way that adults and students take action and expect immediate intervention, investigation, and confrontation of students engaged in bullying behavior.

- To implement nonphysical and nonhostile strategies for changing the behavior of students engaged in bullying and follow through with disciplinary actions if the bullying behavior persists.

- To provide intervention for children who are bullied and who bully.

What Is the Bully Free Program's Philosophy?

The philosophy of the Bully Free Program is based on child development research; social psychology; research regarding school climate and development of a peaceful, safe, and meaningful community; effective teaching; learning principles; behavior and classroom management; and current thinking regarding effective anti-bullying programs. The Bully Free Program is based on and maintains the following:

- Bullying is a form of overt and aggressive behavior that is intentional, hurtful (physical or psychological, or both), and persistent (repeated). Bullied students are teased, harassed, and assaulted verbally or physically by one or more peers and often socially rejected by their peers. There has to be an imbalance of power. Although this definition of bullying is well accepted, some children may be hurt so much by a single event that they are changed for life. Therefore, it is not as important to label an event as bullying as it is to help children who are being hurt, regardless of the number of times they have been mistreated.

- Bullying is violence and is a heart problem. Students need to have more empathy and sensitivity regarding the needs and experiences of others. They must overcome their desire to be accepted by those who seem popular and powerful and who mistreat others. They also must have the courage to intervene in bullying situations, when there is no danger of being harmed themselves. An effective program also maintains that children basically have good hearts and that an effective program should emphasize their potential for future leadership, affirm their strengths, and encourage them to do good and remarkable things. Therefore, an effective anti-bullying program discourages labeling children as *victims* or *bullies*. There are simply children who are mistreated (bullied) and children who mistreat others (bullies). Both groups need help.

- Bullying behavior should not be labeled as mild, moderate, and severe. How children respond to mistreatment varies too greatly. One child, because of his or her past life experiences (psychological and relational), temperament, personality, sensitivity, and other characteristics, may consider a bullying behavior moderate or severe bullying while another child considers the same behavior as a mild form of bullying.

- An effective program:
  - Should include not only a framework, policies, and procedures but also proactive prevention strategies and intervention strategies that are administrative, teacher centered, student centered, and parent centered, as well as an age-appropriate curriculum (lesson plans, materials, and resources for each grade level) with an appropriate scope and sequence. This eliminates the need for schools to take the time to determine what must be taught at each grade level.
  - Has been systematically implemented districtwide and schoolwide and the coordinating team is provided a manual and tools to ensure such systematic implementation. The program must be continuous and become a way of living every day in the school for all school personnel. It's not enough to have a few teachers or the counselor teaching lessons and responding to bullying.
  - Helps prevent students from becoming targets of bullying, helps those who are bullied, helps children who bully change the way they act, empowers bystanders, and educates all stakeholders (for example, school personnel, parents, and community representatives).
  - Has implementation flexibility that does not jeopardize effectiveness. One size does not fit all. All schools and communities are different, and schools should be allowed to select strategies that are most appropriate for them.
  - Maintains that the main responsibility of a program rests with adults, but also maintains that student-initiated change is critical, beginning with school personnel seeking input from all students and listening to students. An effective program harnesses the knowledge, experience, and energy of the students.
  - Maintains that, when appropriate, students who are bullied need to learn how to clearly state their disapproval of their mistreatment and help themselves in other ways, but it is mainly the responsibility of adults to prevent and stop bullying.
  - Maintains that it is important not to minimize any problem, such as sexual harassment or racism, by classifying it under the umbrella term *bullying*. Although an effective anti-bullying program will attack these problems, additional efforts are required to prevent and reduce these problems.
  - Maintains that peer mediation and conflict resolution are not usually effective in helping true aggressive bullies to change. These are just important skills to teach students in order to have a more peaceful school.
  - Endorses that consistent application of consequences is important (negative for inappropriate behavior and positive for desired new behavior) but also encourages a healthy dialogue regarding norms, rules, and issues between

school personnel, students, and parents that stimulates creativity and solutions to life problems, especially bullying. Prosocial (nonpunitive) strategies should also be used. Also, improvement in behavior should be rewarded.

○ Places great value on quality and sufficient adult supervision. Each school should develop a supervision plan that includes strategies for each high-risk area identified and provides training for supervisors. Therefore, the program should include a bank of ideas for increasing and improving the quality of supervision and adding structure to unstructured times. To support these efforts, the program should include behavioral expectations for each high-risk area.

○ Seeks to change the culture of the school and create a "telling environment." To change the culture of a school, all faculty, staff, and students need to be involved in the program. There must also be strong parent involvement. Students need to see and experience activities and visuals (such as bully free posters, banners, bulletin boards, and bracelets) that communicate that the school is serious about preventing and stopping bullying. These serve as visual safety cues. Students also see an appropriate response to bullying and need to feel that teachers and staff care about their hurt, understand their hurt, and know how to respond in a way that will not make it worse for them.

○ Rewards efforts to make the school bully free and celebrates successful efforts and the achievement of program goals.

For Whom Is the Program Designed?

Any anti-bullying program should be used in every school and have a broad base of impact. The Bully Free Program targets students in preschool, elementary, middle or junior high, and high school and, to some extent, the community. Some of the strategies are designed specifically for children who are bullied and children who bully others, while other strategies are designed for all students in a school. Parents, law enforcement officers, and community representatives also play a role in the program. Systemwide, schoolwide, classroom, and individual components interrelate throughout the program.

What Are the Major Components of the Bully Free Program?

The Bully Free Program includes the following major components that should be present in any anti-bullying program:

• Each school forms and trains a coordinating committee called the Bully Free Program team. The team is a working committee that meets on a regular basis. When the program is implemented in several schools, a district steering committee is encouraged.

- One member of the team serves as the director or coordinator of the program. This person selects a team member to serve as the team's recorder or secretary, and another member is asked to coordinate the evaluation of the program (determining effectiveness).

- Mission statement, goals, objectives, a slogan, and logo are established by the Bully Free Program team.

- There is an ongoing effort to promote acceptance and a sense of belonging in all students by encouraging them to treat others the way they would want to be treated.

- Anti-bullying policies, procedures, rules, discipline rubrics, and behavioral expectations are established.

- Response plans are developed to allow immediate, consistent intervention by adults.

- Appropriate progressive negative or reductive consequences and positive consequences are used as well as nonpunitive, nonblaming approaches.

- A comprehensive bank of research-based and proven prevention and intervention strategies is provided. The components are:
  - System centered (districtwide and schoolwide)
  - Child centered (the bullied, the child who bullies, followers, bystanders)
  - Peer centered (empowerment of bystanders)
  - Family centered
  - Personnel centered
  - Community centered

- Bullying awareness training and program implementation training are provided for all school personnel.

- Bully free awareness presentation is held for parents and community representatives.

- A bully free awareness assembly is held for students.

- There is an assembly for students to increase awareness and their involvement.

- There is a meeting for parents, school personnel, and community representatives to increase awareness and their involvement.

- Serious talks or interviews are conducted with children who are bullied, children who bully, followers, and bystanders.

- Bully free lesson plans are provided for every grade level, from preschool to high school.

- Classroom meetings are used for reviewing lessons and problem-solving.

- Reporting systems and bulletin boards, posters, banners, pamphlets, and bracelets designed to help change the culture of the school are provided.

- Adults model treating others the way you want to be treated. There are consequences when they are not good models.

- Strategies are included for a:
    - Student involvement and empowerment plan
    - Parent involvement and education plan
    - Community involvement and education plan

- Strategies are included for:
    - Identifying children who are bullied, children who bully, and followers
    - Ongoing communication with stakeholders
    - Maintaining the program's momentum
    - Communicating leadership's commitment
    - Creating a "telling environment": school personnel and parents must become "safe places" to tell about bullying
    - Identifying high-risk areas
    - Developing and monitoring a supervision plan, supervision schedule, and information exchange system
    - Evaluating the effectiveness of the program

- Ongoing review and monitoring of program implementation and effectiveness are conducted through surveys, examining existing data, staff focus meetings, student focus meetings, and parent focus meetings.

- Strategies for maintaining momentum throughout the school year and each following year are provided.

- Intervention plans are provided for children who are bullied and children who bully.

What Are the Major Elements of the Bully Free Program?

The components of the program include the following critical elements:

- Addresses all forms of bullying: physical, verbal, social, relational, and electronic.

- Uses research-based strategies and an age-appropriate curriculum, with lesson plans for each grade level from preschool through high school.

- Recognizes and allows the creativity and preferences of schools yet ensures systematic and consistent implementation.

- Includes curriculum and a multitude of strategies that promote acceptance and a sense of belonging, empower bystanders, and address all forms of bullying behavior: physical, verbal, social-relational, and electronic.

- Addresses empathy, impulse control, anger management, friendship, supporting children who are bullied, changing the behavior of children who bully, empowerment of bystanders, parent education, community involvement, and much more.

- Provides instruction in peer mediation and conflict resolution. Although these are not usually effective in resolving bullying problems, they are important skills to give children.

- Empowers school personnel, parents, volunteers, community representatives, and students.

- Is process oriented (as opposed to conducting only special events). It maintains that the little things done every day—for example, letting others hear you compliment a student who is bullied, helping students identify what they have in common, and giving a student a list of his or her positive characteristics—are what make a difference in attitudes, thinking, and behavior.

- Includes an ongoing effort to encourage students to treat others the way they would want to be treated.

- Includes student-initiated activities.

- Includes systematic implementation of prevention and intervention strategies that are administrative, teacher centered, student centered, and parent centered and are coupled with curriculum.

- Includes policies and procedures for investigating rumors and unverified reports of bullying, as well as responding to bullying when it is observed.

- Seeks to help all stakeholders (school personnel, students, parents, community representatives) understand the nature of bullying.

- Harnesses the energy and commitment of students and empowers them as bystanders.

- Encourages adults to model treating others the way they want to be treated.

- Identifies high-risk areas and includes supervision strategies and supportive supervisory strategies to be used (for example, adding structure to unstructured activities).

- Recognizes that boys and girls from all walks of life bully and is sensitive to the differences in their behavior.

- Creates a "telling environment": all adults must be "safe places" to tell about bullying.

- Does not minimize any forms of bullying behavior and does not classify such behaviors as mild, moderate, and severe because the impact varies too much from one student to another.

- Includes several student-to-student and student-to-adult activities focusing on student thinking, input, and feedback, including student focus meetings and lesson plan activities requiring students to discuss questions, reach consensus, express orally and in writing their thoughts and feelings, and so on.

What Materials and Resources Are Included in the Program?

Materials to Guide the Bully Free Program Team

Each team member is provided a copy of *Bullying Prevention for Schools: A Step-by-Step Guide to Implementing the Bully Free Program.* The team is also given access at www.bully free.com to numerous helpful Microsoft Word files of materials, handouts, and examples of such documents as discipline rubrics, policies, and supervision plans, and much more.

Instructional Materials and Resources

Teachers, counselors, parents, and students are provided a variety of instructional and support materials and resources. The Bully Free Program includes a comprehensive scope and sequence of lesson plans for every level from preschool through high school and books for teachers, counselors, parents, and students. The program includes supportive materials such as pamphlets, posters, bulletin boards, banners, bracelets, a card game, a CD, and many other materials. Ideally, every teacher and counselor will be given a kit of materials and resources. All materials and resources are available in kits or as individual items. For more information, visit www.bullyfree.com.

School Support Materials

Each school receives the school support materials kit. This kit contains manuals, several Bully Free Zone posters for high-risk areas and two PDF files, a book of helpful facts for parents, and a book for students. The school can print an unlimited number of these books and distribute them to the school's personnel, parents, and students or place them on the school's Web site.

What Are the Effects of the Bully Free Program?

This program is research based and integrates the latest research with proven prevention and intervention strategies. Prior to developing the program, Bully Free Systems LLC carefully conducted an analysis of the current research on the topic and related topics (promoting acceptance, hate, prejudice, discrimination, peer rejection, empathy, impulse control, conflict, anger, behavior management, violence, assimilation, sense of community, school climate) and effective instructional practices. Current educational standards were also analyzed.

Research was conducted to develop an appropriate scope and sequence of the knowledge and skills to be learned. Many of the strategies and much of the curriculum (lesson plans for preschool to high school) were developed and tested in several schools. Many of the strategies were developed through problem-solving teacher and administrator focus groups and workshops. Since 1999, teachers and other professionals have reported the educational effectiveness of materials included in the Bully Free Program.

The effectiveness of the Bully Free Program has been reported in *School Violence and Primary Prevention* (Miller, 2008). Visit www.bullyfree.com for an example of the effectiveness data.

Rick Spurling (2006) tested the effectiveness of the Bully Free Program in five western North Carolina middle schools (grades 5 to 8). Fifty-four participants (administrators, teachers, and parents) were involved in this study with in-depth interviews. The following summary of his findings in the five schools reflects the variety of areas that can be affected by the Bully Free Program:

- Improved the dynamics of interpersonal relationships in the school community (student-student, student-teacher, teacher-teacher, parent-teacher, parent-parent, and school-community)

- Improved lines of communication among all stakeholders

- Significantly decreased incidences of aggressive and violent behavior

- Improved school attendance

- Improved state test scores

- Created trust among personnel working on the program

- Increased interactions between teachers and students during nonclass times

- Increased awareness of the need for and importance of adults modeling positive interactions, as well as made adults more conscious of their behavior

- Increased students' understanding of their role in preventing and stopping bullying

- Increased the comfort level and confidence of personnel in their ability to deal with bullying

- Dramatically decreased fighting among boys

- Changed how discipline was administered

- Increased a sense of security

- Increased school attendance and involvement of students in after-school events

- Dramatic decrease in vandalism

Major Components and Elements of the Bully Free Program

(Handout)

School-Level Components and Elements

- Bully Free Program team (coordinating committee), program coordinator, and implementation guide

- Policies, procedures, rules, behavior expectations, and discipline rubric

- Professional development

- Pre- and postprogram assessment (program evaluation plan and evaluation coordinator)

- Bully Free Surveys (for students, faculty, and parents)

- Program's mission statement, goals, slogan, and logo

- Campaign against bullying (activities harnessing the energy of students)

- Bully free school assembly program

- Focus meetings with school personnel, parents, and students

- Student involvement and empowerment plan (a bank of strategies and activities)

- Parent involvement and education plan (a bank of strategies and activities)

- Community involvement plan (a bank of strategies and activities)

- Bank of administrative strategies for creating a caring, safe, and peaceful school

- Bully free pledge for students, school personnel, parents, and community representatives

- School support materials kit (PDF files for parents and students placed on school's server) and several Bully Free Zone posters for high-risk areas

- Supervision plan, schedule, and professional development

  - Strategies for providing quality supervision

  - Strategies for information sharing and exchange

  - Supportive supervision strategies (technology, adding structure, etc.)

- Bully free bulletin boards, posters, and banners for high-risk areas

- Strategies for connecting students to school

- Celebration of program's success

(continued on next page)

Parent- and Community-Level Components and Elements

- Strategies for developing a parent and community involvement and education plan

- Awareness presentation for parents and community representatives

- Educational pamphlets

- Committee representation

- Bully free pledge for parents and community representatives

- Focus meetings and bully free pledges

- Bully Free Survey

Individual-Level, Response-Level, and Intervention-Level Components and Elements

- Improved supervision and on-the-spot response plan (responding when it is seen)

- Procedures for investigating rumors and unverified reports

- Response plan (responding after the on-the-spot response)

- Discipline rubrics with progressive consequences and behavioral expectations for high-risk areas

- Pro-social and nonpunitive strategies

- Intervention plan to help students (who are bullied, and who bully others)

Classroom-Level Components and Elements

- A comprehensive scope and sequence of bully free lesson plans (preschool through high school) and classroom meetings

- Grade-specific bully free classroom kit of materials and resources

    ○ Supportive instructional materials for the teacher

    ○ Bully free classroom poster, bully free bracelets, and pamphlets and brochures (for school personnel, students, and parents)

    ○ Instructional materials for students and book for parents

- Bully free bulletin boards, banners, and posters (for the classroom)

- Posted and enforced bully free classroom rules and behavioral expectations

Appendix B

Overview of Bullying— Handouts and Fact Sheets

The materials in this appendix are available in the files located at www.bullyfree.com. After entering the Web site, click on "Click here to access our training resources." Then click on "Resources for Bully Free Program Committee." Then type *bfp1* when you are asked your user name and *bullyfree* when you are asked your password.

Fact Sheet 1:
What Is Bullying?

Bullying is a form of overt and aggressive behavior that is intentional, hurtful, and persistent (repeated). Bullied students are teased, harassed, rejected, and assaulted (verbally or physically, or both) by one or more individuals. There is an imbalance of strength (power and dominance).

The above definition includes the following criteria that will help you determine if a student is being bullied:

1. The mistreatment must be *intentional*.

2. The mistreatment must be *hurtful* (physical or psychological).

3. The mistreatment must *occur more than once*. However, some disagree about this. They say one very hurtful event is enough to label it bullying.

4. There must be a *power imbalance*.

Of course, all inappropriate behavior should be prevented and stopped.

Fact Sheet 2:
What Does Bullying Look Like?

Direct Bullying Behaviors

Physical Bullying (a few examples)

- Hitting, slapping, elbowing, shouldering (slamming someone with your shoulder)
- Shoving in a hurtful or embarrassing way
- Kicking
- Taking, stealing, damaging or defacing belongings or other property
- Restraining
- Pinching
- Flushing someone's head in the toilet
- Cramming someone into his or her locker
- Attacking with spit wads or food

Verbal Bullying (a few examples)

- Name-calling
- Insulting remarks and put-downs
- Repeated teasing
- Racist remarks or other harassment
- Threats and intimidation
- Whispering behind someone's back

Indirect Bullying Behaviors (a few examples)

- Destroying and manipulating relationships (turning your best friend against you)
- Destroying status within a peer group
- Destroying reputations
- Humiliation and embarrassment
- Intimidation
- Gossiping, spreading nasty and malicious rumors and lies about someone
- Hurtful graffiti
- Excluding someone from a group (social rejection or isolation)
- Stealing boyfriends or girlfriends to hurt someone

- Negative body language (facial expressions, turning your back to someone)
- Threatening gestures, taunting, pestering, insulting remarks and gestures
- Glares and dirty looks, nasty jokes, notes passed around, anonymous notes
- Hate petitions (promising to hate someone)

Other Bullying Behaviors

- Cyberbullying: negative text messages on cell phones, e-mail, voice-mail messages, Web pages, and so on

Direct and indirect forms of bullying often occur together. All of these behaviors can be interrelated.

Fact Sheet 3:
How Are Boys and Girls
Different in Their Bullying?

Both boys and girls use verbal aggression (such as mocking, name-calling, teasing, mean telephone calls, verbal threats of aggression) and intimidation (such as graffiti, publicly challenging someone to do something, playing a dirty trick, taking possessions, coercion) (Garrity, Jens, Porter, Sager, and Short-Camilli, 1996). Nevertheless, there are some differences.

Boy Bullies

- Boys may bully more than girls. However, some question this.
- Boys bully both boys and girls (Olweus, 1993).
- Boys use more direct behaviors (physical and verbal bullying) than girls do. They usually use more indirect bullying as their verbal skills increase (Mullin-Rindler, 2002).
- Boys may use more physical aggression than girls (Espelage, Bosworth, & Simon, 2000; Hyde, 1986; McDermott, 1966). However, more research is needed to verify this, and the research indicates that assumptions should not be made about the nature of their aggression (Espelage & Swearer, 2004).
- Boys are just as likely as girls to use social and emotional taunting.

Girl Bullies

- Girls are aggressive, but may use more indirect behaviors to damage relationships and can be sneaky and nasty.
- Girls are becoming more physical in bullying than in the past.
- Girls are more likely to bully other girls, but sometimes they bully boys (Olweus, 1993).
- Girls bully in groups more than boys do.
- Girls seek to inflict psychological pain on their victims, which hurts as much as, if not more than, physical attacks and has long-lasting effects.
- Girls behave well around adults but can be cruel and mean to peers.
- Girls target weaknesses in others.
- Girls frequently make comments regarding the sexual behavior of girls they don't like (Byrne, 1994a, 1994b).
- Girls attack within tightly knit networks of friends, which intensifies the hurt.

Fact Sheet 4:
How Frequently Does Bullying Occur?

There are different estimates of how often children are bullied or engage in bullying:

- According to the American Medical Association, 3.7 million youths engage in bullying, and more than 3.2 million are victims of "moderate" or "serious" bullying each year (Cohn & Canter, 2003).

- Some studies have shown that between 15 and 25 percent of U.S. students are frequently bullied; 15 to 20 percent report that they bully others frequently (Nansel et al., 2001; Melton et al., 1998; Geffner, Loring, & Young, 2001).

- Over the course of a year, nearly one-fourth of students across grades reported that they had been harassed or bullied on school property because of their race, ethnicity, gender, religion, sexual orientation, or disability (Austin, Huh-Kim, Skage, & Furlong, 2002).

- Almost 30 percent of youth in the United States (or over 5.7 million) are estimated to be involved in bullying as either a bully, a target of bullying, or both. In a national survey of students in grades 6 to 10, 13 percent reported bullying others, 11 percent reported being the target of bullies, and another 6 percent said that they bullied others and were bullied themselves (Nansel et al., 2001).

- Seventy-four percent of eight- to eleven-year-old students said teasing and bullying occur at their schools (Kaiser Family Foundation & Nickelodeon, 2001).

- Every seven minutes, a child on an elementary playground is bullied (Pepler, Craig, & Roberts, 1998).

Fact Sheet 5:
When and Where Does
Bullying Usually Occur?

- It occurs at early ages and in all grades, with an onset between three and four years of age (Byrne, 1994a, 1994b).

- In the United States, it increases for boys and girls during late elementary years, peaks during the middle school years, and decreases in high school (Hoover, Oliver, & Hazler, 1992; Banks, 1997; Garrett, 2003).

- Physical severity may decrease with age (Sharp & Smith, 1994).

- At the start of the school year, bullies begin looking for easy targets.

- It occurs two to three times more often at school than on the trip to and from school (Olweus, 1995).

- It is most likely to occur where there is no adult supervision, inadequate adult supervision, poor supervision, a lack of structure, and few or no anti-bullying rules; it is also more likely to occur where teachers and students accept bullying or are indifferent to it (Beane, 2008).

- It occurs virtually everywhere: in homes, nursery schools, preschools, elementary schools, middle schools, high schools, neighborhoods, churches, city parks, on the trip to and from school, on the streets, and in the workplace, for example. It occurs in large cities and small towns, large schools and small schools—and even one-room schools in other countries (Olweus, 1995).

- It occurs mainly in hidden areas and areas lacking adult supervision: halls, stairwells, the playground, areas where students take brief breaks, between buildings, restrooms, locker rooms, the cafeteria, on buses, and parking lots; it occurs when students are walking to and from school, but also in classrooms.

Fact Sheet 6:
Why Do Students Keep Bullying a Secret?

- They are taught not to "tattle." They think telling someone they are being hurt or someone else is being hurt is wrong.

- They have told or heard someone else tell adults about bullying before, and nothing was done about it.

- They are afraid adults will make the situation worse.

- They are embarrassed or feel shame because they feel no one likes them; they feel defective.

- They feel shame because they cannot stand up for themselves as they have been taught.

- They do not want to worry their parents. They love their parents and want to protect them from worry and anxiety.

Fact Sheet 7:
Why Must Bullying Be Stopped?

- It is more prevalent today than in the past and occurs in more serious forms today.
- The intensity of bullying has increased because more students join in.
- More kids are participating—and even encouraging bullies to victimize others.
- It creates a fearful school climate.
    - Other students worry they may become victims.
    - Twenty percent of students are scared throughout much of the school day (Garrity, Jens, Porter, Sager, & Short-Camilli, 1997).
    - It causes confusion and fear in bystanders (Pepler, Craig, Ziegler, & Charach, 1993). It intensifies normal fears of being laughed at, losing what they have, rejection, fear of the unknown, and exposure.
- It is a common theme in school shootings as students retaliate for the bullying.
    - It is a path taken by students who retaliate: they are hurt, are fearful, overwhelmed by anxiety, angry, and filled with hate and rage, and have a desire for revenge.
    - Roughly two-thirds of school shooters "felt persecuted, bullied, threatened, attacked, or injured by others" (Bowman, 2001, p. 11).
- It causes stress in students.
- It causes a lack of trust in oneself to cope appropriately, in adults to help, and in life to be good to them in the future.
- It causes "toxic shame," which is destructive to one's sense of worth (Garbarino, 1999).
- It causes some students to harm themselves, cutting themselves, for example.
- Thirty percent of all child suicides can be directly related to bullying (Hawker & Boulton, 2000).
- It may raise suicide risk in bystanders who are considering suicide for other reasons.
- Every environment is social, and there seems to be no escape.
- "Every day of school can be a new social mine field" (Simmons, 2002).
- Rejected students may withdraw and commit social suicide, and in the process they are robbed of opportunities to develop needed social skills.
- It encourages students to run away from home.
- It encourages gang membership. Victims may find acceptance, security, and a sense of family. Bullies who over time lose their peer group status may seek association with other aggressive students found in gangs (Cairns, Cairns, Neckerman, Gest, & Gariepy, 1988).
- Some victims join a cult, drug group, or hate group to find acceptance and a sense of belonging.

- It encourages teen pregnancies. Rejected girls may seek someone to love, and someone to love them unconditionally.
- It encourages dropping out of school. Ten percent of dropouts do so because of repeated bullying (Weinhold & Weinhold, 1998).
- It contributes to poor school attendance. According to the National Association of School Psychologists, 160,000 students per day stay home from school because of bullying (Fried & Fried, 2003).
  - Seven percent of eighth graders stay home at least once a month because of bullies (Banks, 2000).
  - Twenty-five percent of girls grades 8 to 12 don't want to attend school and stay home or skip classes because of sexual bullying (American Association of University Women, 1993).
- It leads to loneliness, low self-esteem, depression and anxiety disorders, post-traumatic stress, eating disorders, and other long-lasting harmful emotional effects in the adult years (Olweus, 1993; McMaster, Connolly, Pepler, & Craig, 1998; Rigby, 2001).
- It has a negative impact on student morale and learning and achievement.
  - Fourteen percent of surveyed students in grades 8 to 12 and 22 percent in grades 4 to 8 reported that "bullying diminished their ability to learn in school" (Hoover & Oliver, 1996, p. 10).
  - Seventeen percent of students said bullying interfered with academic performance (Hazler, Hoover, & Oliver, 1992).
- It is a root cause of discipline problems for both the victim and bully.
  - Bullied students have behavior problems after the bullying, and those problems get worse over time (Schwartz, McFayden-Ketchum, Dodge, Pettit, & Bates, 1998).
- Hostile children are more likely to develop diabetes and develop cardiac problems as they age (Elias, 2002).
- It prevents the full inclusion of students with disabilities.
- It creates societal problems.
  - Bullies identified by age eight are six times more likely to be convicted of a crime by age twenty-four and five times more likely than nonbullies to end up with serious criminal records by age thirty (Maine Project Against Bullying, 2000).
  - Sixty percent of students characterized as bullies in grades 6 to 9 had at least one criminal conviction by age twenty-four and 40 percent had three or more arrests by that age (Banks, 2000; Olweus, 1993).
  - Chronic bullies often bully in their adult years, which hinders their ability to develop and maintain positive relationships (Oliver, Hoover, & Hazler, 1994)
  - Bullies may grow up to abuse their spouse, children, and coworkers (Beane, 2008).

Fact Sheet 8:
Are There Different Types of Victims?

There are two types of victims. Parents and school personnel should avoid speaking about these characteristics as weaknesses.

Typical Characteristics of Passive or Submissive Victims

- They are generally quiet, cautious, sensitive, and perhaps easily moved to tears.
- They are insecure and have little self-confidence (negative self-esteem), perhaps as the result of bullying.
- If boys, they are usually physically weaker than their classmates, particularly the bullies, and they do not like to fight.
- They have few or no friends, perhaps as a result of bullying.
- They may be afraid of getting hurt or hurting themselves.
- They find it easier to associate with adults than peers.

Provocative Victims

- Only 15 to 20 percent of victims are of this type.
- They are often bullied more often and by more peers than passive or submissive victims.
- They have tempers and may try to fight back if bullied, but usually without success.
- They are restless, clumsy, immature, unfocused, and generally perceived as awkward or tiresome. Some are hyperactive; they may be fidgety, impulsive, or restless and have difficulty concentrating.
- They may have reading and writing problems.
- They may be disliked by adults because of their often irritating behavior.
- They may try to bully weaker students and therefore may be both victims and bullies.
- Some are popular, and some are not. Their popularity may decrease in higher grades, but it never reaches the lowest popularity levels.

For a detailed description of these types, see Olweus (1993).

Fact Sheet 9:
Possible Warning Signs of Victims

- Sudden decrease in school attendance or skipping certain classes
- Decline in quality of academic performance
- Difficulty concentrating in class and easily distracted
- Wants to take a different route to school or different transportation to school
- Sudden lack of interest in school-sponsored activities and events
- Seems happy on weekends but unhappy and preoccupied or tense on Sundays
- Uses "victim" body language: hunches shoulders, hangs head, will not look people in the eye, and backs off from others
- Suddenly prefers the company of adults
- Frequent illness or fakes illness (headaches, stomachaches, pains)
- Nightmares and insomnia
- Comes home with unexplainable scratches and bruises
- Suddenly develops a stammer or stutter
- Angry, irritable, disruptive, aggressive, quick-tempered, and fights back (but always loses)
- Cautious, clingy, nervous, anxious, worried, fearful, and insecure
- Overly concerned about personal safety; spends a lot of time and effort thinking or worrying about getting safely to and from school and getting around in the school (to and from lunch, to and from recess, to and from the bathroom, to and from the lockers); wants to stay in at night and prefers to stay home on weekends
- Talks about avoiding certain areas of the school
- Carries protection devices (knife, box opener, fork, gun)
- Frequently asks for extra money, saying it is for lunch or school supplies
- Possessions (books, money, clothing) are often "lost," damaged, or destroyed without an explanation
- Sudden change in behavior (bed-wetting, nail-biting, tics)
- Cries easily or often, becomes emotionally distraught and has extreme mood swings
- Blames self for problems or difficulties; feels defective and inadequate.
- Talks about being made fun of, laughed at, picked on, teased, put down, pushed around, threatened, kicked, hit, called names, or students telling lies about them, gossiping about them, or excluding them from a group, and other bullying behaviors

- Talks about not being able to stand up for himself or herself
- Expresses lack of self value and self confidence
- Talks about dropping out of school
- Expresses lack of trust in and respect for school personnel
- Suddenly starts bullying other students, siblings, or children in the neighborhood
- Becomes overly aggressive, rebellious, and unreasonable
- Sudden loss of respect for authority figures
- Seeks the wrong friends in the wrong places
- Talks about joining or forming a cult
- Sudden interest in violent movies, video games, and books
- Talks about running away
- Talks about feeling depressed
- Talks about or attempts suicide
- Self harms (cutting, no eating, overeating)
- Drastic change in appearance

Fact Sheet 10:
Possible Characteristics of Bullies

- Enjoys feeling powerful and in control (Olweus, 1993)
- Seeks to dominate or manipulate others (Olweus, 1993)
- May be popular with other students, who envy his or her power
- Is physically larger or makes himself or herself seem larger than his or her peers; exhibits physical or psychological power, or both
- Is impulsive (Olweus, 1993)
- Exhibits low tolerance of frustration (Olweus, 1993)
- Loves to win at everything; hates to lose at anything and is a poor winner; can be boastful
- Seems to derive satisfaction or pleasure from others' fear, discomfort, or pain
- Seems overly concerned with others "disrespecting" him or her; equates respect with fear
- Expects to be "misunderstood," "disrespected," and picked on; attacks before he or she can be attacked
- Interprets ambiguous or innocent acts as purposeful and hostile; uses these as excuses to strike out at others verbally or physically
- Seems to have little or no empathy or compassion for others (Olweus, 1993)
- Seems unable or unwilling to see things from another person's perspective
- Seems willing to use and abuse other people to get what he or she wants
- Defends his or her negative actions by insisting that others "deserve it," "asked for it," or "provoked it"; often describes a conflict as someone else's "fault"
- Is good at hiding negative behaviors or doing them where adults cannot see them
- Gets excited when conflicts arise between others
- Is more likely to get into trouble, smoke, drink, and fight (Nansel et al., 2001; Ericson, 2001)
- Stays cool during conflicts in which he or she is directly involved
- Exhibits little or no emotion when talking about his or her part in a conflict
- Blames other people for his or her problems
- Refuses to accept responsibility for his or her negative behaviors
- Shows little or no remorse for his or her negative behaviors
- Lies in an attempt to stay out of trouble

- "Tests" authority by committing minor infractions, then waits to see what will happen
- Disregards or breaks school or class rules
- Is generally defiant or oppositional toward adults
- Seeks, even craves, attention; seems just as satisfied with negative attention as positive attention
- Attracts more than the usual amount of negative attention from others and is therefore disciplined more often than most other students
- Is street-smart
- Tends to be confident, with high self-esteem (Nansel et al., 2001)
- Seems mainly concerned with his or her own pleasure and well-being
- Seems antisocial or lacks social skills
- Has difficulty fitting into groups; may experience loneliness (Ericson, 2001)
- Has a close network of friends (actually "henchmen" or "lieutenants") who follow along with whatever he or she wants to do
- Has average or above-average performance in school (Olweus, 1993); however, some studies say they may do poorly (Schwartz, 2006; Ericson, 2001)
- May have problems at school or at home
- Lacks coping skills
- Average in anxiety and uncertainty
- May be a victim of bullying (Nansel et al., 2001; Crawford, 2002)

Fact Sheet 11:
The Responses of Adults

- Forty percent of bullied students in elementary and 60 percent of bullied students in middle school report that teachers intervene in bullying incidents "once in a while" or "almost never" (Olweus, 1993; Charach, Pepler, & Ziegler, 1995).

- Twenty-five percent of teachers see nothing wrong with bullying or put-downs and consequently intervene in only 4 percent of bullying incidents (Cohn & Canter, 2003).

- Researchers Craig and Pepler (1995) have found that adults are often unaware of bullying problems (Mullin-Rindler, 2002).

- In an initial survey of students in fourteen Massachusetts schools, over 30 percent believed that adults did little or nothing to help with bullying (Mullin-Rindler, 2002).

- Almost 25 percent of the more than twenty-three hundred girls surveyed felt that they did not know three adults they could go to for support if they were bullied (Girl Scout Research Institute, 2003).

- Students often feel that adult intervention is infrequent and unhelpful, and fear that telling adults will only bring more harassment from bullies (Banks 1997; Cohn & Canter, 2003).

Appendix C

Bully Free Survey Instruments

The materials in this appendix are available in the files located at www.bullyfree.com. After entering the Web site, click on "Click here to access our training resources." Then click on "Resources for Bully Free Program Committee." Type *bfp1* when you are asked your user name and *bullyfree* when you are asked your password.

Instructions for the Teacher:
Bully Free Survey (for Preschool to Grade 2)

Because administering the survey does not involve bubble or scan sheets, changes in the survey may be made, and items can be added. A Microsoft Word file of the survey can be accessed at www.bullyfree.com. If you do not make changes in the survey, students completing the surveys should be told to skip items (for example, about stairwells or walking to school) that are not relevant to them.

Administering the Test

- Because students may want to change their responses, only black lead pencils should be used. Instruct those taking the survey not to use crayons, ink, or ballpoint pens.

- Tell students to completely fill in the face circle when responding.

- Tell them to cleanly erase any answer they wish to change.

- Help students complete the five questions.

- Read the items in the table to students and ask them to color in the face that best describes how they feel when they are in one of these places. They should skip places they do not go.

After you analyze their responses, engage students in a discussion about how they feel in each of the listed areas. For example, you might ask, "Why do you sometimes feel happy in the lunchroom?" and "Why do you sometimes feel sad in the lunchroom?"

Make a note of any concerns you have for specific students. Also note any issues that need to be addressed. Present your findings to the Bully Free Program team.

Bully Free Survey (for Preschool to Grade 2)

Name of student (optional): _____ Grade: ___

Sex: ___ Boy ___ Girl

Child's teacher: _____

1. Does anyone at school make you feel sad or afraid because they hurt you or scare you? ___ Yes ___ No

2. Has anyone at school ever called you a mean name or said mean things to you? ___ Yes ___ No

3. Has anyone at school ever hurt your body? ___ Yes ___ No

4. If someone was mean to you, would you tell your teacher? ___ Yes ___ No

5. If you saw someone being mean to someone, would you tell your teacher? ___ Yes ___ No

Color in the face that best describes how you feel when you are in one of these places.

Waiting for the school bus to take me to school	☺ ☹	Stairs	☺ ☹
Riding the bus to school	☺ ☹	Bathroom	☺ ☹
Walking to school	☺ ☹	Library	☺ ☹
Front door of school	☺ ☹	Back door of school	☺ ☹
Classroom	☺ ☹	Between buildings at school	☺ ☹
Lunchroom	☺ ☹	Waiting for bus to take me home	☺ ☹
Playground	☺ ☹	Riding the bus home	☺ ☹
Gym	☺ ☹	Walking home after school	☺ ☹
Hallway	☺ ☹	In my neighborhood	☺ ☹

Instructions for the Teacher:
Bully Free Surveys for Grades 3 to 12

- No names or identifying information should be recorded.

- The demographic information starts with item 1 on the bubble sheet.

- Do not make any changes in the surveys, including adding items. Those completing the surveys should be told to skip items that are not relevant (as indicated on the surveys). The survey items must not be renumbered. Changes in the surveys require additional work and alterations in the software used by Bully Free Systems LLC to analyze the data.

- Prior to administering the survey, it is important for those completing it to understand the definition of bullying. Therefore, make sure that those who administer the survey read the instructions to the students.

Administering the Survey

- Only no. 2 black lead pencils should be used. Instruct those taking the survey not to use ink or ballpoint pens.

- Tell students to make heavy black marks that fill in the circle completely.

- Tell students to cleanly erase any answer they wish to change.

- Tell students that no stray marks should be made on the answer sheet.

- Read the definition of bullying that appears at the top of the survey to students: "All students should feel safe and accepted, and have a sense of belonging at our school. For this to happen, we need your help to prevent and stop bullying. Bullying is when a more powerful person (or persons) mistreats someone *over and over* on purpose. It is not hurting someone accidentally. Examples of bullying are hitting, pushing, tripping, shoving someone into his or her locker, name-calling, teasing, making fun of someone because of looks or skin color or dress, rejecting someone, spreading rumors and lies about someone, writing mean notes, turning others against someone, threatening someone, embarrassing someone, and stealing or damaging things that belong to someone."

- For younger students, you may read each item of the survey aloud, then pause long enough for them to ask questions.

- Instruct those taking the survey not to write their name anywhere on the survey instrument or bubble sheet.

Interpreting the Survey Data: Bully Free Surveys for Grades 3 to 12

Interpreting the Survey Data

Interpreting the Means

- Any item with a mean below 3 is a problem that should be a priority for program improvement plans.

- Any item with a mean near 3 should be of some concern. Attention should be given to the frequency data. There should be an effort to rid the school of all negative behaviors.

- Any item with a mean of 4 or greater may not be a great concern, but needs some attention. Attention should be given to the frequency data, which may indicate that something is occurring that cannot be tolerated. There should be an effort to rid the school of all negative behaviors. For example, a mean of 4.75 might indicate that overall, bullying on buses is not a problem. But the frequency data may indicate that twelve students are almost always bullied on the bus. That is a problem that needs attention.

Interpreting the Frequencies

- For positive behavior items (for example, "Most students try to help other students who are being bullied"), the frequency indicates the number of students who responded to the item with either "almost never" or "a little."

- For negative behavior items (for example, "When students see someone bullied, most of them ignore it"), the frequency indicates the number of students who said "almost always" or "a lot."

Examples

In the following example, the item is considered a positive one (it's what you want to see in your school). We read from this that 129 students said that when students see someone bullied, most students "almost never" try to help that person or students try "a little" to help that student. We also see that the mean is 2.37. Because the mean is below 3.0, this item indicates a problem and should be a priority to improve.

Frequency	Mean	Item Number	Item
129	2.37	32	Most students try to help other students who are being bullied.

Interpreting the Survey Data:
Bully Free Surveys for Grades 3 to 12, Continued

In the next example, the item is negative: it's not what you want to see in your school. We read that eighty-seven students said that when students see someone bullied, most of them "almost always" ignore it or ignore it "a lot." The mean is 3.03. Since the mean is near 3.0, this item is of some concern.

Frequency	Mean	Item Number	Item
87	3.03	33	When students see someone bullied, most of them ignore it.

In the next table, we see the importance of looking at frequency data and the mean of an item. The item is a negative one: it's not what you want to see in your school. We read that twelve students said they are bullied in the classroom "almost always" or "a lot." The mean is 4.54. Because the mean is 4 or above, the item appears not to be as great concern, but the frequency data indicate that it needs attention because twelve students almost always are bullied in the classroom or are bullied a lot in the classroom.

Frequency	Mean	Item Number	Item
12	4.54	20	I am bullied in the classroom.

Bully Free Survey
(for Elementary Students, Grades 3 to 6)

Instructions: Do not write your name anywhere on this questionnaire or on the bubble sheet (or other answer sheets).

All students should feel safe and accepted, and have a sense of belonging at our school. For this to happen, we need your help to prevent and stop bullying. Bullying is when a more powerful person (or persons) mistreats someone *over and over* on purpose. It is not hurting someone accidentally. Examples of bullying are hitting, pushing, tripping, shoving someone into his or her locker, name-calling, teasing, making fun of someone because of looks or skin color or dress, rejecting someone, spreading rumors and lies about someone, writing mean notes, turning others against someone, threatening someone, embarrassing someone, and stealing or damaging things that belong to someone.

Respond to each statement by shading in the appropriate bubble (with a no. 2 pencil) on the computer scan sheet that best describes you.

1. I am in the _____ grade.

    a. 3rd

    b. 4th

    c. 5th

    d. 6th

2. I am a _____ .

    a. Female

    b. Male

3. I live with _____ .

    a. Both parents

    b. One parent

    c. A relative

    d. A friend

    e. A foster parent

4. My parents are _____ .

    a. Married

    b. Separated

    c. Divorced

    d. Don't know

    e. Other

5. What is your ethnic group?

    a. African American

    b. Asian

    c. Caucasian

    d. Hispanic

    e. Other

6. I feel taken care of at home.

    a. Yes

    b. No

Use the scale below, and respond to each item by shading in the appropriate bubble (with a no. 2 pencil) on the computer scan sheet for the response that comes closest to describing what you see and experience. The scale indicates the frequency of which something occurs or would occur.

A Almost Never	B A Little	C Sometimes	D A Lot	E Almost Always

Bully Free Survey
(for Elementary Students, Grades 3 to 6), Continued

A Almost Never	B A Little	C Sometimes	D A Lot	E Almost Always

What Bullying Looks Like

7	I see other students hit, pinched, kicked, tripped, pushed, elbowed, touched, or grabbed in a hurtful or embarrassing way.
8	I am hit, pinched, kicked, tripped, pushed, elbowed, touched, or grabbed in a hurtful or embarrassing way.
9	I see other students ignored, rejected, or lied about, have rumors told about them, or have hurtful and mean notes written about them.
10	I am ignored, rejected, or lied about, have rumors told about me, or have hurtful and mean notes written about me.
11	I see other students called names, teased, made fun of for the way they look or dress, or put down in a hurtful way.
12	I am called names, teased, made fun of for the way I look or dress, or put down in a hurtful way.
13	I see other students forced to do things they don't want to do.
14	I am forced to do things I don't want to do.
15	I see other students have things damaged or stolen from them.
16	I have things damaged or stolen from me.
17	I see other students bullied in other ways.
18	I am bullied in other ways.

Bullied in the School

19	I am bullied in the classroom.
20	I am bullied in the hall.
21	I am bullied in the lunchroom.
22	I am bullied in the gym or locker room.
23	I am bullied in the bathroom.
24	I am bullied in other places in the school.

Bullied Outside School Building

25	I am bullied in the parking lot.
26	I am bullied during recess.
27	I am bullied outside the school building before school starts.

Bully Free Survey
(for Elementary Students, Grades 3 to 6), Continued

A Almost Never	B A Little	C Sometimes	D A Lot	E Almost Always

Who Is Bullying?

28	I am bullied by one student.
29	I am bullied by more than one student.

Bystanders

30	Most students try to help other students who are bullied.
31	When students see someone bullied, most of them ignore it.
32	When students see someone bullied, most of them join in by laughing or other ways.

How I Feel

33	I feel safe at school.
34	I feel safe at home.
35	I feel safe in my neighborhood.
36	I feel unhappy at school because I am being bullied.
37	I feel angry at school because I am being bullied.
38	I feel lonely at school because no one likes me.
39	I feel upset because I see students being bullied.
40	I feel afraid because I am bullied.
41	I feel afraid because I see other students bullied.
42	I sometimes stay home because of bullying at school.

Reporting Bullying

43	If I were bullied, I would tell an adult at school.
44	If I heard about or saw someone bullied, I would tell an adult at school.
45	If I were bullied at school, I would tell an adult at home.

Friends at School

46	If I were mistreated by other students, my friends would help me.
47	I am able to make friends at school.

Bully Free Survey
(for Elementary Students, Grades 3 to 6), Continued

A Almost Never	B A Little	C Sometimes	D A Lot	E Almost Always

Adults as Models and Helpers

48	If an adult at school saw bullying, he or she would try to stop the bullying without making it worse for the student being bullied.
49	If an adult at my house reported that I am being bullied at school, someone at my school would try to stop it without making it worse for me.
50	My principal and/or assistant principal try to stop students from bullying.
51	I am bullied by one or more adults at school.
52	There are some adults at school who bully students.
53	There are some adults at school who bully other adults.

Rules and Instruction

54	My teacher(s) have classroom rules against bullying.
55	The punishment for breaking classroom rules about bullying is clear.
56	Some adults at school talk to us about bullying.
57	Some adults at school talk to us about the Golden Rule—treating others the way we want to be treated.

Riding the Bus
(Answer these questions only if you ride the bus to school and/or ride the bus home from school.)

58	I am bullied while waiting for the bus to arrive to take me to school.
59	I am bullied on the bus going to school.
60	I am bullied while waiting for the bus to arrive to take me home.
61	I am bullied while riding the bus home from school.

Walking to and from School
(Answer these questions only if you walk to and/or from school.)

62	I am bullied while walking to school.
63	I am bullied while walking home from school.

Bully Free Survey (for Middle and High School Students, Grades 6 to 12)

Instructions: Do not write your name anywhere on this questionnaire or on the bubble sheet (or other answer sheets).

All students should feel safe and accepted, and have a sense of belonging at our school. For this to happen, we need your help to prevent and stop bullying. Bullying is when a more powerful person (or persons) mistreats someone *over and over* on purpose. It is not hurting someone accidentally. Examples of bullying are hitting, pushing, tripping, shoving someone into his or her locker, name-calling, teasing, making fun of someone because of looks or skin color or dress, rejecting someone, spreading rumors and lies about someone, writing mean notes, turning others against someone, threatening someone, embarrassing someone, stealing or damaging things that belong to someone, and so on.

Respond to each statement by shading in the appropriate bubble (with a no. 2 pencil) on the computer scan sheet that best describes you.

1. **I am in the _____.**

   A. 6th grade   B. 7th grade   C. 8th grade

2. **I am in the _____.**

   A. 9th grade   B. 10th grade   C. 11th grade   D. 12th grade

3. **I live with _____.**

   A. Both parents   B. One parent   C. A relative   D. A friend   E. A foster parent

4. **My parents are _____.**

   A. Married   B. Separated   C. Divorced   D. Don't know   E. Other

5. **What is your ethnic group?**

   A. African American   B. Asian   C. Caucasian   D. Hispanic   E. Other

6. **I feel taken care of at home.**

   A. No   B. Yes

7. **I am a _____.**

   A. Female   B. Male

Use the scale below, and respond to each item by shading in the appropriate bubble (with a no. 2 pencil) on the computer scan sheet for the response that comes closest to describing your opinion about what you see and experience. The scale indicates the frequency of which something occurs or would occur.

A Almost Never	B A Little	C Sometimes	D A Lot	E Almost Always

What Bullying Looks Like

8	I see other students hit, pinched, kicked, tripped, pushed, elbowed, touched, or grabbed in a hurtful or embarrassing way.
9	I am hit, pinched, kicked, tripped, pushed, elbowed, touched, or grabbed in a hurtful or embarrassing way.

Bully Free Survey (for Middle and High School Students, Grades 6 to 12), Continued

A Almost Never	B A Little	C Sometimes	D A Lot	E Almost Always

What Bullying Looks Like, Continued

10	I see other students ignored, rejected, or lied about, have rumors told about them, or have hurtful and mean notes written about them.
11	I am ignored, rejected, or lied about, have rumors told about me, or have hurtful and mean notes written about me.
12	I see other students called names, teased, made fun of for the way they look or dress, or put down in a hurtful way.
13	I am called names, teased, made fun of for the way I look or dress, or put down in a hurtful way.
14	I see other students forced to do things they don't want to do.
15	I am forced to do things I don't want to do.
16	I see other students' things damaged or stolen from them.
17	I have had things damaged or stolen from me.
18	I see other students bullied in other ways.
19	I am bullied in other ways.

Bullied in the School

20	I am bullied in the classroom.
21	I am bullied in the hall.
22	I am bullied in the lunchroom.
23	I am bullied in the gym or locker room.
24	I am bullied in the bathroom.
25	I am bullied in other places in the school.

Bullied Outside the School Building

26	I am bullied in the parking lot.
27	I am bullied outside during physical education classes.
28	I am bullied outside the school building before school starts.
29	I am bullied on an athletic field.

Bully Free Survey (for Middle and High School Students, Grades 6 to 12), Continued

A Almost Never	B A Little	C Sometimes	D A Lot	E Almost Always

Who Is Bullying?

30	I am bullied by one student.
31	I am bullied by more than one student.

Bystanders

32	Most students try to help other students who are being bullied.
33	When students see someone bullied, most of them ignore it.
34	When students see someone bullied, most of them join in by laughing or other ways.

How I Feel

35	I feel safe at school.
36	I feel safe at home.
37	I feel safe in my neighborhood.
38	I feel unhappy at school because I am being bullied.
39	I feel angry at school because I am being bullied.
40	I feel lonely at school because no one likes me.
41	I feel upset because I see students being bullied.
42	I feel afraid because I am bullied.
43	I feel afraid because I see other students bullied.
44	I sometimes stay home because of bullying at school.

Reporting Bullying

45	If I were bullied, I would tell an adult at school.
46	If I heard about or saw someone bullied at school, I would tell an adult at school.
47	If I were bullied at school, I would tell an adult at home.

Friends at School

48	If I were mistreated by other students, my friends would help me.
49	I am able to make friends at school.

Bully Free Survey (for Middle and High School Students, Grades 6 to 12), Continued

A Almost Never	B A Little	C Sometimes	D A Lot	E Almost Always

Adults as Models and Helpers

50	If an adult at school saw bullying, he or she would try to stop the bullying without making it worse for the student being bullied.
51	If an adult at my house reported that I am being bullied, someone at my school would try to stop it without making it worse for me.
52	My principal and/or assistant principal try to stop students from bullying.
53	I am bullied by one or more adults at school.
54	There are some adults at school who bully students.
55	There are some adults at school who bully other adults.

Rules and Instruction

56	My teacher(s) have classroom rules against bullying.
57	The punishment for breaking classroom rules about bullying is clear.
58	Some adults at school talk to us about bullying.
59	Some adults at school talk to us about the Golden Rule—treating others the way we want to be treated.

Walking to and from School
(Answer these questions only if you walk to and/or from school. If you ride the bus, go to item 62.)

60	I am bullied while walking to school.
61	I am bullied while walking home from school.

Riding the Bus
(Answer these questions only if you ride the bus to school and/or ride the bus home from school.)

62	I am bullied while waiting for the bus to arrive to take me to school.
63	I am bullied on the bus going to school.
64	I am bullied while waiting for the bus to arrive to take me home.
65	I am bullied while riding the bus home from school.

Bully Free Survey (for School Personnel)

Instructions: Read each item of the survey, and respond to it by shading in the appropriate bubble (with a no. 2 pencil) on the computer scan sheet (or other answer sheet) that best describes you. Do not write your name on the survey or bubble sheet.

We are interested in making our schools a place where all students feel safe, have a sense of belonging, and feel accepted. For this to happen, we need your help. We want to create a school environment where no one is mistreated. We want to prevent bullying. If it is happening, we want it to stop. Bullying is when someone is intentionally mistreated *over and over* on purpose. It can be physical (hitting, pushing, shoving, pinching, tripping, and so on), verbal (name-calling, teasing), or relational (rejecting someone, spreading rumors and lies about someone, turning others against another). The items on this survey address these kinds of behavior.

1. **I am a teacher in the _____.**

   A. 3rd grade   B. 4th grade   C. 5th grade

2. **I am a teacher in the _____.**

   A. 6th grade   B. 7th grade   C. 8th grade

3. **I am a teacher in the _____.**

   A. 9th grade   B. 10th grade   C. 11th grade   D. 12th grade

4. **What is your ethnic group?**

   A. African American   B. Asian   C. Caucasian   D. Hispanic   E. Other

5. **I am a _____.**

   A. Female   B. Male

Use the scale below and respond to each item by shading in the appropriate bubble (with a no. 2 pencil) on the computer scan sheet (or other answer sheet) for the response that comes closest to describing your opinion about what you see and experience. The scale indicates the frequency of which something occurs or would occur.

A Almost Never	B A Little	C Sometimes	D A Lot	E Almost Always

What Bullying Looks Like

6	I see students hit, pinched, kicked, tripped, pushed, elbowed, touched, or grabbed in a hurtful or embarrassing way.
7	I see students ignored, rejected, or lied about, have rumors told about them, or have hurtful and mean notes written about them.
8	I see students threatened.
9	I see students called names, teased, made fun of for the way they look or dress, or put down in a hurtful way.
10	I see students forced to do things they do not want to do.
11	I see students who have things damaged or stolen.
12	I see students bullied in other ways.

Bully Free Survey (for School Personnel), Continued

A Almost Never	B A Little	C Sometimes	D A Lot	E Almost Always

Bullied in the School

13	I see students bullied in the classroom.
14	I see students bullied in the hall.
15	I see students bullied in the lunchroom.
16	I see students bullied in the gym or locker room.
17	I see students bullied in the bathroom.
18	I see students bullied in other places in the school.

Bullied Outside the School Building

19	I see students bullied in the parking lot.
20	I see students bullied outside during physical education classes.
21	I see students bullied outside the school building before school starts.
22	I see students bullied on an athletic field.

Who Is Bullying?

23	I see students being bullied by one student.
24	I see students being bullied by more than one student.

Bystanders

25	Most students try to help other students who are being bullied.
26	When students see someone bullied, most of them ignore it.
27	When students see someone bullied, most of them join in by laughing, or other ways.

Reporting Bullying

28	If students were bullied, they would tell an adult at school.
29	If students heard or saw someone bullied at school, they would tell an adult at school.
30	If students were bullied at school, they would tell an adult at home.

Bully Free Survey (for School Personnel), Continued

A Almost Never	B A Little	C Sometimes	D A Lot	E Almost Always

Friends at School

31	Students who are mistreated by other students have friends who will help them.
32	It is easy for students to make friends at school.

Adults as Models and Helpers

33	If adults at school saw bullying, they would try to stop the bullying without making it worse for the student being bullied.
34	If parents reported that their child was being bullied, the school would try to stop it without making it worse for them.
35	The principal and/or assistant principal try to stop students from bullying.
36	One or more adults at school bully students.
37	One or more adults at the school bully other adults at school.

Rules and Instruction

38	I have classroom rules against bullying.
39	The punishment for breaking classroom rules about bullying is clear.
40	I have talked to students about bullying.
41	I have talked to students about the Golden Rule—treating others the way we want to be treated.

Riding the Bus

42	I see students bullied while waiting for the bus to arrive to take them to school.
43	I see students bullied on the bus going to school.
44	I see students bullied while waiting for the bus to arrive to take them home.
45	I see students bullied while riding the bus home from school.

Walking to and from School

46	I see students bullied while walking to school.
47	I see students bullied while walking home from school.

Bully Free Survey (for Parents)

Instructions: Read each item of the survey and respond to each statement by shading in the appropriate bubble (with a no. 2 pencil) on the computer scan sheet (or other answer sheet) that best describes you and your child. Do not write your name on the survey or bubble sheet.

We are interested in making our schools a place where all students feel safe, have a sense of belonging, and feel accepted. For this to happen, we need your help. We want to create a school environment where no one is mistreated. We want to prevent bullying. If it is happening, we want it to stop. Bullying is when someone is intentionally mistreated *over and over*. It can be physical (hitting, pushing, shoving, pinching, tripping, and so on), verbal (name-calling, teasing), or relational (rejecting someone, spreading rumors and lies about someone, turning others against another). The items on this survey address this kind of behavior.

This form has been sent to the family of each student in our school. If you have more than one child in our school, you should receive more than one copy. Please complete this form for each child.

1. What is your relationship to the child?

A. Parent   B. Guardian   C. Grandparent   D. Foster parent   E. Other

2. What is your ethnic group?

A. African
   American   B. Asian   C. Caucasian   D. Hispanic   E. Other

3. I am a _____.

A. Female   B. Male

A Almost Never	B A Little	C Sometimes	D A Lot	E Almost Always

What Bullying Looks Like

4	My child is hit, pinched, kicked, tripped, pushed, elbowed, touched, or grabbed in a hurtful or embarrassing way.
5	My child is ignored, rejected, or lied about, has rumors told about him or her, or has hurtful and mean notes written about him or her.
6	My child is threatened.
7	My child is called names, teased, made fun of for the way he or she looks or dresses, or put down in a hurtful way.
8	My child is forced to do things he or she doesn't want to do.
9	My child has things damaged or stolen.
10	My child is bullied in other ways.
11	My child has seen other students bullied.

Bully Free Survey (for Parents), Continued

A Almost Never	B A Little	C Sometimes	D A Lot	E Almost Always

Bullied in the School

12	My child is bullied in the classroom.
13	My child is bullied in the hall.
14	My child is bullied in the lunchroom.
15	My child is bullied in the gym or locker room.
16	My child is bullied in the bathroom.
17	My child is bullied in other places in the school.

Bullied Outside the School Building

18	My child is bullied in the parking lot.
19	My child is bullied outside during physical education classes.
20	My child is bullied outside the school building before school starts.
21	My child is bullied on an athletic field.

Who Is Bullying?

22	My child is bullied by one student.
23	My child is bullied by more than one student.

Bystanders

24	If my child were bullied, most students would try to help him or her.
25	If my child were bullied, most students would ignore it.
26	If my child were bullied, most students would join in by laughing or other ways.

Reporting Bullying

27	If my child were bullied, she or he would tell an adult at school.
28	If my child heard or saw someone bullied at school, she or he would tell an adult at school.
29	If my child were bullied at school, she or he would tell me.

Friends at School

30	If my child were mistreated by other students, his or her friends would help.
31	My child is able to make friends at school.

Bully Free Survey (for Parents), Continued

A Almost Never	B A Little	C Sometimes	D A Lot	E Almost Always

Adults as Models and Helpers

32	If adults at school saw bullying, they would try to stop the bullying without making it worse for the student being bullied.
33	If we reported that our child was being bullied, the school would try to stop it without making it worse for him or her.
34	The principal and/or assistant principal try to stop students from bullying.
35	One or more adults at school bully my child.
36	I have heard about one or more adults at the school who bully other adults at school.
37	I have heard about one or more adults at the school who bully other students at school.

Rules and Instruction

38	My child's teacher has classroom rules against bullying.
39	My child knows the punishment for breaking classroom rules about bullying.
40	One or more adults at school have talked to my child about bullying.
41	One or more adults at school have talked to my child about the Golden Rule—treating others the way we want to be treated.

Riding the Bus
(Answer these questions only if your child rides the bus to school and/or rides the bus home from school.)

42	My child is bullied while waiting for the bus to arrive to take him or her to school.
43	My child is bullied on the bus going to school.
44	My child is bulled while waiting for the bus to arrive to take him or her home.
45	My child is bullied while riding the bus home from school.

Walking to and from School
(Answer these questions only if your child walks to and/or from school.)

46	My child is bullied while walking to school.
47	My child is bullied while walking home from school.

Appendix D

Example Anti-Bullying Policy

The following is just one example of several excellent anti-bullying policies available on the Internet that your team should examine before developing one for your school or school system. This example also appears in the files located at www.bullyfree.com. After entering the Web site, click on "Click here to access our training resources." Then click on "Resources for Bully Free Program Committee." Type *bfp1* when you are asked your user name and *bullyfree* when you are asked your password.

The school board of Broward County Schools, Florida, adopted the following policy on July 22, 2008 (www.browardschools.com). It was the first school district anti-bullying policy in Florida. The policy was designed by the district's Office of Prevention Programs and Student Support Services, under the Safe Schools Healthy Students Grant initiative.

The Florida Department of Education has utilized this policy as a model for the state's sixty-six other school districts. The policy was developed prior to the passage of House Bill 669, which mandated that all districts in the state adopt anti-bullying policies by December 1, 2008.

A district's anti-bullying policy should specifically prohibit bullying of or by any district student or employee, with consequences for those acts that meet the definition of bullying as defined in the policy.

As you modify or adapt the following example policy, review and adhere to the policy guidelines discussed in Step 8.

Sample Anti-Bullying Policy

The school board of Broward County, Florida, is committed to protecting its students, employees, and applicants for admission from bullying, harassment, or discrimination for any reason and of any type. The school board believes that all students and employees are entitled to a safe, equitable, and harassment-free school experience. Bullying, harassment, or discrimination will not be tolerated and shall be just cause for disciplinary action. This policy shall be interpreted and applied consistently with all applicable state and federal laws and the board's collective bargaining agreements. Conduct that constitutes bullying, harassment or discrimination, as defined herein, is prohibited. Policy 4001.1, *Nondiscrimination Statement Policy,* addresses requirements for discrimination against defined federal, state, and local protected categories of persons.

It is essential that a basic universal prevention curriculum be in place so that every school will receive a foundation of prevention upon which to build a culture of health, wellness, safety, respect and excellence.

The standards of this policy constitute a specific, focused, coordinated, integrated, culturally sensitive system of supports for all students, staff, families, and community agencies that will improve relations within each school. It is designed to ensure that every school has staff that have been trained and are supported in their school's efforts to provide awareness, intervention training, and instructional strategies on prevention, including violence prevention, to each staff, parent, and student in the District and to direct follow up when incidents are reported and/or occur.

I. Definitions

A. *"Bullying"* means systematically and chronically inflicting physical hurt or psychological distress on one or more students or employees. It is further defined as: unwanted purposeful written, verbal, nonverbal, or physical behavior, including but not limited to any threatening, insulting, or dehumanizing gesture, by an adult or student, that has the potential to create an intimidating, hostile, or offensive educational environment or cause long-term damage; cause discomfort or humiliation; or unreasonably interfere with the individual's school performance or participation, is carried out repeatedly and is often characterized by an imbalance of power.

Bullying may involve, but is not limited to:

1. unwanted teasing
2. threatening
3. intimidating
4. stalking

5. cyberstalking

6. cyberbullying

7. physical violence

8. theft

9. sexual, religious, or racial harassment

10. public humiliation

11. destruction of school or personal property

12. social exclusion, including incitement and/or coercion

13. rumor or spreading of falsehoods

B. *"Harassment"* means any threatening, insulting, or dehumanizing gesture, use of technology, computer software, or written, verbal or physical conduct directed against a student or school employee that:

1. places a student or school employee in reasonable fear of harm to his or her person or damage to his or her property;

2. has the effect of substantially interfering with a student's educational performance, or employee's work performance, or either's opportunities, or benefits;

3. has the effect of substantially negatively impacting a student's or employee's emotional or mental well-being; or

4. has the effect of substantially disrupting the orderly operation of a school.

C. *"Cyberstalking,"* as defined in Florida State Statute 784.048(d), means to engage in a course of conduct to communicate, or to cause to be communicated, words, images, or language by or through the use of electronic mail or electronic communication, directed at or about a specific person, causing substantial emotional distress to that person and serving no legitimate purpose.

D. *"Cyberbullying"* is defined as the willful and repeated harassment and intimidation of a person through the use of digital technologies, including, but not limited to, e-mail, blogs, social Web sites (e.g., MySpace, Facebook), chat rooms, and instant messaging.

E. *"Bullying," "Cyberbullying,"* and/or *"Harassment"* also encompass:

1. retaliation against a student or school employee by another student or school employee for asserting or alleging an act of bullying, harassment, or discrimination.

2. retaliation also includes reporting a baseless act of bullying, harassment, or discrimination that is not made in good faith.

3. perpetuation of conduct listed in the definition of bullying, harassment, and/or discrimination by an individual or group with intent to demean, dehumanize, embarrass, or cause emotional or physical harm to a student or school employee by:

a. incitement or coercion;

b. accessing or knowingly and willingly causing or providing access to data or computer software through a computer, computer system, or computer network within the scope of the District school system; or

c. acting in a manner that has an effect substantially similar to the effect of bullying, harassment, or discrimination.

F. *"Bullying," "Cyberbullying," "Harassment,"* and *"Discrimination"* (hereinafter referred to as bullying, as defined in Section A, for the purpose of this Policy) also encompass, but are not limited to, unwanted harm towards a student or employee in regard to their real or perceived: sex, race, color, religion, national origin, age, disability (physical, mental, or educational), marital status, socio-economic background, ancestry, ethnicity, gender, gender identity or expression, linguistic preference, political beliefs, sexual orientation, or social/family background or being viewed as different in its education programs or admissions to education programs and therefore prohibits bullying of any student or employee by any Board member, District employee, consultant, contractor, agent, visitor, volunteer, student, or other person in the school or outside the school at school-sponsored events, on school buses, and at training facilities or training programs sponsored by the District. For Federal requirements when these acts are against Federally identified protected categories, refer to Policy 4001.1.

G. *"Accused"* is defined as any District employee, consultant, contractor, agent, visitor, volunteer, student, or other person in the school or outside the school at school-sponsored events, on school buses, and at training facilities or training programs sponsored by the District who is reported to have committed an act of bullying, whether formally or informally, verbally or in writing, of bullying.

H. *"Complainant"* is defined as any District employee, consultant, contractor, agent, visitor, volunteer, student, or other person who formally or informally makes a report of bullying, orally or in writing.

II. Expectations

The Broward County School District expects students and employees to conduct themselves in keeping with their levels of development, maturity, and demonstrated capabilities with a proper regard for the rights and welfare of other students and school staff, the educational purpose underlying all school activities, and the care of school facilities and equipment.

A. The School District prohibits the bullying of any student or school employee:

1. during any educational program or activity conducted by SBBC;

2. during any school-related or school-sponsored program or activity or on a SBBC school bus;

3. through the use of any electronic device or data while on school grounds or on a SBBC school bus, computer software that is accessed through a computer, computer system, or computer network of the SBBC. The physical location or time of access of a computer-related incident cannot be raised as a defense in any disciplinary action initiated under this section.

4. through threats using the above to be carried out on school grounds. This includes threats made outside of school hours, which are intended to be carried out during any school-related or school-sponsored program or activity, or on a SBBC school bus.

5. while the District does not assume any liability for incidences that occur at a bus stop or en route to and from school, a student or witness may file a complaint following the same procedures for bullying against a student and the school will investigate and/or provide assistance and intervention as the principal/designee deems appropriate, which may include the use of the School Resource Officer. The principal/designee shall use all District Reporting Systems to log all reports and interventions.

B. All administrators, faculty, and staff, in collaboration with parents, students, and community members, will incorporate systemic methods for student and staff recognition through positive reinforcement for good conduct, self discipline, good citizenship, and academic success, as seen in the required school plan to address positive school culture and behavior (aka Discipline Plan).

C. Student rights shall be explained as outlined in this policy and in the Student Code of Conduct: Respect for Persons and Property.

D. Proper prevention and intervention steps shall be taken based on the level of severity of infraction as outlined in the Student Code of Conduct, the Discipline Matrix, and this Policy.

III. Stakeholder responsibilities

A. Student Support Services' Office of Prevention

Student Support Services professionals, in collaboration with other District departments, will collaborate with school-based staff members, families, and community stakeholders to utilize this Policy and associated procedures to promote academic success, enhance resiliency, build developmental assets, and promote protective factors within each school by ensuring that each and every staff member and student is trained on violence prevention. These trainings will work to create a climate within each school and within the District that fosters the safety and respect of children and the belief that adults are there to protect and help them. Additionally, students and staff (including but not limited to school-based employees, administrators, area/district personnel, counseling staff, bus drivers) will be given the skills, training, and tools needed to create the foundation for preventing, identifying, investigating, and intervening when issues of bullying arise.

B. Schools

By August 2011, each school principal shall designate a Prevention Liaison who shall serve on existing teams that address acts of violence and school safety, e.g., threat assessment teams, SAFE Teams, and act as the Student Support Service's Office of Prevention contact. At minimum, this team should include staff members from administration, guidance, and instruction. These designees are the key school-based personnel who will receive prevention training and assist in the dissemination of prevention methods, intervention, and curriculum, for bullying and other issues that impact the school culture and welfare of students and staff.

C. Community Resources

Student Support Services professionals, in collaboration with other District departments, will train a wide range of community stakeholders, profit, non-profit, School Resource Officers, and faith-based agencies to provide the dissemination and support of violence prevention curriculums to students, their families and school staff. This collaboration will make effective use of available school district and community resources while ensuring seamless service delivery in which each and every school and student receives an equitable foundation of violence prevention.

D. Evidence-Based Interventions and Curriculum

Student Support Services' Office of Prevention staff members will serve as the coordinators and trainers of prevention for all designated school staff and outside agencies/community partners. Those trained in Prevention (e.g., Prevention Liaisons, Office of Prevention staff and Community Partners) will then collaborate as "violence prevention partners" to implement the evidence-based interventions and proven programs within each of their schools. Training will focus on prevention and evidence-based programs.

E. Parent Participation and Partnership

Student Support Services professionals, in collaboration with other District departments, will provide opportunities and encourage parents to participate in prevention efforts with their children in meaningful and relevant ways that address the academic, social, and health needs of their children. The District will offer parents and parent associations' trainings on violence prevention as well as knowledge of and/or opportunity to participate in any violence prevention initiatives currently taking place in their school via the District school Web site, Broward Education Communication Network (BECON), open houses, and parent/school newsletters. Training will provide resources and support for parents by linking them with internal supports as well as referral to community-based resources as needed.

F. Evaluation of Service Effectiveness

Evaluations to determine the effectiveness and efficiency of the services being provided will be conducted at least every three years and shall include data-based outcomes.

G. Accountability

The Superintendent, other district administrators, the Area Superintendents and their staffs, as well as school principals, share accountability for implementation of these student support services consistent with the standards of this policy. These administrators will take steps to assure that student support services are fully integrated with their instructional components at each school and are pursued with equal effort in policy and practice.

IV. Training for students, parents, teachers, area/district staff, school administrators, student support staff, counseling staff, bus drivers, School Resource Officers/Deputies, contractors and school volunteers on identifying, preventing, and responding to bullying will be conducted

At the beginning of each school year, the school principal/designee and or appropriate area/district administrator shall provide awareness of this policy, as well as the process for reporting incidents, investigation and appeal, to students, school staff, parents, or other persons responsible for the welfare of a pupil through appropriate references in the Student Code of Conduct, Employee Handbooks, the school Web site, and/or through other reasonable means.

V. Disciplinary sanctions (consequences) and due processes for a person who commits an act of bullying under this policy

Concluding whether a particular action or incident constitutes a violation of this policy requires a determination based on all of the facts and surrounding circumstances, followed by the determination of disciplinary sanctions appropriate to the perpetrator's position within the District.

1. Consequences and appropriate interventions for students who commit acts of bullying may range from positive behavioral interventions up to, but not limited

to suspension, as outlined in the Student Code of Conduct, the Discipline Matrix, and this Policy.

2. Consequences and appropriate interventions for a school/district employee found to have committed an act of bullying will be instituted in accordance with District policies, procedures, and agreements (Policy 4.9, Employee Disciplinary Guidelines, Part I, Section b and Policy 2410, Workplace Violence, Rules) and the Education Professionals' Contract Agreement (BTU). Additionally, egregious acts of bullying by certified educators may result in a sanction against an educator's state-issued certificate (Rule 6B-1.006 F.A.C.).

3. Consequences and appropriate intervention for a visitor or volunteer, found to have committed an act of bullying shall be determined by the school administrator after consideration of the nature and circumstances of the act, including reports to appropriate law enforcement officials.

4. These same actions will apply to persons, whether they be students, school employees, or visitors/volunteers/independent contractors, who are found to have made wrongful and intentional accusations of another as a means of bullying.

VI. Reporting an act of bullying

A. At each school, the principal/designee is responsible for receiving oral or written complaints alleging violations of this policy, as with all infractions from the Student Code of Conduct.

B. All District faculty and staff are required and must report, in writing, any allegations of bullying or violations of this Policy to the principal/designee or appropriate area/district administrator. Failure to report will result in action(s) or discipline, consistent with the collective bargaining agreement provisions, up to and including termination of employment (SBBC Policy 2410, section 1).

C. Any other members of the school community who have credible information that an act of bullying has taken place may file a report of bullying, whether a victim or witness.

D. Any student (and/or the parent on that complainant's behalf if the complainant is a minor) who believes he/she is a victim of bullying (or any individual, including any student who has knowledge of any incident(s) involving bullying of students) is strongly encouraged to report the incident(s) in writing to a school official. Complaints should be filed as soon as possible after the alleged incident and noted on the specified data system, but must be filed within ninety (90) school days after the alleged incident (i.e., within 90 school days of the last act of alleged bullying). Failure on the part of the complainant to initiate and/or follow up on the complaint within this period may result in the complaint being deemed abandoned. For protected categories covered under Policy 4001.1, a different timeline may apply.

E. The principal of each school in the District shall establish, and prominently publicize to students, staff, volunteers, and parents, how a report of bullying may be filed and how this report will be acted upon.

F. A school district employee, school volunteer, contractor, student, parent/or other persons who promptly reports in good faith an act of bullying to the appropriate school official, and who makes this report in compliance with the procedures set forth in this District Policy, is immune from a cause of action for damages arising out of the reporting itself or any failure to remedy the reported incident. Submission of a good faith complaint or report of bullying will not affect the complainant or reporter's future employment, grades, learning or working environment, or work assignments within the SBBC.

G. Administrators/principal/designee(s) shall document in writing and/or via the specified data system all complaints regarding bullying, as with all infractions of the Code of Student Conduct, to ensure that problems are appropriately addressed in a timely manner, whether the report is made verbally or in writing.

H. Anonymous reports may be made utilizing the Broward County Public Schools Anonymous Bullying Report Form. This reporting form can be found on the School District's Web site www.browardschools.com (click on special investigative unit; click on report anonymous tips), at each school's front office, or at each area/district/ department site. Anonymous reports may be delivered to the school administration's front office, put in the school's reporting box, or through the Special Investigative Unit (herein after to be referred to as SIU) via their Internet Web site www.broward.k12.fl .us/siu or Emergency/Silence Hurts Tipline at (754) 321-0911. Administrators shall use the specified data system to log all reports and interventions. Formal disciplinary action may not be based solely on the basis of an anonymous report.

VII. Bullying complaints and resolution

A. The investigation of a reported act of bullying of a student, school-based employee, or other persons providing service to the school is deemed to be a school-related activity and begins with a report of such an act.

B. The principal/designee shall document all complaints in writing and/or through the appropriate data system to ensure that problems are addressed in a timely manner. Although this Policy encourages students to use the formal written complaint process, school officials "should investigate all complaints and reports of harassment, whether or not the complaint is in writing," as stated by the Office for Civil Rights in *Protecting Students from Harassment and Hate Crime: A Guide for Schools, Part II* (1999).

C. If the complaint is about the principal or an area/district's staff member's direct supervisor, then the Area Superintendent/Designee or appropriate district administrator shall be asked to address the complaint.

D. Informal Resolution - where the administrator, along with the complainant and the accused/student, may agree to informally resolve the complaint. The incident and the resolution must be documented on the appropriate data system.

- If a mutual resolution has not been achieved, a formal written appeal must be filed within five (5) work days after the informal meeting and submitted to the principal or appropriate area/district supervisor.

E. Formal Resolution - the complainant/student/employee or parent(s), on behalf of the student, may file a written complaint with the principal/designee or appropriate area/district administrator by utilizing the Broward County Public Schools Bullying Complaint Report Form. Said form is available on the School District's Web site www.browardschools.com, at each school's front office, or area/district/department site. According to the level of infraction, parents will be promptly notified of any actions being taken to protect the victim via telephone or personal conference; the frequency of notification will depend on the seriousness of the bullying incident.

F. The resolution, all interviews and interventions that take place and the corresponding dates shall be documented in writing and/or noted in the district specified data system.

VIII. Investigation requirements for reported acts of bullying under this policy

A. The procedures for investigating school-based bullying may include the principal/designee and/or the utilization of a Prevention Liaison, in the case of student-to-student bullying. The principal or designee and Prevention Liaison shall be trained in investigative procedures and interventions as outlined in this Policy. For incidents at the area/district level, the appropriate administrator will be responsible for the investigation as outlined in this policy.

B. The investigator may not be the accused or the alleged victim.

C. The principal/designee or appropriate area/district administrator shall begin a thorough investigation and interviews with the complainant(s), accused, and witnesses within two (2) school days of receiving a notification of complaint. (The Florida Department of Education requires that school administrators/designees provide immediate notification to the parents of both the victim and the alleged perpetrator of an act of bullying or harassment.)

D. During the investigation, the principal/designee or appropriate area/district administrator may take any action necessary to protect the complainant, other students or employees consistent with the requirements of applicable regulations and statutes.

1. In general, student complainants will continue attendance at the same school and pursue their studies as directed while the investigation is conducted and the complaint is pending resolution. Any legal order of a court will prevail.

2. When necessary to carry out the investigation or for other good reasons, and consistent with federal and state privacy laws, the principal/designee or appropriate area/district administrator also may discuss the complaint with any school district employee, the parent of the complainant or accused, if one or both is a minor (or has given consent or is an adult who has been determined to be incompetent or unable to give informed consent due to disability), and/or child protective agencies responsible for investigating child abuse.

3. During the investigation where an employee is the accused, the principal/designee or the appropriate area/district administrator may recommend to the Associate Superintendent of Human Resources/designee, any action necessary to protect the complainant, or other students or employees, consistent with the requirements of applicable statutes, State Board of Education Rules, School Board Policies, and collective bargaining agreements.

E. Within ten (10) school days of the filing of the complaint, there shall be a written decision by the Principal/Designee or appropriate area/district administrator regarding the completion of the investigation. The principal/designee shall make a decision about the validity of the allegations in the complaint and about any corrective action, if applicable, consistent with the Discipline Matrix.

F. The Principal/Designee or appropriate area/district administrator will inform all relevant parties in writing of the decision and the right to appeal. A copy of the decision will be sent to the originating school and be noted in all relevant data tracking systems including, but not limited to the SESIR and the Statewide Report on School Safety and Discipline Data system.

G. If the accused is an employee, discipline may be taken, consistent with any applicable collective bargaining agreement provisions, to resolve a complaint of bullying (Policy 4.9, Employee Disciplinary Guidelines). The supervisor/designee (e.g., principal/designee for school-based employees) of the employee shall discuss the determination and any recommended corrective action with the Area Director, for school-based actions, or the appropriate area/district supervisor, for area/district actions, and the Associate Superintendent of Human Resources.

H. No retaliation of any kind is permitted in connection with an individual's having made a bullying complaint and if it occurs, it shall be deemed an additional act of bullying as stated herein this Policy.

IX. Referral for intervention

A. Referral of a student to the collaborative problem-solving team (or equivalent school-based team with a problem-solving focus) for consideration of appropriate services is made through the school problem-solving process by school personnel or parent to the principal/designee. Parent notification is required. When such a report of formal discipline or formal complaint is made, the principal/designee shall refer the student(s) to the collaborative problem-solving team for determination of need for counseling support and interventions.

B. Referral of school or area/district personnel to the Employee Assistance Program (EAP) for consideration of appropriate services will be made by the administrator.

C. School-based intervention and assistance will be determined by the collaborative problem-solving team and may include, but is not limited to:

1. counseling and support to address the needs of the victims of bullying.

2. counseling interventions to address the behavior of the students who bully (e.g., empathy training, anger management).

3. intervention which includes assistance and support provided to parents.

4. analysis and evaluation of school culture with resulting recommendations for interventions aimed at increasing peer ownership and support.

D. Self referral for informal consultation: District staff, students or parents may request informal consultation with school staff (e.g., school social worker, school counselor, school psychologist, Prevention Liaison, EAP, etc.) to determine the severity of concern and appropriate steps to address the concern of bullying (the involved students' parents may be included) orally or in writing to the principal/designee.

E. Any investigations and interventions shall be recorded on the District specified data system.

X. Incident reporting requirements

A. The procedure for including incidents of bullying in the school's report of safety and discipline data is required under F.S. 1006.09(6). The report must include each incident of bullying and the resulting consequences, including discipline, interventions and referrals. In a separate section, the report must include each reported incident of bullying or harassment that does not meet the criteria of a prohibited act under this policy, with recommendations regarding said incident.

B. The School District will utilize Florida's School Environmental Safety Incident Reporting (SESIR) Statewide Report on School Safety and Discipline Data, which includes bullying/harassment in its codes.

C. Discipline, referral data, investigations, interventions, and actions of discipline shall be recorded on the specified data system, as with other infractions from the Code of Student Conduct.

XI. Process for referral for external investigation

A. If the act is outside the scope of the District, and determined a criminal act, referral to appropriate law enforcement shall be made immediately, the parent will be notified, and the referral documented by the principal/designee in the specified data system.

B. While the District does not assume any liability for incidences that must be referred for external investigation, it encourages the provision of assistance and intervention as the principal/designee deems appropriate, including the use of the School Resource Officer and other personnel. The principal/designee shall use District Reporting Systems to log all reports and interventions.

XII. Appeals process

A. Appeal procedure for bullying by a student will follow the steps outlined in the Code of Student Conduct – "Right to Appeal Unfair Penalties."

B. Appeal procedure for an accused/employee:

1. If the accused/employee wishes to appeal the action taken in resolution of the complaint, such appeal shall be filed either in accordance with SBBC Board Policy 4015 or pursuant to the relevant collective bargaining agreement.

2. For those employees not in a bargaining unit, the appeal shall be filed in accordance with SBBC Policy 4015. In reaching a decision about the complaint, the following should be taken into account:

a. SBBC Policy 4.9, Employee Disciplinary Guidelines; and

b. Case law, state and federal laws and regulations, and the Board's Policies prohibiting bullying and discrimination, including Policy 4001.1.

XIII. Confidentiality

A. To the greatest extent possible, all complaints will be treated as confidential and in accordance with SBBC Policy 5100.1, F.S. § 1002.22(3)(d); the Family Educational Rights and Privacy Act ("FERPA"); the Health Insurance Portability and Accountability Act ("HIPAA") and any other applicable law, such as F.S. § 119.07(1); 1012.31(3)(a); or 1012.796(1)(c).

B. Limited disclosure may be necessary to complete a thorough investigation as described above. The District's obligation to investigate and take corrective action may supersede an individual's right to privacy.

C. The complainant's identity shall be protected, but absolute confidentiality cannot be guaranteed. The identity of the victim of the reported act shall be protected to the extent possible.

XIV. Retaliation prohibited

A. Retaliation includes, but is not limited to, any form of intimidation, reprisal or harassment in connection with filing a complaint or assisting with an investigation under this Policy.

B. Retaliatory or intimidating conduct against any individual who has made a bullying complaint or any individual who has testified, assisted, or participated, in any manner, in an investigation is specifically prohibited and as detailed in this Policy shall be treated as another incidence of bullying.

XV. Additional referral

In all cases, the District reserves the right to refer the results of its own investigation to the State Attorney for the Seventeenth Judicial Circuit of Florida for possible criminal charges, whether or not the District takes any other action.

XVI. Constitutional safeguard

This policy does not imply to prohibit expressive activity protected by the First Amendment of the United States Constitution or Article I, Section 4 of the Florida Constitution.

XVII. Preclusion

This policy should not be interpreted as to prevent a victim or accused from seeking redress under any other available law either civil or criminal.

XVIII. Severability

If a provision of this policy is or becomes illegal, invalid or unenforceable in any jurisdiction, that shall not affect the validity or enforceability in that jurisdiction of any other provision of this policy.

AUTHORITY: F.S. 1006.147

POLICY ADOPTED AS AMENDED: 7/22/08* Broward County Schools, Florida

Appendix E

Bully Free Discipline Rubrics and Blank Rubric Forms

The rubrics in this appendix are examples and also appear as Microsoft Word files at www.bullyfree.com. Schools should modify them to match their preferences, needs, policies, and procedures.

Bully Free Discipline Rubrics for Behavior and Consequences, Elementary School

Example 1, Elementary School

Instructions: The behaviors listed in a cell should be considered as a group of behaviors for that cell. Therefore, if any of the behaviors (or similar behaviors) listed in a cell occur, consequences should be applied according to the frequency of behaviors. For example, if you hear a student tease someone in a hurtful way for the first time, *all* of the first-time-offense consequences should be applied. If the next day, you hear the same student hurl insulting remarks at the same or another student, you should apply *all* of the second-time-offense consequences. In other words, the same behavior does not have to be repeated for more severe consequences to be applied.

Example 1, Elementary School

Behavior	First-Time-Offense Consequences *(Apply ALL of the consequences in a cell.)*	Second-Time-Offense Consequences *(Apply ALL of the consequences in a cell.)*	Third-Time-Offense Consequences *(Apply ALL of the consequences in a cell.)*
• Hurtful teasing • Hurtful name-calling • Insulting remarks • Other similar behavior (physical, verbal, written, electronic, or nonverbal) that intentionally hurts a person	1. Student receives verbal reprimand and warning, and behavior is recorded in grade book or discipline book. 2. Student must apologize in writing to the student and ask forgiveness. Letter should also make positive comments about the student. 3. Student must participate in a behavioral conference with the teacher. 4. Student loses one recess and not play with anyone. Student is required to exercise in some way.	1. Student receives verbal reprimand, and behavior is recorded in grade book or discipline book. 2. Student must call his or her parents, if appropriate. 3. Student must participate in a behavioral conference with counselor. 4. Student loses two recesses and not allowed to play with anyone. Student is required to exercise in some way, or must sit near the teacher's desk for two days, or eat lunch in isolation for two days.	1. Student receives verbal reprimand, and behavior is recorded in grade book or discipline book. 2. Student must call his or her parents, if appropriate. 3. Student must participate in a behavioral conference with assistant principal and/or principal. 4. Required parent conference. 5. Student loses three recesses and not allowed to play with anyone. Student is required to exercise in some way or given detention.
• Spreading lies, destroying reputations • Socially rejecting • Sending nasty notes or hate notes • Stealing or damaging property • Other similar behavior (physical, verbal, written, electronic, or nonverbal) that intentionally hurts a person	1. Student receives verbal reprimand and warning, and behavior is recorded in grade book or discipline book. 2. Student must apologize in writing to the student and ask forgiveness. Letter should also make positive comments about the student. 3. Student must call his or her parents if property is stolen or damaged and if appropriate. 4. Student must participate in a behavioral conference with the teacher. 5. Student loses two recesses. Student is required to exercise in some way. 6. Student must make restitution for any property stolen or damaged.	1. Student receives verbal reprimand, and behavior is recorded in grade book or discipline book. 2. Student must call his or her parents if property is stolen or damaged and if appropriate. 3. Student must participate in a behavioral conference with counselor. 4. Student loses three recesses (student is required to exercise in some way), or must sit near the teacher's desk for three days, or eat lunch in isolation for three days. 5. Student must make restitution for any property stolen or damaged.	1. Student receives verbal reprimand, and behavior is recorded in grade book or discipline book. 2. Student must call his or her parents if property is stolen or damaged and if appropriate. 3. Student must participate in a behavioral conference with assistant principal and/or principal. 4. Required parent conference. 5. Student loses four recesses (student is required to exercise in some way) or given detention. 6. Student must make restitution for any property stolen or damaged.

Example 1, Elementary School, Continued

Behavior	First-Time-Offense Consequences (Apply ALL of the consequences in a cell.)	Second-Time-Offense Consequences (Apply ALL of the consequences in a cell.)	Third-Time-Offense Consequences (Apply ALL of the consequences in a cell.)
• Pushing • Tripping • Grabbing • Pinching • Restraining • Other similar behavior (physical, verbal, written, electronic, or nonverbal) that intentionally hurts a person	1. Student receives verbal reprimand and warning, and behavior is recorded in grade book or discipline book. 2. Student must apologize in writing to the student and ask forgiveness. Letter should also make positive comments about the student. 3. Student must call his or her parents, if appropriate. 4. Student must participate in a behavioral conference with the teacher. 5. Student loses three recesses and not allowed to play with others. Student is required to exercise in some way.	1. Student receives verbal reprimand, and behavior is recorded in grade book or discipline book. 2. Student must call his or her parents, if appropriate. 3. Student must participate in a behavioral conference with counselor. 4. Student loses four recesses and not allowed to play with others. Student is required to exercise in some way, or must sit near the teacher's desk for four days, or eat lunch in isolation for four days.	1. Student receives verbal reprimand, and behavior is recorded in grade book or discipline book. 2. Student must call his or her parents, if appropriate. 3. Student must participate in a behavioral conference with assistant principal and/or principal. 4. Required parent conference. 5. Student loses five recesses and not allowed to play with others. Student is required to exercise in some way or given detention.

Example 1, Elementary School, Continued

Behavior	First-Time-Offense Consequences (Apply ALL of the consequences in a cell.)	Second-Time-Offense Consequences (Apply ALL of the consequences in a cell.)	Third-Time-Offense Consequences (Apply ALL of the consequences in a cell.)
• Spitting on someone • Hitting and punching • Slapping • Slamming with shoulder • Kicking • Threats • Other similar behavior (physical, verbal, written, electronic, or nonverbal) that intentionally hurts a person	1. Student receives verbal reprimand, and behavior is recorded in grade book or discipline book. 2. Student must apologize in writing to the student and ask forgiveness. Letter should also make positive comments about the student. 3. Student must call his or her parents, if appropriate. 4. Student must participate in a behavioral conference with the teacher. 5. Student given detention.	1. Student receives verbal reprimand, and behavior is recorded in grade book or discipline book. 2. Student must call his or her parents, if appropriate. 3. Student must participate in a behavioral conference with counselor. 4. Student given detention (for longer period) or Saturday school.	1. Student receives verbal reprimand, and behavior is recorded in grade book or discipline book. 2. Student must call his or her parents, if appropriate. 3. Student must participate in a behavioral conference with assistant principal and/or principal. 4. Required parent conference. 5. Student suspended.

Note: The negative consequences should be applied consistently. Consequences greater than those listed in the rubric may be applied and will be based on the type of misbehavior, the frequency of the mistreatment, the attitude and cooperation of the student, the school's discipline plan, harassment and anti-bullying policies, and relevant board policies. Negative consequences should be applied with statements regarding inappropriate behavior and the behavior desired. Also, for a time period, the student should receive positive reinforcement for self-control and modeling the desired behavior.

Bully Free Discipline Rubrics for Behavior and Consequences, Elementary School

Example 2, Elementary School

Instructions: The behaviors listed in a cell should be considered as a group of behaviors for that cell. The menu of consequences is progressive in that the further you go down the list, the more significant or severe the consequences. For example, if you hear a student tease someone in a hurtful way for the first time, you should *select one or more* of the consequences appearing first in the menu of consequences. If the next day, you hear the same student hurl insulting remarks at the same or another student, you should apply more severe consequences located further down the list. In other words, the same behavior does not have to be repeated to receive more severe consequences.

Example 2, Elementary School

Behavior	Menu of Consequences *(ONE or MORE of the following may be applied according to the frequency of mistreatment, the student's attitude, and the student's cooperation.)*
• Hurtful teasing • Hurtful name-calling • Insulting remarks • Other similar behavior (physical, verbal, written, electronic, or nonverbal) that intentionally hurts a person	1. Student receives verbal reprimand and warning, and behavior is recorded in grade book or discipline book. 2. Student must in writing apologize to the student and ask forgiveness. The letter should also make positive comments about the student. 3. Student must call his or her parents, if appropriate. 4. Student must participate in a behavioral conference with the teacher. 5. Student loses one recess and not allowed to play with others. Student is required to exercise in some way. 6. Student must participate in a behavioral conference with counselor. 7. Student loses two recesses (required to exercise in some way), or must sit near the teacher's desk for two days, or eat lunch in isolation for two days. 8. Student must participate in a behavioral conference with assistant principal and/or principal. 9. Required parent conference. 10. Student loses three recesses and not allowed to play with anyone. Student is required to exercise in some way or given detention.
• Spreading lies, destroying reputations • Socially rejecting • Sending nasty notes or hate notes • Stealing or damaging property • Other similar behavior (physical, verbal, written, electronic, or nonverbal) that intentionally hurts a person	1. Student receives verbal reprimand and warning, and behavior is recorded in grade book or discipline book. 2. Student must apologize in writing to the student and ask forgiveness. Letter should also make positive comments about the student. 3. Student must call his or her parents, if property is stolen or damaged and if appropriate. 4. Student must participate in a behavioral conference with the teacher. 5. Student loses two recesses and is not allowed to play with others. He or she is required to exercise in some way. 6. Student must participate in a behavioral conference with counselor. 7. Student must participate in a behavioral conference with assistant principal and/or principal. 8. Student loses three recesses and not allowed to play with others. Student is required to exercise in some way or must sit near the teacher's desk for three days, or eat lunch in isolation for three days. 9. Required parent conference. 10. Student loses four recesses and not allowed to play with anyone. Student required to exercise in some way or given detention. 11. Student must make restitution for any property stolen or damaged.

Example 2, Elementary School, Continued

Behavior	Menu of Consequences *(ONE or MORE of the following may be applied according to the frequency of mistreatment, the student's attitude, and the student's cooperation.)*
• Pushing • Tripping • Grabbing • Pinching • Restraining • Other similar behavior (physical, verbal, written, electronic, or nonverbal) that intentionally hurts a person	1. Student receives verbal reprimand and warning, and behavior is recorded in grade book or discipline book. 2. Student must apologize in writing to the student and ask forgiveness. Letter should also make positive comments about the student. 3. Student must call his or her parents, if appropriate. 4. Student must participate in a behavioral conference with the teacher. 5. Student loses three recesses and not allowed to play with others. He or she is required to exercise in some way. 6. Student must participate in a behavioral conference with counselor. 7. Student loses four recesses and not allowed to play with others (required to exercise in some way), or must sit near the teacher's desk for four days, or eat lunch in isolation for four days. 8. Student must participate in a behavioral conference with assistant principal and/or principal. 9. Required parent conference. 10. Student loses five recesses (required to exercise in some way) or given detention.

Example 2, Elementary School, Continued

Behavior	Menu of Consequences *(ONE or MORE of the following may be applied according to the frequency of mistreatment, the student's attitude, and the student's cooperation.)*
• Spitting on someone • Hitting and punching • Slapping • Slamming with shoulder • Kicking • Threats • Other similar behavior (physical, verbal, written, electronic, or nonverbal) that intentionally hurts a person	1. Student receives verbal reprimand and warning, and behavior is recorded in grade book or discipline book. 2. Student must apologize in writing to the student and ask forgiveness. The letter should also make positive comments about the student. 3. Student must call his or her parents, if appropriate. 4. Student must participate in a behavioral conference with the teacher. 5. Student given detention. 6. Student must participate in a behavioral conference with the counselor. 7. Student given detention for a longer period of time than previous detention or Saturday school. 8. Student must participate in a behavioral conference with assistant principal and/or principal. 9. Required parent conference. 10. Student suspended.

Note: The negative consequences should be applied consistently. Consequences greater than those listed in the rubric may be applied and will be based on the type of misbehavior, the frequency of the mistreatment, the attitude and cooperation of the student, the school's discipline plan, harassment and anti-bullying policies, and relevant board policies. Negative consequences should be applied with statements regarding inappropriate behavior and the behavior desired. Also, for a time period, the student should receive positive reinforcement for self-control and modeling the desired behavior.

Bully Free Discipline Rubrics for Behavior and Consequences, Elementary School

Example 3, Elementary School

Instructions: The behaviors listed in a cell should be considered as a group of behaviors for that cell. Therefore, if any of the behaviors (or similar behaviors) listed in a cell occur, the appropriate consequences should be applied. For example, if you hear a student tease someone in a hurtful way for the first time, *all* of the first-time-offense consequences should be applied. If the next day, you hear the same student hurl insulting remarks at the same or another student, you should *select one or more* of the more significant or severe consequences from the column labeled Menu of Consequences for Repeated Offenses. In other words, the same behavior does not have to be repeated to receive more severe consequences. If the student continues to mistreat others, select the most severe consequences listed in the last column. The consequences for repeated offenses are progressive in that as you move down the list, they are more severe.

Example 3, Elementary School

Behavior	Consequences for First Offense (Apply ALL of the consequences in a cell.)	Menu of Consequences for Repeated Offenses (ONE or MORE of the following may be applied according to the frequency of mistreatment, the student's attitude, and the student's cooperation.)
• Hurtful teasing • Hurtful name-calling • Insulting remarks • Other similar behavior (physical, verbal, written, electronic, or nonverbal) that intentionally hurts a person	1. Student receives verbal reprimand and warning, and behavior is recorded in grade book or discipline book. 2. Student must apologize in writing to the student and ask forgiveness. The letter should also make positive comments about the student. 3. Student must participate in a behavioral conference with the teacher. 4. Student loses one recess and not allowed to play with others. He or she is required to exercise in some way.	1. Student receives verbal reprimand, behavior is recorded, and he or she must participate in a behavioral conference with counselor. 2. Student loses two recesses and not allowed to play with anyone. Student is required to exercise in some way, or must sit near the teacher's desk for two days, or eat lunch in isolation for two days. 3. Student must call his or her parents, if appropriate. 4. Student must participate in a behavioral conference with assistant principal and/or principal. 5. Required parent conference. 6. Student loses three recesses and not allowed to play with anyone. Student is required to exercise in some way.
• Spreading lies, destroying reputations • Socially rejecting • Sending nasty notes or hate notes • Stealing or damaging property • Other similar behavior (physical, verbal, written, electronic, or nonverbal) that intentionally hurts a person	1. Student receives verbal reprimand and warning, and behavior is recorded in grade book or discipline book. 2. Student must apologize in writing to the student and ask forgiveness. The letter should also make positive comments about the student. 3. Student must call his or her parents if property is stolen or damaged and if appropriate. 4. Student must participate in a behavioral conference with the teacher. 5. Student loses two recesses and not allowed to play with others. He or she is required to exercise in some way. 6. Student must make restitution for any property stolen or damaged.	1. Student receives verbal reprimand, behavior is recorded, and he or she must participate in a behavioral conference with counselor. 2. Student must call his or her parents if property is stolen or damaged and if appropriate. 3. Student loses three recesses (required to exercise in some way), or must sit near the teacher's desk for three days, or eat lunch in isolation for three days. 4. Student must participate in a behavioral conference with assistant principal and/or principal. 5. Required parent conference. 6. Student loses four recesses (required to exercise in some way) or given detention. 7. Student must make restitution for any property stolen or damaged.

Example 3, Elementary School, Continued

Behavior	Consequences for First Offense (Apply ALL of the consequences in a cell.)	Menu of Consequences for Repeated Offenses (ONE or MORE of the following may be applied according to the frequency of mistreatment, the student's attitude, and the student's cooperation.)
• Pushing • Tripping • Grabbing • Pinching • Restraining • Other similar behavior (physical, verbal, written, electronic, or nonverbal) that intentionally hurts a person	1. Student receives verbal reprimand and warning, and behavior is recorded in grade book or discipline book. 2. Student must apologize in writing to the student and ask forgiveness. The letter should also make positive comments about the student. 3. Student must call his or her parents, if appropriate. 4. Student must participate in a behavioral conference with the teacher. 5. Student loses three recesses and is not allowed to play with others. He or she is required to exercise in some way.	1. Student receives verbal reprimand, behavior is recorded, and he or she must participate in a behavioral conference with counselor. 2. Student must call his or her parents, if appropriate. 3. Student loses four recesses (he or she is required to exercise in some way), or must sit near the teacher's desk for four days, or eat lunch in isolation for four days. 4. Student must participate in a behavioral conference with assistant principal and/or principal. 5. Student loses five recesses and cannot play with anyone. Student is required to exercise in some way or given detention.
• Spitting on someone • Hitting and punching • Slapping • Slamming with shoulder • Kicking • Threats • Other similar behavior (physical, verbal, written, electronic, or nonverbal) that intentionally hurts a person	1. Student receives verbal reprimand and warning, and behavior is recorded in grade book or discipline book. 2. Student must apologize in writing to the student and ask forgiveness. The letter should also make positive comments about the student. 3. Student must call his or her parents, if appropriate. 4. Student must participate in a behavioral conference with the teacher. 5. Student given detention.	1. Student receives verbal reprimand, behavior is recorded, and he or she must participate in a behavioral conference with counselor. 2. Student must call his or her parents, if appropriate. 3. Detention (for longer period) or Saturday school. 4. Student must participate in a behavioral conference with assistant principal and/or principal. 5. Required parent conference. 6. Student suspended.

Note: The negative consequences should be applied consistently. Consequences greater than those listed in the rubric may be applied and will be based on the type of misbehavior, the frequency of the mistreatment, the attitude and cooperation of the student, the school's discipline plan, harassment and anti-bullying policies, and relevant board policies. Negative consequences should be applied with statements regarding inappropriate behavior and the behavior desired. Also, for a time period, the student should receive positive reinforcement for self-control and modeling the desired behavior.

Bully Free Discipline Rubrics for Behavior and Consequences, Middle School

Example 1, Middle School

Instructions: The behaviors listed in a cell should be considered as a group of behaviors for that cell. Therefore, if any of the behaviors (or similar behaviors) listed in a cell occur, consequences should be applied according to the frequency of behaviors. For example, if you hear a student tease someone in a hurtful way for the first time, *all* of the first-time-offense consequences should be applied. If the next day, you hear the same student hurl insulting remarks at the same or another student, you should apply *all* of the second-time-offense consequences. In other words, the same behavior does not have to be repeated for more severe consequences to be applied.

Example 1, Middle School

Behavior	First-Time Offense (Apply ALL the consequences in a cell.)	Second-Time Offense (Apply ALL the consequences in a cell.)	Third-Time Offense (Apply ALL the consequences in a cell.)
• Hurtful teasing • Hurtful name-calling • Insulting remarks • Other similar behavior (physical, verbal, written, electronic, or nonverbal) that intentionally hurts a person	1. Student receives verbal reprimand and warning, and behavior is recorded in grade book or discipline book. 2. Student must apologize in writing to the student and ask forgiveness. The letter should also make positive comments about the student. 3. Student must participate in a behavioral conference with the teacher. 4. Student must sit in isolation during one lunch period.	1. Student receives verbal reprimand, and behavior is recorded in grade book or discipline book. 2. Student must call his or her parents, if appropriate. 3. Student must participate in a behavioral conference with counselor. 4. Student must sit in isolation during two lunch periods.	1. Student receives verbal reprimand, and behavior is recorded in grade book or discipline book. 2. Student must call his or her parents, if appropriate. 3. Student must participate in a behavioral conference with assistant principal and/or principal. 4. Required parent conference. 5. Student must sit in isolation during three lunch periods or given detention.
• Spreading lies, destroying reputations • Socially rejecting • Sending nasty notes or hate notes • Stealing or damaging property • Other similar behavior (physical, verbal, written, electronic, or nonverbal) that intentionally hurts a person	1. Student receives verbal reprimand and warning, and behavior is recorded in grade book or discipline book. 2. Student must apologize in writing to the student and ask forgiveness. The letter should also make positive comments about the student. 3. Student must call his or her parents if property is stolen or damaged and if appropriate. 4. Student must participate in a behavioral conference with the teacher. 5. Student must stay after school one hour for one day. 6. Student must make restitution for any property stolen or damaged.	1. Student receives verbal reprimand, and behavior is recorded in grade book or discipline book. 2. Student must call his or her parents, if property is stolen or damaged and if appropriate. 3. Student must participate in a behavioral conference with counselor. 4. Student must stay after school one hour for two days or eat lunch in isolation for three days. 5. Student must make restitution for any property stolen or damaged.	1. Student receives verbal reprimand, and behavior is recorded in grade book or discipline book. 2. Student must call his or her parents, if property is stolen or damaged and if appropriate. 3. Student must participate in a behavioral conference with assistant principal and/or principal who completes the Safe School Report. 4. Required parent conference. 5. Student receives detention. 6. Student must make restitution for any property stolen or damaged.

Example 1, Middle School, Continued

Behavior	First-Time Offense (Apply ALL the consequences in a cell.)	Second-Time Offense (Apply ALL the consequences in a cell.)	Third-Time Offense (Apply ALL the consequences in a cell.)
• Pushing • Tripping • Grabbing • Pinching • Restraining • Other similar behavior (physical, verbal, written, electronic, or nonverbal) that intentionally hurts a person	1. Student receives verbal reprimand and warning, and behavior is recorded in grade book or discipline book. 2. Student must apologize in writing to the student and ask forgiveness. The letter should also make positive comments about the student. 3. Student must call his or her parents, if appropriate. 4. Student must participate in a behavioral conference with the teacher. 5. Student must eat lunch in isolation for two days.	1. Student receives verbal reprimand, and behavior is recorded in grade book or discipline book. 2. Student must call his or her parents, if appropriate. 3. Student must meet with the counselor once a day for a few days to discuss his or her behavior. 4. Student must eat lunch in isolation for four days.	1. Student receives verbal reprimand, and behavior is recorded in grade book or discipline book. 2. Student must call his or her parents, if appropriate. 3. Student must participate in a behavioral conference with assistant principal and/or principal. 4. Required parent conference. 5. Student given detention or in-school suspension.

Example 1, Middle School, Continued

Behavior	First-Time Offense (Apply ALL the consequences in a cell.)	Second-Time Offense (Apply ALL the consequences in a cell.)	Third-Time Offense (Apply ALL the consequences in a cell.)
• Spitting on someone • Hitting and punching • Slapping • Slamming with shoulder • Kicking • Threats • Other similar behavior (physical, verbal, written, electronic, or nonverbal) that intentionally hurts a person	1. Student receives verbal reprimand and warning, and behavior is recorded in grade book or discipline book. 2. Student must apologize in writing to the student and ask forgiveness. The letter should also make positive comments about the student. 3. Student must call his or her parents. 4. Student must participate in a behavioral conference with the teacher. 5. Student given detention.	1. Student receives verbal reprimand, and behavior is recorded in grade book or discipline book. 2. Student must call his or her parents, if appropriate. 3. Student must participate in a behavioral conference with counselor. 4. Detention (for longer period) or Saturday school.	1. Student receives verbal reprimand, and behavior is recorded in grade book or discipline book. 2. Student must call his or her parents, if appropriate. 3. Student must participate in a behavioral conference with assistant principal and/or principal. 4. Required parent conference. 5. Student suspended.

Note: The negative consequences should be applied consistently. Consequences greater than those listed in the rubric may be applied and will be based on the type of misbehavior, the frequency of the mistreatment, the attitude and cooperation of the student, the school's discipline plan, harassment and anti-bullying policies, and relevant board policies. Negative consequences should be applied with statements regarding inappropriate behavior and the behavior desired. Also, for a time period, the student should receive positive reinforcement for self-control and modeling the desired behavior.

Bully Free Discipline Rubrics for Behavior and Consequences, Middle School

Example 2, Middle School

Instructions: The behaviors listed in a cell should be considered as a group of behaviors for that cell. The menu of consequences is progressive in that the further you go down the list, the more significant or severe the consequences. For example, if you hear a student tease someone in a hurtful way for the first time, you should *select one or more* of the consequences appearing first in the menu of consequences. If the next day, you hear the same student hurl insulting remarks at the same or another student, you should apply more severe consequences located further down the list. In other words, the same behavior does not have to be repeated to receive more severe consequences.

Example 2, Middle School

Behavior	Menu of Consequences *(ONE or MORE of the following may be applied according to the frequency of mistreatment, the student's attitude, and the student's cooperation.)*
• Hurtful teasing • Hurtful name-calling • Insulting remarks • Other similar behavior (physical, verbal, written, electronic, or nonverbal) that intentionally hurts a person	1. Student receives verbal reprimand and warning, and behavior is recorded in grade book or discipline book. 2. Student must apologize in writing to the student and ask forgiveness. The letter should also make positive comments about the student. 3. Student must participate in a behavioral conference with the teacher. 4. Student must sit in isolation during one lunch period. 5. Student must call his or her parents, if appropriate. 6. Student must participate in a behavioral conference with counselor. 7. Student must sit in isolation during two lunch periods. 8. Student must participate in a behavioral conference with assistant principal and/or principal. 9. Required parent conference. 10. Student must sit in isolation during three lunch periods or given detention.
• Spreading lies, destroying reputations • Socially rejecting • Sending nasty notes or hate notes • Stealing or damaging property • Other similar behavior (physical, verbal, written, electronic, or nonverbal) that intentionally hurts a person	1. Student receives verbal reprimand and warning, and behavior is recorded in grade book or discipline book. 2. Student must apologize in writing to the student and ask forgiveness. The letter should also make positive comments about the student. 3. Student must call his or her parents, if property is stolen or damaged and if appropriate. 4. Student must participate in a behavioral conference with the teacher. 5. Student must stay after school one hour for one day. 6. Student must participate in a behavioral conference with counselor. 7. Student must stay after school one hour for two days, or eat lunch in isolation for three days. 8. Student must participate in a behavioral conference with assistant principal and/or principal. 9. Required parent conference. 10. Student receives detention. 11. Student must make restitution for any property stolen or damaged.

Example 2, Middle School, Continued

Behavior	Menu of Consequences *(ONE or MORE of the following may be applied according to the frequency of mistreatment, the student's attitude, and the student's cooperation.)*
• Pushing • Tripping • Grabbing • Pinching • Restraining • Other similar behavior (physical, verbal, written, electronic, or nonverbal) that intentionally hurts a person	1. Student receives verbal reprimand and warning, and behavior is recorded in grade book or discipline book. 2. Student must apologize in writing to the student and ask forgiveness. The letter should also make positive comments about the student. 3. Student must call his or her parents, if appropriate. 4. Student must participate in a behavioral conference with the teacher. 5. Student must eat lunch in isolation for two days. 6. Student must meet with the counselor once a day for a few days to discuss his or her behavior. 7. Student must eat lunch in isolation for four days. 8. Student must participate in a behavioral conference with assistant principal and/or principal. 9. Required parent conference. 10. Student given detention or in-school suspension.

Example 2, Middle School, Continued

Behavior	**Menu of Consequences** *(ONE or MORE of the following may be applied according to the frequency of mistreatment, the student's attitude, and the student's cooperation.)*
• Spitting on someone • Hitting and punching • Slapping • Slamming with shoulder • Kicking • Threats • Other similar behavior (physical, verbal, written, electronic, or nonverbal) that intentionally hurts a person	1. Student receives verbal reprimand and warning, and behavior is recorded in grade book or discipline book. 2. Student must apologize in writing to the student and ask forgiveness. The letter should also make positive comments about the student. 3. Student must call his or her parents, if appropriate. 4. Student must participate in a behavioral conference with the teacher. 5. Student given detention. 6. Student must participate in a behavioral conference with counselor. 7. Student given detention (for longer period) or Saturday school. 8. Student must participate in a behavioral conference with assistant principal and/or principal. 9. Required parent conference. 10. Student suspended.

Note: The negative consequences should be applied consistently. Consequences greater than those listed in the rubric may be applied and will be based on the type of misbehavior, the frequency of the mistreatment, the attitude and cooperation of the student, the school's discipline plan, harassment and anti-bullying policies, and relevant board policies. Negative consequences should be applied with statements regarding inappropriate behavior and the behavior desired. Also, for a time period, the student should receive positive reinforcement for self-control and modeling the desired behavior.

Bully Free Discipline Rubrics for Behavior and Consequences, Middle School

Example 3, Middle School

Instructions: The behaviors listed in a cell should be considered as a group of behaviors for that cell. Therefore, if any of the behaviors (or similar behaviors) listed in a cell occur, the appropriate consequences should be applied. For example, if you hear a student tease someone in a hurtful way for the first time, *all* of the first-time-offense consequences should be applied. If the next day, you hear the same student hurl insulting remarks at the same or another student, you should *select one or more* of the more significant or severe consequences from the column labeled Menu of Consequences for Repeated Offenses. In other words, the same behavior does not have to be repeated to receive more severe consequences. If the student continues to mistreat others, select the most severe consequences listed in the last column. The consequences for repeated offenses are progressive in that as you move down the list, they are more severe.

Example 3, Middle School

Behavior	Consequences for First Offense (Apply ALL of the consequences in a cell.)	Menu of Consequences for Repeated Offenses (ONE or MORE of the following may be applied according to the frequency of mistreatment, the student's attitude, and the student's cooperation.)
• Hurtful teasing • Hurtful name-calling • Insulting remarks • Other similar behavior (physical, verbal, written, electronic, or nonverbal) that intentionally hurts a person	1. Student receives verbal reprimand and warning, and behavior is recorded in grade book or discipline book. 2. Student must apologize in writing to the student and ask forgiveness. The letter should also make positive comments about the student. 3. Student must participate in a behavioral conference with the teacher. 4. Student must sit in isolation during one lunch period.	1. Student receives verbal reprimand, behavior is recorded, and he or she must participate in a behavioral conference with counselor. 2. Student must sit in isolation during two lunch periods. 3. Student must call his or her parents. 4. Student must participate in a behavioral conference with assistant principal and/or principal. 5. Required parent conference. 6. Student must sit in isolation during three lunch periods or given detention.
• Spreading lies, destroying reputations • Socially rejecting • Sending nasty notes or hate notes • Stealing or damaging property • Other similar behavior (physical, verbal, written, electronic, or nonverbal) that intentionally hurts a person	1. Student receives verbal reprimand and warning, and behavior is recorded in grade book or discipline book. 2. Student must apologize in writing to the student and ask forgiveness. The letter should also make positive comments about the student. 3. Student must call his or her parents if property is stolen or damaged and if appropriate. 4. Student must participate in a behavioral conference with the teacher. 5. Student must stay after school one hour for one day. 6. Student must make restitution for any property stolen or damaged.	1. Student receives verbal reprimand, behavior is recorded, and he or she must participate in a behavioral conference with counselor. 2. Student must call his or her parents, if property is stolen or damaged and if appropriate. 3. Student must stay after school one hour for two days, or eat lunch in isolation for three days. 4. Student must participate in a behavioral conference with assistant principal and/or principal. 5. Required parent conference. 6. Student receives detention. 7. Student must make restitution for any property stolen or damaged.

Example 3, Middle School, Continued

Behavior	Consequences for First Offense (Apply ALL of the consequences in a cell.)	Menu of Consequences for Repeated Offenses (ONE or MORE of the following may be applied according to the frequency of mistreatment, the student's attitude, and the student's cooperation.)
• Pushing • Tripping • Grabbing • Pinching • Restraining • Other similar behavior (physical, verbal, written, electronic, or nonverbal) that intentionally hurts a person	1. Student receives verbal reprimand and warning, and behavior is recorded in grade book or discipline book. 2. Student must apologize in writing to the student and ask forgiveness. The letter should also make positive comments about the student. 3. Student must call his or her parents, if appropriate. 4. Student must participate in a behavioral conference with the teacher. 5. Student must eat lunch in isolation for two days.	1. Student must call his or her parents, if appropriate. 2. Student receives reprimand, behavior is recorded, and he or she must participate in a behavioral conference with assistant principal and/or principal. 3. Required parent conference. 4. Student given detention or in-school suspension.
• Spitting on someone • Hitting and punching • Slapping • Slamming with shoulder • Kicking • Threats • Other similar behavior (physical, verbal, written, electronic, or nonverbal) that intentionally hurts a person	1. Student receives verbal reprimand and warning, and behavior is recorded in grade book or discipline book. 2. Student must apologize in writing to the student and ask forgiveness. The letter should also make positive comments about the student. 3. Student must call his or her parents, if appropriate. 4. Student must participate in a behavioral conference with the teacher. 5. Student receives detention.	1. Student must call his or her parents, if appropriate. 2. Student receives verbal reprimand, behavior is recorded, and he or she must participate in a behavioral conference with counselor. 3. Student receives detention (for longer period) or Saturday school. 4. Student must participate in a behavioral conference with assistant principal and/or principal. 5. Required parent conference. 6. Student suspended.

Note: The negative consequences should be applied consistently. Consequences greater than those listed in the rubric may be applied and will be based on the type of misbehavior, the frequency of the mistreatment, the attitude and cooperation of the student, the school's discipline plan, harassment and anti-bullying policies, and relevant board policies. Negative consequences should be applied with statements regarding inappropriate behavior and the behavior desired. Also, for a time period, the student should receive positive reinforcement for self-control and modeling the desired behavior.

Bully Free Discipline Rubrics for Behavior and Consequences, High School

Example 1, High School

Instructions: The behaviors listed in a cell should be considered as a group of behaviors for that cell. Therefore, if any of the behaviors (or similar behaviors) listed in a cell occur, consequences should be applied according to the frequency of behaviors. For example, if you hear a student tease someone in a hurtful way for the first time, *all* of the first-time-offense consequences should be applied. If the next day, you hear the same student hurl insulting remarks at the same or another student, you should apply *all* of the second-time-offense consequences. In other words, the same behavior does not have to be repeated for more severe consequences to be applied.

Example 1, High School

Behavior	First-Time Offense (Apply ALL of the consequences in the cell.)	Second-Time Offense (Apply ALL of the consequences in the cell.)	Third-Time Offense (Apply ALL of the consequences in the cell.)
• Hurtful teasing • Hurtful name-calling • Insulting remarks • Other similar behavior (physical, verbal, written, electronic, or nonverbal) that intentionally hurts a person	1. Student receives verbal reprimand and warning, and behavior is recorded in grade book or discipline book. 2. Student must apologize in writing to the student and ask forgiveness. The letter should also make positive comments about the student. 3. Student must participate in a behavioral conference with the teacher. 4. Student must sit in isolation during one lunch period.	1. Student receives verbal reprimand, and behavior is recorded in grade book or discipline book. 2. Student must call his or her parents, if appropriate. 3. Student must participate in a behavioral conference with counselor. 4. Student must sit in isolation during two or three lunch periods. 5. Student must stay after school one hour for one day.	1. Student must call his or her parents. 2. Student receives verbal reprimand, and behavior is recorded in grade book or discipline book. 3. Student must participate in a behavioral conference with assistant principal and/or principal. 4. Required parent conference. 5. Student receives detention.
• Spreading lies, destroying reputations • Socially rejecting • Sending nasty notes or hate notes • Stealing or damaging property • Other similar behavior (physical, verbal, written, electronic, or nonverbal) that intentionally hurts a person	1. Student receives verbal reprimand and warning, and behavior is recorded in grade book or discipline book. 2. Student must apologize in writing to the student and ask forgiveness. The letter should also make positive comments about the student. 3. Student must call his or her parents if property is stolen or damaged. 4. Student must participate in a behavioral conference with the teacher. 5. Student must stay after school one hour for one day. 6. Student must make restitution for any property stolen or damaged.	1. Student receives verbal reprimand, and behavior is recorded in grade book or discipline book. 2. Student must call his or her parents. 3. Student must participate in a behavioral conference with counselor. 4. Student must stay after school one hour for two days, or eat lunch in isolation for three or four days. 5. Student must make restitution for any property stolen or damaged.	1. Student must call his or her parents. 2. Student receives verbal reprimand, and behavior is recorded in grade book or discipline book. 3. Student must participate in a behavioral conference with assistant principal and/or principal. 4. Required parent conference. 5. Student receives detention. 6. Student must make restitution for any property stolen or damaged.

Example 1, High School, Continued

Behavior	First-Time Offense (Apply ALL of the consequences in the cell.)	Second-Time Offense (Apply ALL of the consequences in the cell.)	Third-Time Offense (Apply ALL of the consequences in the cell.)
• Pushing • Tripping • Grabbing • Pinching • Restraining • Other similar behavior (physical, verbal, written, electronic, or nonverbal) that intentionally hurts a person	1. Student receives verbal reprimand and warning, and behavior is recorded in grade book or discipline book. 2. Student must apologize in writing to the student and ask forgiveness. The letter should also make positive comments about the student. 3. Student must call his or her parents, if appropriate. 4. Student must participate in a behavioral conference with the teacher. 5. Student must stay after school two days, one hour each day.	1. Student receives verbal reprimand, and behavior is recorded in grade book or discipline book. 2. Student must call his or her parents, if appropriate. 3. Student must meet with the counselor once a day for a few days to discuss his or her behavior. 4. Student must stay after school three days, one hour each day.	1. Student must call his or her parents, if appropriate. 2. Student receives verbal reprimand, and behavior is recorded in grade book or discipline book. 3. Student must participate in a behavioral conference with assistant principal and/or principal. 4. Required parent conference. 5. Student given detention or in-school suspension.

Example 1, High School, Continued

Behavior	First-Time Offense *(Apply ALL of the consequences in the cell.)*	Second-Time Offense *(Apply ALL of the consequences in the cell.)*	Third-Time Offense *(Apply ALL of the consequences in the cell.)*
• Spitting on someone • Hitting and punching • Slapping • Slamming with shoulder • Kicking • Threats • Other similar behavior (physical, verbal, written, electronic, or nonverbal) that intentionally hurts a person	1. Student receives verbal reprimand and warning, and behavior is recorded in grade book or discipline book. 2. Student must apologize in writing to the student and ask forgiveness. The letter should also make positive comments about the student. 3. Student must call his or her parents. 4. Student must participate in a behavioral conference with the teacher. 5. Student receives one day out-of-school suspension.	1. Student receives verbal reprimand, and behavior is recorded in grade book or discipline book. 2. Student must call his or her parents. 3. Student must participate in a behavioral conference with counselor. 4. Student receives three days out-of-school suspension.	1. Student must call his or her parents, if appropriate. 2. Student receives verbal reprimand, and behavior is recorded in grade book or discipline book. 3. Student must participate in a behavioral conference with assistant principal and/or principal. 4. Required parent conference. 5. Student receives five days out-of-school suspension.

Note: The negative consequences should be applied consistently. Consequences greater than those listed in the rubric may be applied and will be based on the type of misbehavior, the frequency of the mistreatment, the attitude and cooperation of the student, the school's discipline plan, harassment and anti-bullying policies, and relevant board policies. Negative consequences should be applied with statements regarding inappropriate behavior and the behavior desired. Also, for a time period, the student should receive positive reinforcement for self-control and modeling the desired behavior.

Bully Free Discipline Rubrics for Behavior and Consequences, High School

Example 2, High School

Instructions: The behaviors listed in a cell should be considered as a group of behaviors for that cell. The menu of consequences is progressive in that the further you go down the list, the more significant or severe the consequences. For example, if you hear a student tease someone in a hurtful way for the first time, you should *select one or more* of the consequences appearing first in the menu of consequences. If the next day, you hear the same student hurl insulting remarks at the same or another student, you should apply more severe consequences located further down the list. In other words, the same behavior does not have to be repeated to receive more severe consequences.

Example 2, High School

Behavior	Menu of Consequences (ONE or MORE of the following may be applied according to the frequency of mistreatment, the student's attitude, and the student's cooperation.)
• Hurtful teasing • Hurtful name-calling • Insulting remarks • Other similar behavior (physical, verbal, written, electronic, or nonverbal) that intentionally hurts a person	1. Student receives verbal reprimand and warning, and behavior is recorded in grade book or discipline book. 2. Student must apologize in writing to the student and ask forgiveness. The letter should also make positive comments about the student. 3. Student must call his or her parents, if appropriate. 4. Student must participate in a behavioral conference with the teacher. 5. Student must sit in isolation during one lunch period. 6. Student must participate in a behavioral conference with counselor. 7. Student must sit in isolation during two or three lunch periods. 8. Student must stay after school one hour for one day. 9. Student must participate in a behavioral conference with assistant principal and/or principal. 10. Required parent conference. 11. Student receives detention.
• Spreading lies, destroying reputations • Socially rejecting • Sending nasty notes or hate notes • Stealing or damaging property • Other similar behavior (physical, verbal, written, electronic, or nonverbal) that intentionally hurts a person	1. Student receives verbal reprimand and warning, and behavior is recorded in grade book or discipline book. 2. Student must apologize in writing to the student and ask forgiveness. The letter should also make positive comments about the student. 3. Student must call his or her parents. 4. Student must participate in a behavioral conference with the teacher. 5. Student must stay after school one hour for one day. 6. Student must participate in a behavioral conference with counselor. 7. Student must stay after school one hour for two days, or eat lunch in isolation for three or four days. 8. Student must participate in a behavioral conference with assistant principal and/or principal. 9. Required parent conference. 10. Student receives detention. 11. Student must make restitution for any property stolen or damaged.

Example 2, High School, Continued

Behavior	Menu of Consequences *(ONE or MORE of the following may be applied according to the frequency of mistreatment, the student's attitude, and the student's cooperation.)*
• Pushing • Tripping • Grabbing • Pinching • Restraining • Other similar behavior (physical, verbal, written, electronic, or nonverbal) that intentionally hurts a person	1. Student receives verbal reprimand and warning, and behavior is recorded in discipline book. 2. Student must call his or her parents, if appropriate. 3. Student must apologize in writing to the student and ask forgiveness. The letter should also make positive comments about the student. 4. Student must participate in a behavioral conference with the teacher. 5. Student must stay after school two days, one hour each day. 6. Student must meet with the counselor once a day for a few days to discuss his or her behavior. 7. Student must stay after school three days, one hour each day. 8. Student must participate in a behavioral conference with assistant and/or principal. 9. Required parent conference. 10. Student given detention or in-school suspension.

Example 2, High School, Continued

Behavior	Menu of Consequences *(ONE or MORE of the following may be applied according to the frequency of mistreatment, the student's attitude, and the student's cooperation.)*
• Spitting on someone • Hitting and punching • Slapping • Slamming with shoulder • Kicking • Threats • Other similar behavior (physical, verbal, written, electronic, or nonverbal) that intentionally hurts a person	1. Student receives verbal reprimand and warning, and behavior is recorded in grade book or discipline book. 2. Student must apologize in writing to the student and ask forgiveness. The letter should also make positive comments about the student. 3. Student must call his or her parents, if appropriate. 4. Student must participate in a behavioral conference with the teacher. 5. Student receives one day out-of-school suspension. 6. Student must participate in a behavioral conference with counselor. 7. Student receives three days out-of-school suspension. 8. Student must participate in a behavioral conference with assistant principal and/or principal. 9. Required parent conference. 10. Student receives five days out-of-school suspension.

Note: The negative consequences should be applied consistently. Consequences greater than those listed in the rubric may be applied and will be based on the type of misbehavior, the frequency of the mistreatment, the attitude and cooperation of the student, the school's discipline plan, harassment and anti-bullying policies, and relevant board policies. Negative consequences should be applied with statements regarding inappropriate behavior and the behavior desired. Also, for a time period, the student should receive positive reinforcement for self-control and modeling the desired behavior.

Bully Free Discipline Rubrics for Behavior and Consequences, High School

Example 3, High School

Instructions: The behaviors listed in each cell should be considered as a group of behaviors for that cell. Therefore, if any of the behaviors (or similar behaviors) listed in a cell occur, the appropriate consequences should be applied. For example, if you hear a student tease someone in a hurtful way for the first time, *all* of the first-time-offense consequences should be applied. If the next day, you hear the same student hurl insulting remarks at the same or another student, you should *select one or more* of the more significant or severe consequences from the column labeled Menu of Consequences for Repeated Offenses. In other words, the same behavior does not have to be repeated to receive more severe consequences. If the student continues to mistreat others, you would select the most severe consequences listed in the last column. The consequences for repeated offenses are progressive in that as you move down the list, they are more severe.

Example 3, High School

Behavior	Consequences for First Offense (Apply ALL of the consequences in a cell.)	Menu of Consequences for Repeated Offenses (ONE or MORE of the following may be applied according to the frequency of mistreatment, the student's attitude, and the student's cooperation.)
• Hurtful teasing • Hurtful name-calling • Insulting remarks • Other similar behavior (physical, verbal, written, electronic, or nonverbal) that intentionally hurts a person	1. Student receives verbal reprimand and warning, and behavior is recorded in grade book or discipline book. 2. Student must apologize in writing to the student and ask forgiveness. The letter should also make positive comments about the student. 3. Student must participate in a behavioral conference with the teacher. 4. Student must sit in isolation during one lunch period.	1. Student receives verbal reprimand, behavior is recorded, and he or she must participate in a behavioral conference with counselor. 2. Student must call his or her parents, if appropriate. 3. Student must sit in isolation during two lunch periods. 4. Student must stay after school one hour for one day. 5. Student must participate in a behavioral conference with assistant principal and/or principal. 6. Required parent conference. 7. Student receives detention.
• Spreading lies, destroying reputations • Socially rejecting • Sending nasty notes or hate notes • Stealing or damaging property • Other similar behavior (physical, verbal, written, electronic, or nonverbal) that intentionally hurts a person	1. Student receives verbal reprimand and warning, and behavior is recorded in grade book or discipline book. 2. Student must apologize in writing to the student and ask forgiveness. The letter should also make positive comments about the student. 3. Student must call his or her parents if property is stolen or damaged and if appropriate. 4. Student must participate in a behavioral conference with the teacher. 5. Student must stay after school one hour for one day. 6. Student must make restitution for any property stolen or damaged.	1. Student receives verbal reprimand, behavior is recorded, and he or she must participate in a behavioral conference with counselor. 2. Student must call his or her parents if property is stolen or damaged and if appropriate. 3. Student must stay after school one hour for two days, or eat lunch in isolation for three days. 4. Student must participate in a behavioral conference with assistant principal and/or principal. 5. Required parent conference. 6. Student receives detention. 7. Student must make restitution for any property stolen or damaged.

Example 3, High School, Continued

Behavior	Consequences for First Offense (Apply ALL of the consequences in a cell.)	Menu of Consequences for Repeated Offenses (ONE or MORE of the following may be applied according to the frequency of mistreatment, the student's attitude, and the student's cooperation.)
• Pushing • Tripping • Grabbing • Pinching • Restraining • Other similar behavior (physical, verbal, written, electronic, or nonverbal) that intentionally hurts a person	1. Student receives verbal reprimand and warning, and behavior is recorded in grade book or discipline book. 2. Student must apologize in writing to the student and ask forgiveness. The letter should also make positive comments about the student. 3. Student must call his or her parents, if appropriate. 4. Student must participate in a behavioral conference with the teacher. 5. Student must stay after school two days, one hour each day.	1. Student receives verbal reprimand, behavior is recorded, and he or she must meet with the counselor once a day for a few days to discuss his or her behavior. 2. Student must call his or her parents, if appropriate. 3. Student must participate in a behavioral conference with assistant principal and/or principal. 4. Required parent conference. 5. Student given detention or in-school suspension.
• Spitting on someone • Hitting and punching • Slapping • Slamming with shoulder • Kicking • Threats • Other similar behavior (physical, verbal, written, electronic, or nonverbal) that intentionally hurts a person	1. Student receives verbal reprimand and warning, and behavior is recorded in grade book or discipline book. 2. Student must apologize in writing to the student and ask forgiveness. The letter should also make positive comments about the student. 3. Student must call his or her parents, if appropriate. 4. Student must participate in a behavioral conference with the teacher. 5. Student receives one day out-of-school suspension.	1. Student receives verbal reprimand, behavior is recorded, and he or she must participate in a behavioral conference with counselor. 2. Student must call his or her parents, if appropriate. 3. Student receives three days out-of-school suspension. 4. Student must participate in a behavioral conference with assistant principal and/or principal. 5. Required parent conference. 6. Student receives five days out-of-school suspension.

Note: The negative consequences should be applied consistently. Consequences greater than those listed in the rubric may be applied and will be based on the type of misbehavior, the frequency of the mistreatment, the attitude and cooperation of the student, the school's discipline plan, harassment and anti-bullying policies, and relevant board policies. Negative consequences should be applied with statements regarding inappropriate behavior and the behavior desired. Also, for a time period, the student should receive positive reinforcement for self-control and modeling the desired behavior.

Bully Free Discipline Rubric Forms

Form for Example 1

Instructions: The behaviors listed in a cell should be considered as a group of behaviors for that cell. Therefore, if *any* of the behaviors (or similar behaviors) listed in a cell occur, consequences should be applied according to the frequency of behaviors. For example, if you hear a student tease someone in a hurtful way for the first time, *all* of the first-time-offense consequences should be applied. If the next day, you hear the same student hurl insulting remarks at the same or another student, you should apply *all* of the second-time-offense consequences. In other words, the same behavior does not have to be repeated for more severe consequences to be applied.

Form for Example 1

Behavior	First-Time Offense (Apply ALL of the consequences in a cell.)	Second-Time Offense (Apply ALL of the consequences in a cell.)	Third-Time Offense (Apply ALL of the consequences in a cell.)

Form for Example 1, Continued

Behavior	First-Time Offense *(Apply ALL of the consequences in a cell.)*	Second-Time Offense *(Apply ALL of the consequences in a cell.)*	Third-Time Offense *(Apply ALL of the consequences in a cell.)*

Note: The negative consequences should be applied consistently. Consequences greater than those listed in the rubric may be applied and will be based on the type of misbehavior, the frequency of the mistreatment, the attitude and cooperation of the student, the school's discipline plan, harassment and anti-bullying policies, and relevant board policies. Negative consequences should be applied with statements regarding inappropriate behavior and the behavior desired. Also, for a time period, the student should receive positive reinforcement for self-control and modeling the desired behavior.

Bully Free Discipline Rubric Forms

Form for Example 2

Instructions: The behaviors listed in a cell should be considered as a group of behaviors for that cell. The menu of consequences is progressive in that the further you go down the list, the more significant or severe the consequences. For example, if you hear a student tease someone in a hurtful way for the first time, you should *select one or more* of the consequences appearing first in the menu of consequences. If the next day, you hear the same student hurl insulting remarks at the same or another student, you should apply more severe consequences located further down the list. In other words, the same behavior does not have to be repeated to receive more severe consequences.

Form for Example 2

Behavior	Menu of Consequences *(ONE or MORE of the following may be applied according to the frequency of mistreatment, the student's attitude, and the student's cooperation.)*

Form for Example 2, Continued

Behavior	Menu of Consequences *(ONE or MORE of the following may be applied according to the frequency of mistreatment, the student's attitude, and the student's cooperation.)*

Note: The negative consequences should be applied consistently. Consequences greater than those listed in the rubric may be applied and will be based on the type of misbehavior, the frequency of the mistreatment, the attitude and cooperation of the student, the school's discipline plan, harassment and anti-bullying policies, and relevant board policies. Negative consequences should be applied with statements regarding inappropriate behavior and the behavior desired. Also, for a time period, the student should receive positive reinforcement for self-control and modeling the desired behavior.

Bully Free Discipline Rubric Forms

Form for Example 3

Instructions: The behaviors listed in a cell should be considered as a group of behaviors for that cell. Therefore, if any of the behaviors (or similar behaviors) listed in a cell occur, the appropriate consequences should be applied. For example, if you hear a student tease someone in a hurtful way for the first time, *all* of the first-time-offense consequences should be applied. If the next day, you hear the same student hurl insulting remarks at the same or another student, you should *select one or more* of the more significant or severe consequences from the column labeled Menu of Consequences for Repeated Offenses. In other words, the same behavior does not have to be repeated to receive more severe consequences. If the student continues to mistreat others, you would select the most severe consequences listed in the last column. The consequences for repeated offenses are progressive in that as you move down the list, they are more severe.

Form for Example 3

Behavior	Consequences for First Offense (Apply ALL of the consequences in a cell.)	Menu of Consequences for Repeated Offenses (ONE or MORE of the following may be applied according to the frequency of mistreatment, the student's attitude, and the student's cooperation.)

Form for Example 3, Continued

Behavior	Consequences for First Offense (Apply ALL of the consequences in a cell.)	Menu of Consequences for Repeated Offenses (ONE or MORE of the following may be applied according to the frequency of mistreatment, the student's attitude, and the student's cooperation.)

Note: The negative consequences should be applied consistently. Consequences greater than those listed in the rubric may be applied and will be based on the type of misbehavior, the frequency of the mistreatment, the attitude and cooperation of the student, the school's discipline plan, harassment and anti-bullying policies, and relevant board policies. Negative consequences should be applied with statements regarding inappropriate behavior and the behavior desired. Also, for a time period, the student should receive positive reinforcement for self-control and modeling the desired behavior.

Appendix F

The Bully Free Response Plan Forms for Students Bullying Students

The response plan discussed in Step 11 and the following response forms are examples that also appear in the files located at www.bullyfree.com. After entering the Web site, click on "Click here to access our training resources." Then click on "Resources for Bully Free Program Committee." Type *bfp1* when you are asked your user name and *bullyfree* when you are asked your password.

These forms are presented as examples. Modify them to meet your needs and the policies and procedures of your school.

Bully Free Statement Sheet—Reported Victim

Name of Student (Print): _____ Date: _____

What is your reaction to the rumor? (Answer only if you have not reported it yourself.)

Is the rumor accurate? (check one) ___ Yes ___ No

Who has been bullying you?

Exactly how has this person bullied you? (If necessary, use the back of this sheet.)

Has this person bullied you before?

How often does it happen?

When and where does the bullying occur?

Who saw it happen, and what did they do?

Have you told any adults (for example, teachers, parents) about it? If so, what was the adult's response?

What did you do?

Signature of Student: _____ Date: _____

Signature of Principal: _____ Date: _____

Note: This form must be filed in a confidential and secured location.

Bully Free Statement Sheet—Accused

Name of Student (Print): _____ Date: _____

What is your reaction to the rumor?

Is the rumor accurate? (check one) ___ Yes ___ No

If the rumor is not accurate, what would you change?

If this was accurate, why would it be bullying, which is against the rules?

What are the consequences for bullying in our school?

Signature of Student: _____ Date: _____

Signature of Principal: _____ Date: _____

Note: This form must be filed in a confidential and secured location.

Bullying Witness Statement Form

This form *must* be completed by witnesses of the alleged bullying. One form must be completed by each witness. All statements that relate to the bullying incident should be attached to the Bullying Situation Report.

Name of Witness: (Print)	Title: (Circle One) Student Parent Staff	Interview Date:
Victim Name: (Print)	Accused Name: (Print)	Incident Date:
Name of Interviewer: (Print)	Title of Interviewer:	

When and where did the incident occur?

What happened?

What was your response, and did your response help the person mistreated?

Who were the other witnesses?

List and attach, if possible, evidence of bullying (for example, photos, notes, letters, damaged property).

I agree that all of the above information is true and accurate to the best of my knowledge.

Signature of Witness: _____ Date: _____

Name of person receiving this form: _____ Date: _____

Bullying Situation Report

Instructions: Complete the form, make a copy, and submit the original to the Principal's Office.
Report Number (assigned by Principal's Office): _____

Check one: ☐ Suspected bullying situation ☐ Confirmed bullying situation
Date: _____
Signature of reporting adult: _____

Name of victim: _____	**Grade of victim:** _____
Name of bully: _____	**Grade of bully:** _____

Names of followers (if any):

Other witnesses/bystanders:

Circle all of the bullying behaviors that the victim has experienced.

Hurtful teasing	Stealing or damaging property	Spitting on him or her
Hurtful name-calling	Pushing	Hitting and punching
Insulting remarks	Tripping	Slapping
Spreading lies and rumors, destroying reputation	Grabbing	Slamming with shoulder
Socially rejecting	Pinching	Kicking
Sending nasty notes or hate notes	Restraining	Threats
Eye-rolling/"the look"	Hurtful graffiti	Stalking
Other (Specify):		

Circle where and when the behaviors have been observed. Circle all that apply.

Bathroom	Hallway	Stairwell
Classroom	Cafeteria	Locker room
Gym	Library	Waiting for bus before school
Waiting for the bus after school	Parking lot	Other

Have you (the reporter) observed any mistreatment of this individual? ___ Yes ___ No
Circle the specific actions taken thus far to prevent and stop the bullying.

Verbal warning and conference with student	Loss of privileges	Restitution
Telephoned parent	Parent conference	Special assignment
Detention	Saturday school	Isolation, time-out
Other:		

Approximately how long has the student been bullied? _____

Parent(s) contacted by: _____ Date: _____ Time: _____

Parent(s) contacted by: _____ Date: _____ Time: _____

Administrative response taken:

Summary of telephone conversation with parent/guardian:

Use the back of this form as necessary for additional comments. If additional pages are needed, number, date, and initial those pages. Attach all relevant notes.

Bully Free Intervention Questionnaire

Date:	Name of School Official Completing Form:		
Student's Name:		Grade:	Age:
Check One: ____Victim ____Bully			

Instructions: Answer the following questions. Some of the questions may require additional research and even testing by the school counselor or psychologist. Do not let having unanswered questions prevent you from completing the Bully Free Intervention Plan Form and implementing prevention and intervention strategies. The plan can be updated.

As you try to help both the victim and bully, seek to answer the following questions that apply to the student. Some of the questions may be more appropriate for the victim or the bully. Most questions are appropriate for both.

Bullying Situation

- What is the nature of the bullying? (Check all that apply.)

  ☐ Physical

  ☐ Verbal

  ☐ Social/relational

  ☐ Cyberbullying

  Comments:

- What is the specific bullying behavior?

- Where and when is the bullying occurring?

- Has a safety plan for the victim been developed?

- Has the safety plan developed earlier for the victim been effective? If not, what changes need to be made?

- Is he or she being abused in other environments (for example, home, neighborhood, scouts, church)?

- Has the student been told to report to an adult on a regular basis regarding his or her treatment? If so, who is the adult, and has the student been making these reports?

- Whom would the student like to report to?

- How often will the student report to an adult?

Bully Free Intervention Questionnaire, Continued

Physical Needs

- Has the student lost weight because of bullying?

- Does the victim have injuries because of bullying?

- Does the student have any features or other characteristics mentioned by those who mistreat him or her?

- Is the student experimenting with alcohol, drugs, or sex to experience pleasure and release from the hurt?

- What are the student's eating habits? Are they healthy habits? Has the student gained or lost weight?

- Does the student exercise? If so, to what extent?

- Is the student physically weak for his or her age?

- What is the student's sleeping pattern?

- How frequently does the student visit the school nurse?

Psychological Needs

- How often has the student visited the school counselor?

- How fearful is the student?

- What is the student's level of anxiety? Is it overwhelming? (Engaging in avoidance—missing school, avoiding going anywhere at night or weekends, unable to sleep)

- Does the student feel helpless?

- Is the student depressed?

- Is the student receiving counseling outside school?

- Does the student have thoughts of suicide? Has the student planned suicide? Has the student attempted suicide?

Bully Free Intervention Questionnaire, Continued

- Does the student seem to expect to be mistreated by others?

- Does the student feel that his or her situation is hopeless?

- Does the student express concern about what he or she might do in response to the bullying?

- Does the student express a lack of trust in adults to help him or her in an appropriate way?

- Does the student feel defective and that he or she deserves to be mistreated?

- Is the student self-harming (cutting, overeating, no eating, and so on)?

- How angry is the student?

- Does the student have feelings of hate?

- Does the student feel rage?

- Does the student desire revenge?

- Does the student have nightmares about the bullying?

- Does the student mentally review or revisit his or her mistreatment? If so, when, and how often?

- Does the student feel humiliated and embarrassed?

- Are there feelings of shame? If so, what are these about? (feels defective, cannot stand up to the bully, and so on)

- How stressed is the student?

- Does the student have an overall positive self-esteem? (positive self statements rather than derogatory statements, expresses self confidence)

- Are there areas (for example, art, music, games, sports) where the student has a positive self-esteem?

- Does the student have adequate self-confidence to be assertive?

Bully Free Intervention Questionnaire, Continued

Social Needs

- Can the student explain the Golden Rule?

- Does the student participate in school activities? If so, which activities?

- What school activities would the student like to be involved in?

- Does the student have a best friend? If so, who is this person?

- What friendships does the student have with adults?

- How do the other students view this student?

- How do personnel view this student?

- Does he or she seek the company of wrong friends (gangs, cults, hate groups, drug groups)?

- Does the student respect authority figures?

- Does the student have any significant relationships with adults at school? If so, who are they?

- Who are the followers of this student?

- How is the student treated in the neighborhood?

Behavioral Needs

- Has the student been a discipline problem?

- Does the student have social skills that need to be improved?

- Does the student engage in any behaviors that contribute to his or her mistreatment?

- How does the student use his or her free time (hobbies, sports, clubs, youth groups or organizations)?

- Is the student attracted to violence in books, video games, movies, and other media?

- What assertiveness skills does the student need to learn and use?

Bully Free Intervention Questionnaire, Continued

- What skills, abilities, and talents does the student have?

- Is he or she cruel to animals?

- Does the student demonstrate a lack of empathy?

Academic Needs

- What are the student's grades? Has there been a significant change in grades?

- What has the student's school attendance been like?

Spiritual Needs

- Does the student have personal goals?

- Does the student have connections with any faith-based organizations such as youth groups?

Family

- What is the student's home environment like (relationships with parents and siblings, and level of supervision)?

- What is the discipline style of parents (permissive, overly aggressive)?

- Does the student have any meaningful relationships with extended family such as grandparents, cousins, or aunts or uncles?

- Are there siblings at home? If so, do they mistreat him or her, or does he or she mistreat siblings at home?

- Does the student have older or siblings attending this school?

- Has anyone in the family committed suicide? If so, who?

Other

- Does the student have access to weapons (knives, guns, and so on)?

Instructions for Bully Free
Intervention Plan Form

Complete the demographic data at the top of the Bully Free Intervention Plan Form.

Intervention Strategies: After examining the answers to the questions on the Bully Free Intervention Questionnaire, review some of the prevention and intervention strategies included in the Bully Free Program and other sources, and write down the strategies deemed most appropriate. If additional space is needed, use the back of the form.

Dates to review plan: Indicate the date you wish to review the plan with the student. This will vary according to the student and the intensity of the bullying. Some plans need to be reviewed weekly for a few weeks; some may need to be reviewed less often.

Signature of school official: Sign the plan.

Signature of student (when age appropriate): Ask the student to sign the plan.

Dates reviewed and notes: Each time the plan is reviewed for effectiveness, record the date and notes regarding its effectiveness and any changes that were made.

School official initials: Each time you review the plan with the student and make notes, place your initials in the corresponding column to the right.

Student initials (when age appropriate): Ask the student to write his or her initials to the right of the review notes.

Note: You may find it helpful to involve parents or guardians and other professionals in the development of the intervention plan. Also consider sharing the plan with the parents or guardians—they have an important role to play.

Bully Free Intervention Plan Form

Date:	Name of School Official Completing Form:		
Student's Name:		Grade:	Age:
Check One: _____Victim Plan _____Bully Plan			

Intervention Strategies (may use back of form):

Date(s) to review plan:

Signature of school official:

Signature of student (when age appropriate):

Dates Reviewed and Notes	School Official Initials	Student Initials (when age appropriate)

Note: Once completed, this form should be filed in the designated secured area to ensure confidentiality.

Bibliography

American Association of University Women (AAUW). (1993). *Hostile hallways: The AAUW survey on sexual harassment in America's schools.* Washington, DC: Foundation.

Asher, S. R., & Coie, J. D. (Eds.). (1990). *Peer rejection in childhood.* Cambridge, England: Cambridge University Press.

Austin, G., Huh-Kim, J., Skage, R., & Furlong, M. (2002, Winter). *2001-2002 California student survey.* Jointly sponsored by the California Attorney General's Office, California Department of Education, and Department of Alcohol and Drug Programs. Published by California Attorney General's Office, Bill Lockyer, Attorney General.

Banks, R. (1997). *Bullying in schools* (Report No. EDDY-PS-97-17). Champaign, IL: ERIC Clearinghouse on Elementary and Early Childhood Education. (ERIC Document Reproduction Service No. ED 407 154)

Banks, R. (2000). Bullying in schools. *ERIC Review, 7*(1), 12–14. Retrieved Nov. 19, 2001, from http://ericcass.uncg.edu/virtuallib/bullying/1036.html.

Beane, A. L. (1999). *The bully free classroom.* Minneapolis, MN: Free Spirit.

Beane, A. L. (2003). *Helpful facts for parents.* Murray, KY: Bully Free Systems LLC, www.bullyfree.com.

Beane, A. L. (2004a). *How you can be bully free: For students (Grades 4–8).* Murray, KY: Bully Free Systems LLC, www.bullyfree.com.

Beane, A. L. (2004b). *How you can be bully free: For students (Grades 9–12).* Murray, KY: Bully Free Systems LLC, www.bullyfree.com.

Beane, A. L. (2004c). *Together we can be bully free: A mini-guide for parents.* Minneapolis, MN: Free Spirit.

Beane, A. L. (2004d). *Together we can be bully free: A mini-guide for elementary students.* Minneapolis, MN: Free Spirit.

Beane, A. L. (2004e). *Together we can be bully free: A mini-guide for middle school students.* Minneapolis, MN: Free Spirit.

Beane, A. L. (2004f). *Together we can be bully free: A mini-guide for educators.* Minneapolis, MN: Free Spirit.

Beane, A. L. (2005a). Bully free handbook for student councils. Murray, KY: Bully Free Systems LLC, www.bullyfree.com.

Beane, A. L. (2005b). Establishing a Peers for Peace—Bully Free Club. Murray, KY: Bully Free Systems LLC, www.bullyfree.com.

Beane, A. L. (2008). *Protect your child from bullying*. San Francisco: Jossey-Bass.

Beane, A. L., & Beane, L. (2003). *Bully free bulletin boards, posters, and banners for high school*. Murray, KY: Bully Free Systems LLC, www.bullyfree.com.

Beane, A. L., & Beane, L. (2005). *Bully free bulletin boards, posters, and banners: Creative displays for a safe and caring school grades K–8*. Minneapolis, MN: Free Spirit.

Björkvist, K. (1994). Sex differences in physical, verbal, and indirect aggression: A review of recent research. *Sex Roles: A Journal of Research, 30*(3–4), 177–188.

Bonds, M., & Stoker, S. (2000). *Bully-proofing your school: A comprehensive approach for middle schools*. Longmont, CO: Sopris West.

Bowman, D. H. (2001). Survey of students documents the extent of bullying. *Education Week, 20*(33), 11. Retrieved Nov. 19, 2001, from http://www.edweek.org/newstory.cfm?slug=33bully.h20&keywords=bullying.

Broward County (Florida) Schools. *Anti-bullying policy*. Retrieved Feb. 13, 2009, from http://www.browardschools.com/schools/bullying.htm.

Bullying statistics. (n.d.). Retrieved Nov. 8, 2007, from http://www.atriumsoc.org/pages/bullyingstatistics.html.

Byrne, B. (1994a). *Bullying: A community approach*. Dublin, Ireland: Columbia Press.

Byrne, B. (1994b). *Coping with bullying in schools*. Dublin, Ireland: Columbia Press.

Cairns, R. B., Cairns, B. D., Neckerman, H. J., Gest, S. D., & Gariepy, J. (1988). Social networks and aggressive behavior: Peer support or peer rejection? *Developmental Psychology, 24*, 815–823.

Charach, A., Pepler, D., & Ziegler, S. (1995). Bullying at school—a Canadian perspective: A survey of problems and suggestions for intervention. *Education Canada, 35*(1), 12–18.

Cohn, A., & Canter, A. (2003). *Bullying: Facts for schools and parents*. National Association of School Psychologists. Retrieved Feb. 8, 2009, from http://www.nasponline.org/resources/factsheets/bullying_fs.aspx.

Craig, W. M., & Pepler, D. (1995). Peer processes in bullying and victimization: An observational study. *Exceptionality Education Canada, 5*(3&4), 81–95.

Crawford, N. (2002, October). New ways to stop bullying. *American Psychological Association Monitor on Psychology, 33*(9). Retrieved Feb. 28, 2009, from http://www.apa.org/monitor/oct02/bullying.html.

Duncan, R. D. (1996a). *Prevalence and psychological correlates of bullying in rural America middle schools*. Unpublished manuscript, Murray State University, Murray, KY.

Duncan, R. D. (1996b). *The relationship between child abuse and peer aggression: Further evidence of the revictimization of survivors*. Unpublished manuscript, Murray State University, Murray, KY.

Elias, M. (2002, September 26). Kids' meanness might mean health risks when they grow up. *USA Today*, p. D10.

Elliott, M. (1994). *Keeping safe: A practical book to talking with children*. London: Hodder and Stoughton.

Erickson, K. J. (1994). *Helping your children feel good about themselves: A book to building self-esteem in the Christian family*. Minneapolis, MN: Augsburg.

Ericson, N. (2001, June). *Addressing the problem of juvenile bullying*. Office of Juvenile Justice and Delinquency Prevention. Retrieved Feb. 24, 2009, from http://www.ncjrs.gov/pdffiles1/ojjdp/fs200127.pdf.

Espelage, D. L., Bosworth, K., & Simon, T. R. (2000). Examining the social context of bullying behaviors in early adolescence. *Journal of Counseling and Development, 78*, 326–333.

Espelage, D. L., & Swearer, S. M. (2004). Gender differences in bullying: Moving beyond mean level differences. In D. L. Espelage & S. M. Swearer (Eds.), *Bullying in American schools: A social-ecological perspective on prevention and intervention* (pp. 15–35). Mahwah, NJ: Erlbaum.

Floyd, N. M. (1985). Pick on somebody your own size! Controlling victimization. *Pointer, 29*(2), 9–17.

Floyd, N. M. (1987, Winter). Terrorism in the schools. *School Safety*, 22–25.

Foltz-Gray, D. (1996). The bully trap. *Teaching Tolerance, 5*(2), 19–23.

Fried, S., & Fried, P. (1996). *Bullies and victims: Helping your child survive the schoolyard battlefield*. New York: Evans.

Fried, S., & Fried, P. (2003). *Bullies, targets and witnesses*. New York: Evans.

Garbarino, J. (1999). *Lost Boys*. New York: Free Press.

Garrett, A. G. (2003). *Bullying in American schools*. Jefferson, NC: McFarland.

Garrity, C., Jens, K., Porter, W., Sager, N., & Short-Camilli, C. (1996). *Bully-proofing your school: A comprehensive approach for elementary schools*. Longmont, CO: Sopris West.

Garrity, C., Jens, K., Porter, W., Sager, N., & Short-Camilli, C. (1997, March). Bully proofing your school: Creating a positive climate. *Intervention in School and Clinic, 32*(4), 235–243.

Geffner, R., Loring, M., & Young, C. (Eds.). (2001). *Bullying behavior: Current issues, research and interventions*. Binghamton, NY: Haworth Press.

Girl Scout Research Institute. (2003). *Feeling safe: What girls say*. New York: Girl Scout Research Institute.

Greenbaum, S., Turner, B., & Stephens, R. (1989). *Set straight on bullies*. Malibu, CA: Pepperdine University Press.

Harned, D., & Myers, J. (1994). *Violence: The desensitized generation*. Nashville, TN: Convention Press.

Hawker, D., & Boulton, M. (2000). Twenty years' research on peer victimization and psycho-social maladjustment: A meta-analytic review of cross-sectional studies. *Journal of Child Psychology and Psychiatry and Allied Disciplines, 41*, 441–455.

Hazler, R. J., Hoover, J. H., & Oliver, R. (1992). What kids say about bullying. *Executive Educator, 14*, 20–22.

Hoover, J., & Oliver, R. (1996). *The bullying prevention handbook: A guide for principals, teachers, and counselors.* Bloomington, IN: National Educational Service.

Hoover, J., Oliver, R., & Hazler, R. (1992). Bullying: Perceptions of adolescent victims in the midwestern U.S.A. *School Psychology International, 13*, 5–16.

Hyde, J. S. (1986). Gender differences in aggression. In J. S. Hyde & M. C. Linn (Eds.), *The psychology of gender: Advances through meta-analysis* (pp. 51–66). Baltimore: John Hopkins University Press.

Joiner, L., Beane, A., & Grant, P. (1975). *After desegregation: Suggestions for promoting social integration of handicapped children in regular classes.* Paper presented at the annual convention of the Illinois Council for Exceptional Children, Chicago.

Kaiser Family Foundation & Nickelodeon. (2001). *Talking with kids about tough issues: A national survey of parents and kids.* Menlo Park, CA: Kaiser Family Foundation.

Lajoie, G., McLellan, A., & Seddon, C. (1997). *Take action against bullying.* Coquitlam, BC, Canada: Bully B'Ware Productions.

Maine Project Against Bullying. (2000). Welcome to Maine Project Against Bullying. [Fact sheet]. Retrieved Feb. 28, 2009, from http://lincoln.midcoast.com/~wps/against/bullying.html.

Maines, B., & Robinson, G. (1992). *The no-blame approach.* [Video and training booklet]. Bristol, England: Lucky Duck.

Maines, B., & Robinson, G. (2009). *The Support Group Method Training Pack.* Thousand Oaks, CA: Sage.

Marano, H. E. (1995). Big. Bad. Bully. *Psychology Today, 28*(5), 50–82.

McDermott, P. A. (1966). A nationwide study of developmental and gender prevalence for psychopathology in childhood and adolescence. *Journal of Abnormal Child Psychology, 24*, 53–66.

McMaster, L. E., Connolly, J., Pepler, D., & Craig, W. M. (1998). *Sexual harassment and victimization among early adolescents.* Paper presented at the biennial meeting of the Society for Research on Adolescents, San Diego, CA.

McTaggart, M. (1995, May 5). Signposts on the road to hell. *[London] Times Educational Supplement*, p. FA3. Retrieved Feb. 28, 2009, from https://www.tes.co.uk/article.aspx?storycode=11279.

Mellor, A. *Bullying: Questions and answers.* Anti-Bullying Network. Retrieved Feb. 11, 2009, from http://www.antibullying.net/knowledge/questiontwoamore10.htm.

Melton, G. B., Limber, S., Flerx, V., Cunningham, P., Osgood, D. W., Chambers, J., Henggler, S., & Nation, M. (1998). *Violence among rural youth.* Final report to the Office of Juvenile Justice and Delinquency Prevention.

Miller, T. (Ed.). (2008). *School violence and primary prevention.* New York: Springer.

Minner, S., & Beane, A. L. (1985). Q-sorts for special educators. *Teaching Exceptional Children, 17*(4), 279–281.

Mullin-Rindler, N. (2002). *Teasing and bullying: Facts.* Wellesley Centers for Women. Wellesley, MA. Retrieved Feb. 8, 2009, from http://www.wcwonline.org/content/view/1286/299/.

Nansel, T. R., Overpeck, M., Pilla, R. S., Ruan, W. J., Simons-Morton, B., & Scheidt, P. (2001). Bullying behaviors among US youth: Prevalence and association with psychosocial adjustment. *Journal of the American Medical Association, 285*(16), 2094–2100.

Nebraska Department of Education. Nebraska School Safety Center. Retrieved Feb. 5, 2009, from http://www.nde.state.ne.us/SAFETY/Bullying%20Prevention/BullyingPrevention PolicyDevelopment.htm.

Oliver, R., Hoover, J. H., & Hazler, R. (1994, March/April). The perceived roles of bullying in small-town midwestern schools. *Journal of Counseling and Development, 72*(4), 416–419.

Olweus, D. (1991). Bully/victim problems among schoolchildren: Basic facts and effects of a school based intervention program. In D. J. Pepler & K. H. Rubin (Eds.), *The development and treatment of childhood aggression* (pp. 411–448). Mahwah, NJ: Erlbaum.

Olweus, D. (1993). *Bullying at school: What we know and what we can do.* Cambridge, MA: Blackwell.

Olweus, D. (1995). Bullying or peer abuse at school: Facts and intervention. *Current Directions in Psychological Science, 4*(6), 196–200.

Pepler, D. J., Craig, W. M., & Roberts, W. (1998). Observations of aggressive and nonaggressive children on the school playground. *Merrill Palmer Quarterly, 44,* 55–76.

Pepler, D. J., Craig, W. M., Ziegler, S., & Charach, A. (1993). A school-based anti-bullying intervention: Preliminary evaluation. In D. P. Tattum (Ed.), *Understanding and managing bullying* (pp. 76–91). Oxford, England: Heinemann Educational.

Rigby, K. (2001). Health consequences of bullying and its prevention in schools. In J. Juvonen & S. Graham (Eds.), *Peer harassment in school: The plight of the vulnerable and victimized* (pp. 310–331). New York: Guilford Press.

Rollins, C. E. (1992). *Fifty-two simple ways to encourage others.* Nashville, TN: Thomas Nelson.

Russianoff, P. (1989). *When am I going to be happy?* New York: Bantam Books.

Ryder, V. (1993). *The bully problem: Signs of a victim.* Houston, TX: Ryder Press.

Samenow, S. (1989). *Before it's too late: Why some kids get into trouble and what parents can do about it.* New York: Random House.

Sanford, D. (1995). *How to answer tough questions kids ask.* Nashville, TN: Thomas Nelson.

Schwartz, D., McFayden-Ketchum, S. A., Dodge, K. A., Pettit, G. S., & Bates, J. E. (1998). Peer group victimization as a predictor of children's behavior problems at home and in school. *Development and Psychopathology, 10,* 87–99.

Schwartz, J. (2006, September 12). Violence in the home leads to higher rates of childhood bullying. UPI, via ClariNet. *University of Washington News.* Retrieved Dec. 2, 2008, from http://uwnews.org/article.asp?articleid=26586.

Sharp, S., & Smith, P. K. (Eds.). (1994). *Tackling bullying in your school.* London: Routledge.

Simmons, R. (2002). *Odd girl out.* New York: Harcourt.

Smith, P., & Sharp, S. (Eds.). (1994). *School bullying: Insights and perspectives.* London: Routledge, pp. 88–89.

Spurling, R. (2006). *The Bully-Free School Zone Character Education Program: A study of the impact on five western North Carolina middle schools.* Unpublished doctoral dissertation, East Tennessee State University, Johnson City, TN.

Sullivan, K. (2000). *The anti-bullying handbook.* New York: Oxford University Press.

Sullivan, K., Cleary, M., & Sullivan, G. (2005). *Bullying in secondary schools: What it looks like and how to manage it.* Thousand Oaks, CA: Corwin Press.

Valdez, B. (1993). *I like who I am and it shows.* Carthage, IL: Fearon Teacher Aids.

Waterhouse, T., Sippel, J., Pedrini, L., & Cawley, M. (1998). *Focus on bullying: A prevention program for elementary school communities.* Burnaby, BC, Canada: BC Safe School Centre, British Columbia Ministries of Education and Attorney General. Retrieved Feb. 2008, from http://www.bced.gov.bc.ca/specialed/bullying.pdf.

Weinhold, B. K., & Weinhold, J. B. (1998). Conflict resolution: The partnership way in schools. *Counseling and Human Development, 30*(7), 1–2.

Weisenburger, W., Underwood, K., & Fortune, J. (1995). Are schools safer than we think? *Education Digest, 60*(9), 12–16.

Wolcott, L. (1991, April). Relations: The fourth "R." *Teacher Magazine,* 26–27.

Youngs, B. B. (1992). *The six vital ingredients of self-esteem: How to develop them in your students.* Rolling Hills Estates, CA: Jalmar Press.

Index